Gilmore Girls

POP CULTURE REFERENCE GUIDE

Gilmore Girls

POP CULTURE REFERENCE GUIDE

MATT BROWNING

LYONS PRESS

Essex, Connecticut

An imprint of The Globe Pequot Publishing Group, Inc.
64 South Main St.
Essex, CT 06426
www.globepequot.com

British Library Cataloguing in Publication Information available

Library of Congress Cataloging-in-Publication Data available
ISBN 9781493092444 (paperback) | ISBN 9781493095131 (epub)

The paper used in this publication meets the minimum requirements of American National Standard for Information Sciences—Permanence of Paper for Printed Library Materials, ANSI/NISO Z39.48-1992.

Contents

INTRODUCTION

For more than twenty-five years, viewers have been visiting the fictional village of Stars Hollow, Connecticut, and following along as Lorelai and Rory Gilmore traverse the ups and downs of life. Since its inception—and perhaps even more so as the years have passed—*Gilmore Girls* has provided hours of entertainment. Time and again, we have laughed, cried, celebrated, and mourned along with the residents of Stars Hollow across seven seasons—153 episodes, and a four-part revival series. And we show no signs of slowing down.

In its initial review of the show back in 2000, the *Washington Post* proclaimed that if Lorelai and Rory would stop "zinging one-liners" and "speak more slowly so the audience can understand what they're saying," the show might stand a chance. Imagine if creator Amy Sherman-Palladino and team had actually taken that criticism to heart. The show quickly became known—and beloved—for its rapid-fire dialogue chock full of pop culture references. In part because of the very things the reviewer criticized, *Gilmore Girls* has become a cultural touchstone with an extraordinarily devoted fan base that keeps growing with each generation.

Despite the timelessness of its humor and heart, the *Washington Post* might have had at least a minor point. The sizable cache of pop culture references was topical for the time period but can leave today's viewers, especially those of younger generations, scratching their heads. Every episode is laced with rapid-fire references to people, places, and events that, in many cases, have been blurred, or even forgotten, by time. How many times have you been watching an episode only to furrow your brow at one of Lorelai's random movie quotes, Rory's literary classics, or Lane's obscure punk band shout-outs? With this book, you no longer have to wonder: who was the one-armed surfer girl, what was Enron, or why did Uma wear that dress?

Gilmore Girls Pop Culture Reference Guide is designed as a read-along companion to accompany a viewing of the show. It is structured in episode order, beginning with the pilot and moving through the revival series. When I was writing the book, it became apparent that I would need to develop a working definition of "pop culture." Otherwise, the book would be thousands of pages or multiple volumes long. I decided to adopt the general categories of entertainment (movies, TV, music, literature), sports, news, politics, history, and other odds and ends like fashion or slang terms. I've also incorporated the songs performed by Grant Lee Phillips, the town troubadour, most of which are original compositions by him or his band, Grant Lee Buffalo. You will not find many references to universities, automobiles, companies, or brands unless they are particularly pertinent to the context of the episode. References are also mostly confined to those mentioned in episode dialogue. Books that serve only as props, for example, are not included.

If you come across a reference while viewing that is not in the text, check the index. It was probably already referenced in an earlier episode. Multiple references are repeated and are only defined upon the first mention. If it also is not in the index, then it either did not make the cut of the "pop culture" definition, it is a fictional reference, or I simply missed it. Hopefully there aren't too many occurrences of the last one! I have tried to be quite thorough.

So pour yourself a giant cup of coffee, coffee, coffee; order one of everything on the menu at Al's Pancake World (but don't actually eat any of it); and cozy up for a binge watch of *Gilmore Girls* like you've never experienced before.

Season One: 2000–2001

Episode 1.1: Pilot

Written by Amy Sherman-Palladino. Directed by Lesli Linka Glatter. Aired October 5, 2000.

When Rory is accepted to the prestigious Chilton prep school, Lorelai must swallow her pride and ask her wealthy parents for help paying the tuition.

Jack Kerouac (1922–1969): American novelist and poet, part of a group of writers known as the Beat Generation, a literary subculture movement in the 1950s. He is best known for 1957's *On the Road*.

RuPaul: Drag queen, actor, singer, and television host known for *The RuPaul Show* and *RuPaul's Drag Race*.

Macy Gray: Raspy-voiced singer-songwriter best known for the hit single "I Try."

Officer Krupke: Fictional character in the stage play and films *West Side Story*, a police officer who attempts to keep the street gangs in line. His empty threats lead to the song "Gee, Officer Krupke." William Bramley portrayed the role in the 1961 film; Brian d'Arcy James in the 2021 remake.

Eminem: Born Marshall Mathers in 1972, Eminem is a rapper, songwriter, and producer known for *The Slim Shady LP* (1999), *The Marshall Mathers LP* (2000), and *The Eminem Show* (2002). He also starred in the commercially and critically successful film *8 Mile*.

The Adventures of Huckleberry Finn: Novel by Mark Twain first published in the 1880s. Considered among the Great American Novels, it follows the young titular protagonist who fakes his death to escape an abusive father, befriends a runaway slave named Jim, and embarks on a raft journey down the Mississippi River.

Mark Twain: Born Samuel Clemens, Twain (1835–1910) was an American novelist, humorist, and essayist, considered by many to be among the greatest American authors. His most famous works include *The Adventures of Tom Sawyer*, its sequel *The Adventures of Huckleberry Finn*, and *A Connecticut Yankee in King Arthur's Court*.

Britney Spears: Pop singer whose hits include 1999's "...Baby One More Time," the video for which featured Spears in a Catholic school girl uniform, complete with plaid skirt.

Protestants: Originating in the sixteenth century in Europe, Protestantism is one of the major divisions of Christianity, defined by its reaction to and rebellion against the medieval practices of the Roman Catholic Church. Protestants consider the Bible as the authority on Christian faith and practice.

Stephen King: Author known widely for his successful horror novels, including *Carrie*, *The Shining*, *Misery*, *Pet Sematary*, and many others.

Zsa Zsa Gabor (1917–2016): Hungarian-American actress and socialite known for her extravagant lifestyle, glamorous personality, and multiple marriages. While appearing in a variety of films, it was for her regular appearances as herself on television shows and in cameo roles that more recent audiences remember Gabor best—as well as her exploits like a 1989 accusation of slapping a Beverly Hills police officer who stopped her for a traffic violation.

Amish: Christian subculture with roots in the sixteenth-century Protestant Reformation. While maintaining a degree of separation from surrounding societies and technologies, Amish people are known for simple living, pacifism, and plain dress.

Ruth Gordon, *Rosemary's Baby*: *Rosemary's Baby* is a 1968 psychological horror film written and directed by Roman Polanski and based on a 1967 novel by Ira Levin. The film stars Mia Farrow as Rosemary, a pregnant newlywed who suspects her neighbors, Minnie and Roman Castevet, of being in a Satanic cult and grooming her to use her baby for their rituals. Gordon stars as Minnie, who at one point gifts Rosemary a pendant necklace containing tannis root, a fictional herb used to mind-control the unsuspecting Rosemary. Gordon (1896–1985) won an Academy Award for her role. Her other credits include *Whatever Happened to Aunt Alice?*, *Harold and Maude*, and *Every Which Way But Loose*.

Oprah Winfrey: Talk show host, producer, actress, author, and media mogul. She is best known for her popular talk show, *The Oprah Winfrey*

Show, which was broadcast from Chicago and ran from 1986 to 2011. She has been dubbed the "Queen of All Media" and one of the most influential women in the world.

Broadway: The epitome of American stage performance, Broadway refers to the performances presented in the more than forty theaters making up the Theater District along Broadway in New York City.

Moby-Dick, **Herman Melville**: Melville (1819–1891) was an American novelist and poet whose best-known work is *Moby-Dick*, an 1851 epic novel depicting the sailor Ishmael's narrative of Ahab, a sea captain with a quest for vengeance against the titular giant whale that bit off his leg on a previous voyage.

Madame Bovary: French novel by Gustave Flaubert, published in 1857. Considered the author's masterpiece, the novel centers around Emma, the selfish wife of Charles Bovary, who finds married life dull and empty and craves a life of luxury—going to questionable lengths to achieve it.

Flo-Jo: Florence Griffith Joyner (1959–1998), nicknamed Flo-Jo, was an American track and field athlete who became the fastest woman ever recorded, setting world records in 1988 for the 100-meter dash and 200-meter dash and winning three gold medals at the 1988 Olympics.

Mommie Dearest: A 1981 drama film adapted from Christina Crawford's 1978 autobiography of the same name. The book and film depict the author and her brother's upbringing under their adoptive mother, Joan Crawford, and the volatile relationship between Christina and Joan, who is depicted as abusive and manipulative, valuing career over her children.

The Little Match Girl: Fairy tale by Hans Christian Anderson first published in 1845. It depicts a poor young girl who is afraid to return home to her father after failing to sell matches on the street, instead huddling in an alley on a cold winter night.

Menendez brothers: Lyle and Erik Menendez are brothers convicted of the 1989 shooting murders of their parents, José and Kitty. The subsequent trial became a media sensation. The brothers claimed they feared their father following years of abuse, while prosecutors argued they committed the murders to inherit their father's multimillion dollar estate. Both brothers were sentenced to life in prison without parole. In 2025, they were resentenced to fifty years to life, making them now eligible for parole.

The best laid plans: Common phrase originating in the Robert Burns poem "To a Mouse."

Nick at Nite: A block of nighttime programming on the cable network Nickelodeon launched in the 1980s as a showcase for classic television series, mostly sitcoms. During the 1990s, Nick at Nite had risen in popularity and was home to such classic shows as *The Brady Bunch*, *I Love Lucy*, *The Donna Reed Show*, *The Mary Tyler Moore Show*, *Bewitched*, *I Dream of Jeannie*, and many others.

EPISODE 1.2: THE LORELAIS' FIRST DAY AT CHILTON

Written by Amy Sherman-Palladino. Directed by Arlene Sanford. Aired October 12, 2000.

Rory's first day at Chilton gets off to a rough start.

XTC, *Wasp Star (Apple Venus Volume 2)*: XTC was an English rock band that gained modest popularity and a cult following during the punk and new wave eras of the 1970s. *Wasp Star (Apple Venus Volume 2)* is the band's fourteenth studio album, released in May 2000.

The Hunchback of Notre Dame: French Gothic novel written by Victor Hugo, published in 1831. It is the story of cathedral bell ringer Quasimodo, the titular "hunchback," and his love for the beautiful street dancer, Esmeralda.

The Dukes of Hazzard: Action-comedy TV series that aired on CBS from 1979 to 1985, followed by two made-for-TV movies in 1997 and 2000. The show centered around cousins Bo and Luke Duke, who lived in rural Georgia and were consistently in trouble with the local bumbling sheriff and corrupt county commissioner Boss Hogg. They were aided in their shenanigans by their wise old Uncle Jesse and cousin Daisy (Catherine Bach). Daisy's penchant for wearing very high-cut jean shorts positioned Bach as a bit of a sex symbol for the series, with the style still being referred to as "daisy dukes" today.

Schindler's List: A 1993 epic historical drama film written by Steven Zaillian and directed by Steven Spielberg. It is the tale of German industrialist Oskar Schindler, who saved Jewish refugees from the Holocaust by employing them in his factories during World War II.

Christiane Amanpour: British-Iranian journalist and TV host whose credits include serving as the Chief International Anchor for CNN and hosting the nightly news program *Amanpour*.

Cokie Roberts (1943–2019): American journalist and author whose decades-long career included serving as political reporter and analyst for National Public Radio, PBS, ABC News, and others.

Rosie O'Donnell: Comedian, actress, host, and producer whose film credits include *A League of Their Own*, *Sleepless in Seattle*, and *The Flintstones*. She became a household name in the late 1990s with the launch of her popular daytime variety talk show, *The Rosie O'Donnell Show*, which ran from 1996 to 2002.

The View: Daytime talk show created and originally co-hosted by journalist Barbara Walters. Launched in 1997, the original lineup included a multi-generational panel of women who discussed the hot topics of the day and welcomed a variety of guests. The concept has remained the same for decades, with the panel of hosts alternating over the years. Among the most notable hosts have been Meredith Vieira, Joy Behar, Rosie O'Donnell, Sherri Shepherd, and Whoopi Goldberg.

Dixie Chicks: Known now as The Chicks, this country music trio consists of Natalie Maines and sisters Martie Maguire and Emily Strayer. They rose to fame in the 1990s with albums like *Wide Open Spaces* and *Fly* and hits such as "There's Your Trouble," "Cowboy Take Me Away," and "Goodbye Earl." In 2003, while performing in London, Maines criticized President George W. Bush on stage, which led to strong backlash in the United States. In 2020, the group removed "Dixie" from their name, due to the word's negative connotations.

Leo Tolstoy (1828–1910): Russian writer who received Nobel Prize in Literature nominations every year from 1902 to 1906, as well as three nominations for the Nobel Peace Prize. Among his most enduring works are the novels *War and Peace* and *Anna Karenina*.

Charles Dickens (1812–1870): English author and social critic whose works include *David Copperfield*, *Oliver Twist*, *Great Expectations*, *A Tale of Two Cities*, and *A Christmas Carol*.

Fyodor Dostoevsky (1821–1881): Russian writer often regarded as among the great novelists in literature. His most acclaimed works include *Crime and Punishment* and *The Brothers Karamazov*.

George Sand: Pen name of French writer Amantine Lucile Aurore Dupin de Francueil (1804–1876). She is considered among the most notable authors of the European Romantic era and was an advocate for women's rights and critic of the institution of marriage. Her works include *Indiana* and *Valentine*. She also gained notoriety for her list of romantic involvements, which included such figures as Prosper Mérimée, Alfred de Musset, and Frédéric Chopin.

Honoré de Balzac (1799–1850): French novelist and playwright credited as among the founders of European literary realism. Among his most notable works is *La Comédie humaine* (*The Human Comedy*), a collection of interlinked novels and stories depicting French society during the Restoration and July Monarchy periods.

War and Peace, Anna Karenina: Both classic novels by Russian writer Leo Tolstoy, *War and Peace* chronicles the French invasion of Russia during the Napoleonic era, while *Anna Karenina* is the story of an affair between the titular Anna and cavalry officer Alexei Kirillovich.

David Copperfield, Great Expectations, A Tale of Two Cities, Little Dorrit: Famous works by English author Charles Dickens. *David Copperfield* focuses on the titular character's life from infancy to adulthood. *Great Expectations* is the journey and education of the orphan Pip. Set in London and Paris before and during the French Revolution, *A Tale of Two Cities* is the story of Doctor Manette's imprisonment in the Bastille in Paris and his release to live with his daughter. *Little Dorrit* focuses on Amy Dorrit, who was born and raised in a debtors' prison in London.

Virgin Mary: Mary is an important figure in Christianity as the mother of Jesus. She is described in the Bible as a virgin chosen by God to conceive Jesus through the Holy Spirit.

Quarters: Drinking game in which players attempt to bounce a quarter off a table so that it lands in a cup or shot glass in the center of the table. If the attempt is successful, the player assigns someone at the table to take a drink.

Harry Potter: A series of seven fantasy novels written by British author J. K. Rowling chronicling the life and education of the titular young wizard and his friends, who attend the Hogwarts School of Witchcraft and Wizardry. The primary story arc involves Harry's conflict with the evil Lord Voldemort.

William Shakespeare (1564–1616): English playwright, poet, and actor who is often regarded as among the greatest writers and dramatists in the English language. Among his most notable works are *Hamlet*, *Othello*, *King Lear*, *Macbeth*, and *Romeo and Juliet*.

Martin Luther (1483–1546): German priest, theologian, and professor who became the leader of the Protestant Reformation—a major theological movement that challenged the authority of the Catholic Church in the sixteenth century. Quoted in the scene is a passage of Luther's 1520 address to the Christian Nobility of the German Nation, in which he attacked the corruptions and abuses of the Church's authority and asserted the right to spiritual independence.

The Shining: A 1980 psychological horror film based on the 1977 Stephen King novel of the same name. Produced and directed by Stanley Kubrick, it stars Jack Nicholson and Shelley Duvall, and depicts the descent into insanity of novelist Jack Torrence (Nicholson), who moves his family to a remote mountain-top hotel where he has taken on a winter caretaker position. "All work and no play makes Jack a dull boy" is an old proverb that was popularized when it was included in the film.

Mary Magdalene: Woman depicted in the Bible as a follower of Jesus and witness to his crucifixion and resurrection. According to many popular accounts, she was a sex worker who converted to follow Jesus's teachings.

Episode 1.3: Kill Me Now

Written by Joanne Waters. Directed by Adam Nimoy. Aired October 19, 2000.
Rory takes up golf with the help of her grandfather. Lorelai prepares for a wedding at the inn.

Bob Barker (1923–2023): TV game show host and animal rights activist best known for hosting the CBS daytime series *The Price Is Right* from 1972 to 2007, ending episodes with a plea to have your pets spayed or neutered.

Jocelyn Wildenstein (1940–2024): Swiss socialite known for her extravagant lifestyle, high-profile divorce from billionaire art dealer Alec Wildenstein, and for extensive cosmetic surgery resulting in a catlike appearance and the nickname "Catwoman."

Antonio Banderas: Spanish actor known for such works as *Philadelphia*, *Interview with the Vampire*, *Evita*, *The Mask of Zorro*, and voicing Puss in Boots in the *Shrek* film franchise.

Charlie Brown's teacher: Charlie Brown is the protagonist of the *Peanuts* comic strip, created by Charles M. Schulz. The character is portrayed as a "lovable loser" type, frequently nervous and lacking in self-esteem. He first appeared in 1950. Many of the comic strips—and subsequent cartoon specials and films—feature classroom scenes in which an unseen teacher speaks in a series of sounds ("wah wah wah wah") as opposed to actual words.

Tiger Woods: Professional golfer who rose to fame in the 1990s. By April 1997, the then-twenty-year-old had won three PGA Tour events and the 1997 Masters.

NSYNC: Vocal group that rose to prominence as a boy band in the 1990s. The group consists of Justin Timberlake, Chris Kirkpatrick, Joey Fatone, Lance Bass, and JC Chasez. Their hits include "I Want You Back," "Bye Bye Bye," and "It's Gonna Be Me."

Pepé Le Pew: Animated anthropomorphic French skunk in the Warner Bros. *Looney Tunes* and *Merrie Melodies* series of cartoons. First introduced in 1945, Le Pew's cartoons often feature him in pursuit of romance, with the object of his affections (typically a female black cat that he mistakes for a skunk) fleeing because of his odor.

Peyton Place: Prime-time soap opera that aired on ABC from 1964 to 1969, loosely based on the Grace Metalious novel of the same name. A 1957 film adaptation preceded the series.

Samuel Barber, John Cage, Philip Glass: Musicians and composers considered among the most influential of the twentieth century.

Shania Twain, "Man! I Feel Like a Woman!": Shania Twain is among the most successful singer-songwriters of all time, having sold over 100 million records. "Man! I Feel Like a Woman!" is a 1997 single which won Twain a Grammy for Best Female Country Vocal Performance.

H. L. Mencken, *Chrestomathy*: Henry Louis Mencken (1880–1956) was an American journalist, scholar, and cultural critic. A chrestomathy is a collection of selected literary passages, typically from a single author. *A Mencken Chrestomathy: His Own Selection of His Choicest Writings* was published in 1949.

Thelonious Monk (1917–1982): Pianist and composer known for his many contributions to standard jazz, including "Round Midnight" and "Straight, No Chaser."

Madonna, Sean Penn: Madonna is among the most successful and best-selling singer-songwriters of all time who rose to fame in the 1980s with her infectious pop songs and unapologetic sexualized image. Her hits include "Like a Virgin," "Vogue," "Like a Prayer," and "Holiday." Sean Penn is an actor and director known for such films as *Fast Times at Ridgemont High*, *Mystic River*, *Milk*, and *Dead Man Walking*. Penn and Madonna met in January 1985 and married in August of that year. The marriage provided considerable tabloid fodder, including for Penn's violent outbursts against the press. They divorced in 1989.

Sister Sledge: Musical group from Philadelphia, consisting of sisters Debbie, Joni, Kim, and Kathy Sledge. They rose to fame during the disco era of the 1970s with their breakthrough album *We Are Family*. The album's title track became their signature song.

MTV: Originally standing for Music Television, MTV is a cable television network launched in 1981. It began as a network that solely aired music videos before, over time, shifting its focus less on music and more on reality programming targeting teenagers and young adults.

Episode 1.4: The Deer Hunters

Written by Jed Seidel. Directed by Alan Myerson. Aired October 26, 2000.
Rory struggles to catch up at Chilton.

"To err is human": Famous line from *An Essay on Criticism*, a poem by English author Alexander Pope (1688–1744), published in 1711. The full and often-quoted line is, "To err is human; to forgive, divine."

Maurice Chevalier (1888–1972): French singer and actor known for such songs as "Valentine" and "Thank Heaven for Little Girls" and films such as *The Big Pond* and *Love Me Tonight*.

Versace: Luxury Italian fashion company founded by Gianni Versace in 1978.

Marco Polo: Form of tag typically played in a swimming pool. One player is chosen as "it" and, with closed eyes, tries to find and tag other players by relying on the sound of their voice to find them. The "it" player calls out

"Marco!" while the other players respond "Polo!" If a player is tagged, they become "it." While bearing no direct ties, the game is named after Italian explorer Marco Polo (1254–1324), who traveled Asia along the Silk Road in the thirteenth century.

Black Sabbath: English rock band founded in 1968. Led by vocalist Ozzy Osbourne, they are considered pioneers of heavy metal music.

Steely Dan: Rock band formed in New York in 1971 by Walter Becker and Donald Fagen.

Boston: Rock band formed in Boston in 1975. Their hits include "More Than a Feeling," "Amanda," and "Peace of Mind."

Queen: Band formed in London in 1970. Led by Freddie Mercury, their many hits include "We Will Rock You," "We Are the Champions," and "Bohemian Rhapsody."

Wolfgang Amadeus Mozart (1756–1791): Classical composer who produced more than 800 works in his lifetime. The gifted musician was competent in multiple instruments and had begun composing by the age of five.

Artie Shaw (1910–2004): Bandleader and musician during the Big Band era of the 1930s and 1940s, regarded as among the country's finest jazz clarinetists.

Joan of Arc (1412–1431): Patron saint of France and prominent military leader known for her role in the siege of Orléans during the Hundred Years War. She was captured and put on trial for heresy, where she was found guilty and burned at the stake.

Elizabethan era: Period of the history of England during the reign of Queen Elizabeth I (1558–1603), often cited as a golden age of English history, especially in terms of the arts.

Christopher Marlowe (1564–1593): Prominent Elizabethan era English playwright and poet.

Francis Bacon (1561–1626): English statesman and philosopher cited as the father of empiricism. He served as Attorney General and Lord Chancellor of England under King James I.

Ben Jonson (1572–1637): English poet and playwright known for *The Alchemist* and *Every Man in His Humour*.

John Webster (1578–1632): English playwright known for such works as *The White Devil* and *The Duchess of Malfi*.

"Jesus, Mary, Joseph and the camel": While adding "the camel" for particular dramatic effect, "Jesus, Mary and Joseph!" is a common phrase used to express surprise or shock, referring to the Holy Family of Jesus and his parents.

The B-52s: New wave pop band formed in Athens, Georgia, in 1976, whose original lineup consisted of Fred Schneider, Kate Pierson, Cindy Wilson, Ricky Wilson, and Keith Strickland. Their many hits include "Love Shack," "Rock Lobster," and "Roam."

Saved by the Bell: Teen sitcom that aired on NBC Saturday mornings from 1989 to 1993. It focused on a group of students at the fictional Bayside High in California, and was the launchpad for such stars as Mark-Paul Gosselaar, Mario Lopez, Tiffani-Amber Theissen, and Elizabeth Berkley. Its popularity led to multiple spinoffs and films in the 1990s, as well as a reboot series in 2020.

Sonnet 116: "Let me not to the marriage of true minds admit impediments." Paris is quoting Sonnet 116 by William Shakespeare, first published in 1609.

The Comedy of Errors: Early farcical play by William Shakespeare that tells the story of two sets of identical twins separated at birth.

Richard III (1452–1485): King of England from 1483 until his death.

Iambic pentameter: Type of rhythm used in traditional English poetry and verse.

Pat Benatar: Pop/rock singer-songwriter who rose to fame in the 1980s with hits such as "Heartbreaker," "Hit Me with Your Best Shot," and "Love Is a Battlefield."

Il Duce: Title given to National Fascist Party leader Benito Mussolini (1883–1945), meaning The Leader.

Flashdance: Drama film released in 1983, starring Jennifer Beals as a young dancer who aspires to become a professional ballerina.

Episode 1.5: Cinnamon's Wake

Written by Daniel Palladino. Directed by Michael Katleman. Aired November 2, 2000.

The town mourns the death of Babette's cat.

Nazis: Nazism is a far-right, fascist political ideology that emerged in Germany in the 1920s, led by Adolf Hitler.

Moon landing: The *Apollo 11* spaceflight, led by the United States in July 1969, marked the first time humans landed on the Moon.

Dolly Madison: Bakery brand owned by Hostess that sells packaged snack cakes. It was created in 1937 by Ralph Leroy Nafziger and named after first lady Dolley Madison, wife of President James Madison, who was known for her elegant parties.

Rancid: Punk rock band formed by Tim Armstrong and Matt Freeman in California in 1991.

Henry VIII (1491–1547): King of England from 1509 until 1547. He brought about radical changes during his reign and is also known for his six marriages.

M. Night Shyamalan: Filmmaker known for supernatural plots and twist endings. Among his biggest films are *The Sixth Sense*, *Signs*, and *Unbreakable*.

The Sixth Sense: A 1999 Academy Award–nominated psychological thriller film written and directed by M. Night Shyamalan and starring Bruce Willis as a child psychologist whose patient, played by Haley Joel Osment, claims he can see dead people.

The Bangles: An all-female pop-rock band that rose to fame in the 1980s with a string of hits including "Walk Like an Egyptian," "Eternal Flame," and "Manic Monday."

Jim Carrey: Actor known primarily for his comedic, slapstick performances in such films as *Ace Ventura: Pet Detective*, *Dumb and Dumber*, *The Mask*, *How the Grinch Stole Christmas*, and many others.

Jean Paul Sartre (1905–1980): French philosopher, writer, and activist who was awarded the Nobel Prize in Literature in 1964.

Dalai Lama: The spiritual leader of the Tibetan people.

Hee Haw: Rural-themed television variety show featuring comedy skits and performances by popular country music artists. Set in fictional "Kornfield Kounty," the show aired from 1969 to 1993. It was hosted by Buck Owens and Roy Clark.

Valley of the Dolls: A 1967 drama film based on the 1966 Jacqueline Susann novel of the same name, starring Barbara Parkins, Patty Duke, and Sharon

Tate as three friends attempting to make it in the entertainment industry who descend into barbiturate addiction.

Iran-Contra scandal: US political scandal in which senior officials in the Ronald Reagan administration secretly facilitated the sale of arms to Iran in the 1980s.

Oliver North: American political figure and retired US Marine Corps lieutenant colonel who was a National Security Council staff member during the Iran-Contra affair. In more recent years, he has hosted a Fox News television series and served as president of the National Rifle Association.

Fawn Hall: Secretary to Oliver North during the time of the Iran-Contra affair who gained fame for helping North shred confidential documents. She briefly dated actor Rob Lowe in the late 1980s.

Angelina Jolie, Billy Bob Thornton: Jolie is an actress known for such films as *Girl, Interrupted*, *Lara Croft: Tomb Raider*, and *Mr. & Mrs. Smith*. Thornton is an actor known for *Sling Blade*, *A Simple Plan*, *Tombstone*, and *Bad Santa*. The two were married from 2000 to 2003. Jolie was later married to Brad Pitt.

The Big Dipper: A group of seven bright stars of the constellation Ursa Major that is shaped like a ladle or large dipping spoon.

Episode 1.6: Rory's Birthday Parties
Written by Amy Sherman-Palladino. Directed by Sarah Pia Anderson. Aired November 9, 2000.
Both Lorelai and Emily plan parties for Rory's birthday.

Henny Youngman (1906–1998): Comedian and musician who became known for one-liners like "Take my wife . . . please!"

"Like a Virgin": The title track and lead single from Madonna's second album, released in 1984. It reached the top spot on the Billboard Hot 100 and has become one of her signature songs.

Barbra Streisand: Singer, songwriter, and actress whose hit songs include "The Way We Were," "You Don't Bring Me Flowers," and "Woman in Love." Her film credits include *Funny Girl*, *Hello, Dolly!*, *The Way We Were*, *The Prince of Tides*, and *Meet the Fockers*.

The Pope: The bishop of Rome and the head of the Catholic Church.

Elvis Presley (1935–1977): Singer and actor known as "the King of Rock and Roll" and considered one of the most significant musicians in history. Among his many hits are "Heartbreak Hotel," "Don't Be Cruel," "Hound Dog," "Jailhouse Rock," and many others. He was also an avid collector of police badges, a reference that occurs in a season six episode.

Jim Morrison (1943–1971): Singer and songwriter known for leading the band The Doors. He died unexpectedly at age twenty-seven in a Paris apartment.

Vulcan Death Grip: Fictional maneuver from the *Star Trek* universe where a person is rendered unconscious by pinching a particular pressure point on their neck. Also referred to as the Vulcan Neck Pinch.

The Fly: A 1986 horror/science fiction film loosely based on a 1957 George Langelaan short story and 1958 film. It stars Jeff Goldblum as a scientist who, after an experiment goes wrong, begins to morph into a fly-like creature.

Mother Nature: Personification of nature that embodies its life-giving aspects into a mother goddess figure.

"Lucy, I'm home!": This is an impression of Ricky Ricardo, the fictional Cuban bandleader character played by Desi Arnaz in the television sitcom *I Love Lucy*, which aired from 1951 to 1957. The show was a landmark series starring comedian Lucille Ball and her real-life husband Arnaz.

Justin Timberlake: Pop singer and songwriter who first rose to fame as a member of the boy band NSYNC in the 1990s before embarking on a successful solo career. He had a highly publicized relationship with Britney Spears (see earlier entry) from 1999 to 2002.

Queen of England: Elizabeth II (1926–2022) was Queen of England during the period *Gilmore Girls* was on the air. She reigned from 1952 until her death in 2022.

Barbara Hutton (1912–1979): Socialite and heiress to the Woolworth estate, dubbed the "Poor Little Rich Girl" when she was given a lavish debutante ball during the Great Depression.

Farrah Fawcett (1947–2009): Actress who rose to fame in the 1970s as a cast member of the television series *Charlie's Angels*. A 1976 poster of Fawcett wearing a red bathing suit became one of the most popular pin-up posters of the era. Over twelve million copies of the poster have been sold.

Cinderella: The titular character in an often-adapted folktale about a young girl living in difficult circumstances who finds her happily ever after. The most popular version stems from the 1950 Walt Disney animated film.

The Waltons: Long-running historical drama series about a Virginia family set during the Great Depression and World War II, which aired from 1972 to 1981. Episodes often ended with members of the large family saying goodnight to one another, hence the popular phrase "Goodnight, John-Boy."

Edith Wharton (1862–1937): Writer and designer who became the first woman to win the Pulitzer Prize for Fiction for her novel *The Age of Innocence*.

Shirley Temple-Black, "On the Good Ship Lollipop": Shirley Temple (1928–2014) was an adored child actress in the 1930s who, as an adult, became the United States Ambassador to Ghana and Czechoslovakia and served as Chief of Protocol of the United States. "On the Good Ship Lollipop," written by Richard A. Whiting and Sidney Clare, was a song Temple first sang in 1934's *Bright Eyes*. It would become her signature song.

Freaky Friday: Originally a children's novel by Mary Rodgers, in which a teenage girl awakens one Friday to discover herself in the body of her mother, the story has been adapted into multiple films. Perhaps the most notable adaptation is the 2003 version starring Jamie Lee Curtis and Lindsay Lohan.

The Wall Street Journal: New York City–based newspaper founded in 1889 by Charles Dow, Edward Jones, and Charles Bergstresser, focusing largely on business and finance content.

Episode 1.7: Kiss and Tell

Written by Jenji Kohan. Directed by Rodman Flender. Aired November 16, 2000.
The town is abuzz with news of Rory's first kiss from Dean.

Pilgrims, *Mayflower*, Plymouth Rock: The Pilgrims were a group of English settlers who traveled to North America aboard the *Mayflower* in 1620, establishing the Plymouth Colony in Plymouth, Massachusetts. Plymouth Rock was their disembarkation site.

Members Only: Created in 1975, the clothing brand Members Only rose to popularity in the 1980s for its line of jackets.

Nick Drake (1948–1974): English musician who released his debut album, *Five Leaves Left*, in 1969. He died in 1974 from an overdose of antidepressants.

Liz Phair: Singer-songwriter who rose to fame with her debut album, 1993's *Exile in Guyville*, which was named to *Rolling Stone*'s list of the 500 Greatest Albums of All Time.

The Sugarplastic: Alt-rock band founded in Los Angeles in 1989 by Ben Eshbach and Kiara Geller.

***General Hospital*, Lucky, Liz**: *General Hospital* is an Emmy award–winning daytime soap opera that has aired on ABC since 1963. Lucky and Liz are characters from the show, a "supercouple" who gained popularity in the late 1990s. The roles were originated by actors Jonathan Jackson and Rebecca Herbst. Both have been nominated for Daytime Emmys for their roles, with Jackson winning five.

The Crucible: A 1953 play by Arthur Miller accounting the Salem witch trials that took place in Massachusetts in 1692 and 1693.

Sigmund Freud (1856–1939): Austrian neurologist and founder of psychoanalysis.

9½ Weeks: A 1986 drama film directed by Adrian Lyne and starring Kim Basinger and Mickey Rourke as an art gallery employee and a stockbroker who begin an intense affair. It is based on the 1978 memoir of the same name by Ingeborg Day, written under the pseudonym Elizabeth McNeill.

Willy Wonka & the Chocolate Factory: The fictional character of Willy Wonka first appeared in the 1964 Roald Dahl children's novel *Charlie and the Chocolate Factory*, which was adapted into the beloved 1971 film version referred to in the episode, which starred Gene Wilder in the title role. The story revolves around Wonka, a candy maker who hides five Golden Tickets in his chocolate bars. The recipients of the tickets are rewarded with a special tour of the mysterious factory.

Shaft: A 1971 action film directed by Gordon Parks and written by Ernest Tidyman and John D. F. Black, adapted from the Tidyman novel of the same name. Richard Roundtree stars as the title character, a private detective hired to rescue a man's daughter from mobsters.

Chi-Town: Nickname for the city of Chicago, Illinois.

James Dean (1931–1955): Influential actor during the 1950s who starred in *Rebel Without a Cause*, *East of Eden*, and *Giant*. Dean died in a car accident in 1955 at age twenty-four and has become a symbol of rebellion and youthful defiance.

Nancy Walker (1922–1992): Actress known for roles in *McMillan & Wife* and *Rhoda*.

Fun Dip: Candy first introduced in 1950 as Lik-M-Aid, consisting of pouches of colored and flavored sugar that is consumed by dipping a candy stick into the pouch and licking it.

Gene Hackman (1930–2025): Academy Award–winning actor known for such films as *The French Connection*, *Bonnie and Clyde*, *Mississippi Burning*, and *Unforgiven*.

Gene Wilder (1933–2016): Actor and comedian known for his work in *Willy Wonka & the Chocolate Factory*, *Blazing Saddles*, and *Young Frankenstein*.

Niagara Falls: Group of three waterfalls spanning the border between Ontario and New York.

Elsa Klensch (1930–2022): Journalist, writer, and television personality who hosted *Style with Elsa Klensch*, CNN's fashion program, from 1980 to 2001.

Charlton Heston (1923–2008): Academy Award–winning actor known for such films as *The Ten Commandments*, *Ben-Hur*, *Planet of the Apes*, and *Julius Caesar*.

"Pink Moon": The title track from the third and final album by English musician Nick Drake. The song was used in a 1999 TV ad campaign by the German automobile manufacturer Volkswagen.

The Oompa-Loompas: Small, strange orange human characters from *Willy Wonka & the Chocolate Factory*.

Prince Charming, Sleeping Beauty: Prince Charming is a fairy-tale character often coming to the rescue of damsels in distress and serving as the love interest of characters like Cinderella and Sleeping Beauty, the latter of whom is a princess cursed to sleep for a hundred years.

Ice Castles: A 1978 drama film directed by Donald Wrye and starring Lynn-Holly Johnson and Robby Benson. It details the rise and fall of a young figure skater. Its theme song, "Through the Eyes of Love," performed by Melissa Manchester, was nominated for the Academy Award for Best Original Song.

The Way We Were, **Robert Redford** (1936–2025): A 1973 drama film directed by Sydney Pollack and starring Barbra Streisand (see earlier entry) and Robert Redford, adapted from the 1972 Arthur Laurents novel of the same name. Redford was an Academy Award–winning actor known for such films as *Barefoot in the Park, The Sting,* and *Butch Cassidy and the Sundance Kid.*

Communism: Sociopolitical and economic ideology centered around common ownership of the means of production and distribution.

Boogie Nights: A 1997 drama film written and directed by Paul Thomas Anderson and starring Mark Wahlberg, Julianne Moore, Don Cheadle, and Burt Reynolds. It focuses on a nightclub-employee-turned-pornography actor.

Marky Mark: The former stage name of rapper-turned-actor Mark Wahlberg. He rose to fame in the early 1990s, leading the band Marky Mark and the Funky Bunch and appearing in a series of underwear ads for Calvin Klein before shifting his focus to acting.

Magnolia: A 1999 drama film written and directed by Paul Thomas Anderson and starring Tom Cruise, Melinda Dillon, and Philip Seymour Hoffman. Set in California's San Fernando Valley, it details a series of characters in search of happiness and meaning.

EPISODE 1.8: LOVE AND WAR AND SNOW

Written by Joan Binder Weiss. Directed by Alan Myerson. Aired December 14, 2000. Snow strands Rory at her grandparents' house, while Lorelai gets closer to Max. Lane feels left out of Rory's new life.

Redcoats: Term for British soldiers, particularly those who fought in the American Revolution, derived from the red uniforms they wore.

USSR: Acronym for the Union of Soviet Socialist Republics, commonly known as the Soviet Union, a country that spanned much of Eurasia for most of the twentieth century. It was governed by the Communist Party and was dissolved in 1991.

Emily Dickinson (1830–1886): American poet whose prominent works include "I'm Nobody! Who are you?" and "I felt a Funeral, in my Brain."

Sgt. Pepper's Lonely Hearts Club Band: The eighth album (and a song) by the English rock band the Beatles, released in 1967. It is considered an art rock album and a major work of British psychedelia.

Star Trek: Science-fiction media franchise created by Gene Roddenberry. It began with a television series starring William Shatner and Leonard Nimoy that debuted in 1966 and has since expanded into multiple spinoffs, revivals, movies, books, merchandise, and more.

Jane Austen (1775–1817): English novelist whose enduring works include the classics *Sense and Sensibility*, *Pride and Prejudice*, *Mansfield Park*, and *Emma*.

Hunter S. Thompson (1937–2005): Countercultural journalist and author who rose to fame with 1967's *Hell's Angels*, which recounted his year living with the motorcycle club. He popularized the genre of Gonzo journalism, which is writing that removes objectivity and casts the writer as part of the story via first-person narrative.

Charlotte Brontë (1816–1855): English novelist and poet (along with her two sisters) whose work has come to be considered literary classics. Perhaps her most notable work is the novel *Jane Eyre*.

Noah's Ark: Story from the Bible in which God spares Noah, his family, and a collection of the world's animals from a global flood by instructing Noah to build a massive ark and set sail.

Wonder Woman: Fictional superhero from the DC Comics universe, created by psychologist and writer William Moulton Marston and artist Harry G. Peter in 1941. The character is an Amazonian princess with superpowers who adopts the civilian identity of Diana Prince. She is depicted with long, dark hair and wearing a patriotic costume. The character has become a prominent pop culture figure over the decades, with adaptations to television, film, books, and merchandise.

Junior League: Nonprofit women's volunteer organization founded in 1901.

Bellevue: The actual Bellevue Hospital, located in New York City, is America's oldest public hospital, opening its doors in 1736. It became so heavily associated with its treatment of mentally ill patients that the term "Bellevue" eventually became a slang term for a psychiatric hospital.

Errol Flynn (1909–1959): Actor who rose to fame during the Golden Age of Hollywood who became known for a series of romantic swashbuckling pirate films and for playing the title role in 1938's *The Adventures of Robin Hood*.

The Cure: English rock band formed in 1976 by Robert Smith and Laurence Tolhurst who rose to fame during the new wave, post-punk movements.

Judy Blume: Author of primarily children's and young adult fiction whose notable works include *Are You There God? It's Me, Margaret*, *Tales of a Fourth Grade Nothing*, and *Blubber*.

World Series: Annual championship series of Major League Baseball, held since 1903.

Legos: Popular and enduring line of plastic construction toys debuting in 1949 as basic interlocking bricks. The line has expanded immensely over the years, now including elaborate sets, as well as films, amusement parks, and retail stores.

EPISODE 1.9: RORY'S DANCE

Written by Amy Sherman-Palladino. Directed by Lesli Linka Glatter. Aired December 20, 2000.
Dean accompanies Rory to her first formal dance at Chilton.

Václav Havel (1936–2011): Statesman, author, and poet who served as the president of Czechoslovakia and the Czech Republic. Prior to his presidency, he was a leading dissident whose political activities led to multiple imprisonments by the communist government of then-Czechoslovakia, the longest of which lasted from 1979 to 1983—a period he documented in letters to his wife that were later published as *Letters to Olga*.

Midnight Express: A 1978 drama film, adapted from the Billy Hayes memoir of the same name, about an American student sent to a Turkish prison for trying to smuggle hashish out of the country. The film was directed by Alan Parker and stars Brad Davis as Hayes.

Sixteen Candles: A 1984 John Hughes film starring Molly Ringwald as a suburban teen whose family forgets her sixteenth birthday.

98 Degrees: Boy band that rose to fame in the late 1990s, consisting of brothers Nick and Drew Lachey, Jeff Timmons, and Justin Jeffre. Their hits include "Give Me Just One Night (Una Noche)," "Because of You," "The Hardest Thing," and "Thank God I Found You."

Tom Waits: Singer-songwriter who first rose to fame during the 1970s folk music movement before moving into a variety of genres and establishing himself as a versatile and influential musician.

Blanche: Lane's brief reference to "Blanche" when Rory describes Dean as her gentleman caller has sparked some online fan debate. Most suggest it is a reference to the character Blanche Dubois, an aging Southern belle in the Tennessee Williams play *A Streetcar Named Desire*, who lives in fear of her fading beauty. Others suggest it could refer to another beloved fictional Southern belle, Blanche Devereaux from TV's *The Golden Girls*.

"Babies come from the stork": Stemming from European folklore, and popularized in the 1839 Hans Christian Andersen story "The Storks," the white birds were believed to be responsible for bringing babies to new parents.

V.I.P.: Action-comedy television series that aired in syndication from 1998 to 2002, starring Pamela Anderson as the glamorous figurehead of a bodyguard agency.

Oscar Levant (1906–1972): Actor, comedian, concert pianist, and composer who came to be known for his quick-witted appearances as a radio game show and TV talk show panelist.

Regis Philbin (1931–2020): TV talk show and game show host, known for hosting *Live! with Regis and Kathie Lee* beginning in 1988, which became *Live! with Regis and Kelly* in 2001 until his departure in 2011. He also hosted the original American version of *Who Wants to Be a Millionaire*.

Susan Faludi: Feminist journalist and author whose work won her the Pulitzer Prize for Explanatory Journalism in 1991.

Squeaky Fromme: Lynette Alice "Squeaky" Fromme was a member of the Manson family cult led by Charles Manson, who attempted to assassinate President Gerald Ford in 1975 and was sentenced to life in prison. She was paroled in 2009.

Lambada, Moshing: These are both styles of dancing. The lambada is a partner dance, while moshing refers to an aggressive, frenzied situation where people push and slam into one another in a mosh pit at the front of a concert stage.

Ann Taylor: Brand of women's clothing stores founded by Richard Liebeskind in 1954.

Emily Post (1872–1960): Author and socialite known for writing about etiquette.

***The Outsiders,* Ponyboy**: *The Outsiders* is the 1983 film adaptation of the classic S. E. Hinton 1967 coming-of-age novel of the same name, about two rival gangs divided by socioeconomic status. Ponyboy Curtis is the protagonist and member of one of the gangs. The film was directed by Francis Ford Coppola and stars an impressive roster of then up-and-coming actors, including Rob Lowe, Emilio Estevez, Matt Dillon, Tom Cruise, Patrick Swayze, and C. Thomas Howell as Ponyboy.

Baccarat: French manufacturer of fine crystal.

"Of the manor born": A phrase referring to someone from an upper class family, derived from the line "to the manor born" in William Shakespeare's *Hamlet*.

Barbara Stanwyck, Fred MacMurray: Stanwyck (1907–1990) was a popular actress known for such works as *Ball of Fire* and *The Thorn Birds*. MacMurray (1908–1991) was an actor who appeared in more than a hundred films, his most notable being 1944's *Double Indemnity*, the film referred to in this scene. It stars MacMurray as an insurance salesman who plots with Stanwyck's character to kill her husband and claim a life insurance policy payout.

Dristan: Brand of nasal decongestant.

Dorothy Parker (1893–1967): Poet, writer, and founding member of the Algonquin Round Table, a group of New York City writers who would gather at the Algonquin Hotel. Dean reads an excerpt of the poem *Coda*.

EPISODE 1.10: FORGIVENESS AND STUFF

Written by John Stephens. Directed by Bethany Rooney. Aired December 21, 2000. Lorelai struggles to deal with her father's hospitalization.

"It's Beginning to Look a Lot Like Christmas": Classic holiday song written in 1951 by Meredith Wilson, covered countless times over the years. Notable versions have been sung by Bing Crosby, Perry Como, and Michael Bublé.

The Miracle Worker: Media franchise based on the autobiography of Helen Keller, *The Story of My Life*. It has been adapted for stage and screen, perhaps most notably in the 1962 film version starring Anne Bancroft as Anne

Sullivan, Helen Keller's teacher who struggles to communicate with the deaf, blind, and mute Keller.

***The Metamorphosis*, Franz Kafka**: Kafka (1883–1924) was an Austrian-Czech writer and major literary figure whose works include *The Metamorphosis*, a 1915 novella about a salesman who wakes one morning to discover he's transformed into a giant insect.

Little Bo Peep: The titular character in a children's nursery rhyme dating back to the early 1800s, about a little girl who has lost her sheep.

Tae Bo: Fitness routine developed in the 1970s by Billy Banks, and popularized in the 1990s, which uses martial arts techniques in its workouts.

Razor Scooter: Compact, folding scooter that first hit the market in 2000.

Eric Rudolph: Referred to by Lorelai as the "crazy bomber guy," Rudolph, aka The Olympic Park Bomber, is a domestic terrorist who carried out a series of bombings throughout the American South between 1996 and 1998, including the Centennial Olympic Park bombing at the 1996 Summer Olympics in Atlanta. He spent years as a fugitive hiding in the Appalachian wilderness before being arrested in North Carolina in 2003. He is serving four consecutive life sentences.

Grey Poupon: Brand of Dijon mustard originating in Dijon, France, in 1866. It gained popularity in the 1980s thanks to a memorable ad campaign that positioned it as a high-end, refined product. In the ads, a Rolls-Royce pulls up to another Rolls-Royce, and a person in one car asks the other, "Pardon me, do you have any Grey Poupon?"

Santa Claus: The legendary holiday figure said to bring presents to children on Christmas Eve. The popular version of the character dates back to the folklore surrounding fourth-century bishop Saint Nicholas, the patron saint of children.

Barbie: Fashion doll created by Ruth Handler that first appeared in 1959. The brand has expanded over the years into a multimedia empire with toys, games, and an Academy Award–winning 2023 live-action film.

Barron's: Weekly newspaper covering US financial information, first published in 1921.

Cosmo Woman: *Cosmo* is short for *Cosmopolitan*, a fashion and entertainment magazine targeting women, first published in 1886. Helen Gurley Brown became editor of the magazine in 1965. An outspoken advocate for women's sexual freedom, under Brown's guidance the magazine began to champion glamorous, fashion-focused women who came to be called "Cosmo Girls."

The Scarecrow: A character in the classic L. Frank Baum children's book *The Wonderful Wizard of Oz*, which was adapted into a beloved 1939 musical film, *The Wizard of Oz* (not to mention countless other adaptations). In the film, Dorothy, the young girl transported to the magical land of Oz, is following the Yellow Brick Road in search of Oz's Emerald City when she becomes lost and meets the Scarecrow, who offers some (albeit confused) directions.

Pez: Brand of candy introduced in 1927 that comes in a manually operated dispenser, often designed to depict the heads of popular cartoon and comic book characters.

Jimmy Hoffa: Labor union leader and president of the International Brotherhood of Teamsters who had alleged ties to organized crime and disappeared under mysterious circumstances in 1975. He was never found and declared dead in 1983.

Financial Times: British newspaper focusing on business and economic affairs, first published in 1888.

Charo: Spanish-born entertainer who rose to fame in the 1960s. She's known for her high energy, heavy accent, and the catchphrase "cuchi-cuchi!"

EPISODE 1.11: PARIS IS BURNING

Written by Joan Binder Weiss. Directed by David Petrarca. Aired January 11, 2001.
Paris reveals a shocking secret after Chilton's Parent-Teacher night.

Damien: Fictional antagonist of *The Omen* franchise, considered to be the Antichrist and son of the Devil.

This Old House: Home improvement television series airing on PBS. It debuted in 1979 and was originally hosted by Bob Vila.

Marcel Proust (1871–1922): French writer known for À la recherche du temps perdu (*In Search of Lost Time* or *Remembrance of Things Past*), a novel in seven volumes.

Michael Crichton (1942–2008): Science-fiction writer and filmmaker known for such works as *Jurassic Park* and *The Andromeda Strain*.

Swann's Way: One of the seven-volume Marcel Proust novels mentioned above.

"There's a certain Slant of light": Emily Dickinson poem of which Max recites the first verse.

Marilyn Monroe, Arthur Miller: Monroe (1926–1962) was an actress, model, and popular sex symbol of the 1950s, known for such films as *Gentlemen Prefer Blondes*, *Some Like It Hot*, and *The Seven Year Itch*. Miller (1915–2005) was a renowned playwright and screenwriter known for such works as *Death of a Salesman* and *The Crucible*. In 1956, Miller left his first wife to wed Monroe. They divorced in 1961. Monroe died the following year from a barbiturate overdose.

Psycho: Classic 1960 Alfred Hitchcock horror film starring Anthony Perkins as Norman Bates, the proprietor of the mysterious Bates Motel.

Nancy Kerrigan, Tonya Harding: Kerrigan and Harding were US figure skaters preparing to compete in the 1994 Winter Olympics when Kerrigan was attacked by a man wielding a police baton who struck her in the knee. The man was hired by the ex-husband of Harding, who proclaimed her innocence and non-involvement with the incident. The pair went on to compete in the Olympics, with Kerrigan earning a Silver Medal. During a free skate event, Harding noticed a problem with a loose lace and approached the judges, tearfully requesting a reskate, which she was granted. Following the Kerrigan incident, Harding was banned for life from the US Figure Skating Association.

"Living La Vida Loca," "Shake Your Bon-Bon," Ricky Martin: Martin is Puerto Rican singer, songwriter, and actor who began his career at age twelve as a member of the band Menudo. He reemerged in the 1990s thanks to a string of dance-pop hits, including "Living La Vida Loca" and "Shake Your Bon-Bon," from his 1999 self-titled album. Sookie's line "She's into superstition . . ." comes from "Living La Vida Loca."

Rick James (1948–2004): Singer-songwriter known for hits like "Super Freak" and "Give It to Me Baby." James was convicted in 1993 of two instances involving kidnapping and assaulting two different women while under the influence of cocaine. He served a three-year prison sentence.

Hugh Grant: English actor known for such films as *Sense and Sensibility*, *Four Weddings and a Funeral*, *Bridget Jones's Diary*, and *About a Boy*. He was arrested in 1995 for receiving oral sex in a public place from a Hollywood sex worker.

"Here's Johnny": While popularized as the host's intro on *The Tonight Show Starring Johnny Carson*, which aired from 1962 to 1992, Lorelai is referring here to the version from the 1980 horror film *The Shining*, in which Jack Nicholson's axe-wielding character, the deranged Jack Torrance, utters a frightening version of the phrase after chopping down a door while trying to kill his wife.

Heathers: A 1988 film written by Daniel Waters, directed by Michael Lehmann, and starring Winona Ryder, Christian Slater, and Shannen Doherty. It centers around a quartet of teenage girls, three of whom are named Heather.

Oscar and Felix: The primary characters in *The Odd Couple*, which began as a Neil Simon play about mismatched roommates—the neat and uptight Felix and the messy and lighthearted Oscar. The play has been adapted multiple times, including into a popular 1968 film and a 1970–1975 television sitcom.

Walt Whitman (1819–1892): Renowned poet and essayist whose works include the collection *Leaves of Grass*.

Homer: Ancient Greek poet who wrote the *Iliad* and the *Odyssey*.

Dante (1265–1321): Italian poet known for writing the epic poem *The Divine Comedy*.

Edna O'Brien (1930–2024): Irish novelist whose works included *The Country Girls* and *Down By the River*.

NC-17: A film rating from the Motion Picture Association meaning that a film's content is for adults only, not suitable for anyone under the age of 17.

EPISODE 1.12: DOUBLE DATE

Written by Amy Sherman-Palladino. Directed by Lev L. Spiro. Aired January 18, 2001.

Lorelai begrudgingly accompanies Sookie and Jackson on a double date with Jackson's cousin. Rory sets Lane up with Dean's friend.

Blondie: Rock/new wave band formed in the 1970s by singer Debbie Harry and guitarist Chris Stein. Their many hits include "One Way or Another," "Rapture," "Call Me," and "Heart of Glass."

Kraftwerk: German electronic band formed in the 1970s by Ralf Hütter and Florian Schneider.

Young Marble Giants: A 1970s Welsh post-punk band.

Yoko Ono: Japanese multimedia artist, singer, and activist who became well known when she married John Lennon of the Beatles in 1969.

The Beatles: English rock band formed in the 1960s, consisting of John Lennon, Paul McCartney, George Harrison, and Ringo Starr. Often considered the most influential band in history, they are the best-selling music act of all time.

Julian Lennon, Sean Lennon: The sons of musician John Lennon. Julian's mother is John's first wife, Cynthia. He is a musician and photographer. Sean, a musician, is the son of John and Yoko Ono.

Claudine Longet: French singer/performer popular during the 1960s and 1970s. In 1976, she was arrested and charged with fatally shooting her boyfriend, Olympic skier Vladimir "Spider" Sabich. While claiming it was accidental, she was convicted of negligent homicide, charged a small fine, and spent thirty days in jail.

Grandaddy: California indie rock band formed in 1992.

Thomas Jefferson (1743–1826): American statesman and Founding Father who served as the third president of the United States from 1801 to 1809.

Sylvia Plath (1932–1963): Prominent poet and author who was clinically depressed for much of her life and was treated with early versions of electroconvulsive therapy. She died by suicide in 1963. Her enduring works include *The Colossus and Other Poems* and the semi-autobiographical novel *The Bell Jar*. She was posthumously awarded the Pulitzer Prize in Poetry in 1982.

Beck: Singer-songwriter who rose to fame in the 1990s with an experimental style and hits like "Loser."

Foo Fighters, "Everlong": Foo Fighters are a rock band formed in Seattle, Washington, in 1994, originally as a one-man project by Nirvana drummer Dave Grohl. "Everlong" was the second single from their album *The Colour and the Shape*, released in 1997.

Velvet Underground, Nico: The Velvet Underground was a rock band formed in New York City in the 1960s. Nico was the stage name of German singer and actress Christa Päffgen (1938–1988). The band and Nico collaborated on Velvet Underground's debut album, *The Velvet Underground & Nico*, released in 1967. Despite a poor performance and mixed reviews upon release, it has come to be considered one of the greatest albums of all time.

Fugazi: Post-hardcore punk band formed in Washington, DC, in 1986.

Cher, *Mask*: Cher is an iconic singer and actress who first rose to fame in the 1960s alongside then-husband Sonny Bono with hits like "I Got You Babe" and a popular comedy-variety television series. As a solo artist, her many hits include "If I Could Turn Back Time" and "Believe." She is also an Academy Award–winning actress known for such films as *Moonstruck* and 1985's *Mask*, a biographical drama film in which she played the mother of Rocky Dennis, a boy who had craniodiaphyseal dysplasia, a condition causing disfiguring cranial enlargements.

Beethoven: A 1992 family comedy film directed by Brian Levant and written by John Hughes and Amy Holden Jones about a large St. Bernard, named after the famed German composer, who finds a home with a suburban family. A box-office success, the film spawned several sequels and an animated series.

Richard Simmons (1948–2024): Energetic and flamboyant fitness instructor and television personality who rose to fame with his *Sweatin' to the Oldies* line of workout videos.

Elijah: Biblical prophet who was ordered by God to hide near a brook, where he was continuously fed by ravens and, later, by a widow who has very little food. Elijah informs her that God will not allow the supply of food to run out and, miraculously, it doesn't.

Robert Duvall, *The Great Santini*: Duvall is an Academy Award–winning actor considered by many to be one of the greatest of all time. He's known for such films as *Apocalypse Now*, *To Kill a Mockingbird*, and *The Godfather*. *The Great Santini* is a 1979 drama film, based on the 1976 Pat Conroy novel of the same name, in which Duvall plays a hard-nosed Marine fighter pilot who was a stern disciplinarian as a father.

Rapunzel: Character in an oft-adapted fairy tale about a tower-confined princess with long, flowing hair, who lets it down from the tower window so her suitor can use it to climb up.

Romeo and Juliet: William Shakespeare tragedy about two teenagers from feuding families who fall in love with one another. In the end of the play, mistakenly believing Juliet to be dead, Romeo dies by drinking poison. Juliet, discovering this, dies by stabbing herself.

EPISODE 1.13: CONCERT INTERRUPTUS

Written by Elaine Arata. Directed by Bruce Seth Green. Aired February 15, 2001. Lorelai and Sookie take Rory, Paris, Madeline, and Louise to a Bangles concert.

Grinch: Character created by children's author Dr. Seuss, best known as the titular character in the 1957 book *How the Grinch Stole Christmas.* The Grinch is a green, furry humanoid character who lives on a cliff overlooking the Christmas-loving town of Whoville. A holiday hater, the Grinch conspires to destroy Christmas for the town. It has been adapted multiple times, most notably as voiced by Boris Karloff in an animated 1966 television special and portrayed by Jim Carrey in a 2000 live-action feature film.

Charles I (1600–1649): King of England, Scotland, and Ireland from 1625 until his execution in 1649. An unpopular king, his ruling style and growing unpopularity ultimately led to the English Civil War, marked by years of bloody fighting between the king's supporters and Oliver Cromwell's Parliamentarians. Charles was eventually captured and put on trial for treason against England by using his power to pursue personal interest instead of the greater good. He was declared guilty and executed by beheading.

Harvey Fierstein: Gravelly voiced actor and playwright known for his work in theater and film. His notable works include *Torch Song Trilogy*, *La Cage aux Folles*, and *Hairspray* on the stage, as well as films such as *Mrs. Doubtfire.*

"Very big eyes for you, Grandma": A paraphrasing of the line "Grandma, what big eyes you have," from the fairy tale *Little Red Riding Hood.* The titular Red thinks she is addressing her grandmother, who has actually been eaten by the Big Bad Wolf, who then dons her wardrobe in an effort to trick, and ultimately kill and consume, Red.

"Double, double, toil and trouble," "By the pricking of my thumbs, something wicked this way comes": Both quotes are famous lines from William Shakespeare's *Macbeth*, as said by three witches.

Queen Anne Furniture: Style of decorative furniture developed in the time of Queen Anne, ruler of England, Scotland, and Ireland from 1702 to 1714.

Annie Oakley (1860–1926): American folk heroine and sharpshooter who was part of Buffalo Bill's Wild West show. Her story was adapted into the stage musical *Annie Get Your Gun*.

Copacabana: New York City nightclub that first opened its doors in 1940. It is also the basis for the 1978 Barry Manilow hit "Copacabana."

Pucci: Italian clothing brand created by Emilio Pucci in 1947.

Joanie Loves Chachi: Sitcom that ran on ABC from 1982 to 1983, starring Erin Moran and Scott Baio as the titular characters, which were spun off from the long-running series *Happy Days*.

Paul Bunyan: Folklore hero depicted as a giant lumberjack, often accompanied by his pet, Babe the Blue Ox.

Carrie: Rory's "pig's blood at prom" line is a reference to the 1974 horror novel *Carrie* by Stephen King, in which the titular character, a bullied high school student whose classmates dump a bucket of pig's blood on her at the prom, seeks revenge using her telekinetic powers. It has been adapted into multiple films and a Broadway play, including an Academy Award–nominated 1976 film starring Sissy Spacek in the title role.

Yogi Bear: Paris's reference to picnic baskets in Jellystone Park is a nod to Yogi Bear, an anthropomorphic, tie-wearing bear from a series of Hanna-Barbera cartoons. The character debuted in the late 1950s and was depicted as a bit of a schemer, always attempting to steal the picnic baskets of campers in the fictional Jellystone Park—a play on the real Yellowstone National Park.

Everest: While attempts to climb Mount Everest, the highest mountain peak on Earth, have been the subject of many screen adaptations, including a star-studded 2015 film, given the timing of this episode Sookie is likely referring to the successful 1998 documentary *Everest*, produced by MacGillivray Freeman Films and narrated by Liam Neeson.

Catherine Zeta-Jones: Welsh actress known for such films as *Chicago*, *Intolerable Cruelty*, and *Traffic*. She married actor Michael Douglas, twenty-five years her senior, in 2000.

Michelle Pfieffer: Actress known for such films as *Batman Returns*, *Scarface*, *Dangerous Liaisons*, and *The Fabulous Baker Boys*.

Elle McPherson: Australian model, actress, and TV host known for her record five cover appearances on the *Sports Illustrated Swimsuit Issue*.

Kodak moment: Kodak is a brand that produces a variety of products relating to film photography. Its popular ad tagline, "Kodak moment," which debuted in the 1980s, referred to capturing life's important moments on Kodak film.

Episode 1.14: That Damn Donna Reed

Written by Daniel Palladino and Amy Sherman-Palladino. Directed by Michael Katleman. Aired February 22, 2001.
Rory is bothered by Dean's old-fashioned views of husband and wife roles.

The Donna Reed Show: Family sitcom starring Donna Reed as a middle-class housewife. It aired on ABC from 1958 to 1966. Reed played Donna Stone, and Carl Betz co-starred as her husband, Alex.

"Sister Suffragette": A protest song from the 1964 Disney film *Mary Poppins*. A suffragette refers to a member of an activist women's organization who fought for women's right to vote in the early twentieth century.

"Ya Got Trouble": A song by Meredith Wilson from the 1957 Broadway musical *The Music Man*, as well as its 1962 film version, where the phrase "right here in River City" follows the title in the lyrics.

Lewis Carroll (1832–1898): An English author noted for his wordplay, whose best known works are *Alice's Adventures in Wonderland* and its sequel, *Through the Looking-Glass*.

Catherine the Great (1729–1796): The reigning empress of Russia from 1762 until 1796, having come to power after overthrowing her husband, Peter III.

Sex and the City: Babette's "four girls talking dirty" line refers to this HBO series that starred Sarah Jessica Parker, Kim Cattrall, Cynthia Nixon, and Kristin Davis as four women living and loving in Manhattan. The show ran from 1998 to 2004 and spawned feature films, a prequel series, and a reboot series.

Paul and Linda McCartney: Paul McCartney is an English musician who rose to fame as a member of the Beatles before embarking on a successful solo career. Linda (1941–1998) was a photographer, musician, author, and activist. She was married to Paul from 1969 until her death.

"Sunday Best": A 2001 song by Grant Lee Phillips.

Stella and Stanley Kowalski: Characters in the Tennessee Williams play *A Streetcar Named Desire*.

Martha Stewart: Businesswoman and television personality who founded the home and lifestyle brand Martha Stewart Living Omnimedia. Her magazine, *Martha Stewart Living*, began in 1990, and she hosted a TV show by the same name from 1993 to 2004, as well as *The Martha Stewart Show* from 2005 to 2012. In 2004, she was convicted of insider trading and spent five months in federal prison.

Civil War: The American Civil War was fought from 1861 to 1865 between the Union (North) and Confederacy (South).

Siouxsie and the Banshees: Influential British rock band formed in 1976 by singer Siouxsie Sioux and guitarist Steven Severin. They disbanded in 1996.

Bon Jovi: Rock band led by singer Jon Bon Jovi that rose to fame in the 1980s with hits like "Livin' on a Prayer" and "You Give Love a Bad Name."

Duran Duran: English pop band formed in the 1970s whose hits include "Hungry Like the Wolf" and "Rio."

The Wallflowers: Rock band fronted by Jakob Dylan, son of Bob Dylan, that rose to fame in the 1990s with hits like "One Headlight" and "6th Avenue Heartache."

Bush: British rock band formed in 1992. They disbanded in 2002 and reformed in 2010.

Frank Sinatra, *The Capitol Years*: Sinatra (1915–1998) was a highly influential and successful singer and actor with nicknames like "Chairman of the Board" and "Ol' Blue Eyes." He recorded with Capitol Records from 1953 to 1961. Many of those recordings were compiled into a multi-disc collection titled *The Capitol Years*, which was released in 1990.

William Shatner, "Mr. Tambourine Man," "Lucy in the Sky with Diamonds": Shatner is an actor and entertainer whose best-known role was playing Captain James T. Kirk on the original *Star Trek* series, but he has also occasionally ventured into recording. His debut album, *The Transformed Man*, was released in 1968. It featured Shatner reciting a monologue from classical literature, followed by spoken-word interpretations of popular songs, including the two mentioned by Rory and Lane. "Mr. Tambourine Man" was written by Bob Dylan and appeared on his 1965 album *Bringing It All Back Home*. "Lucy in the Sky with Diamonds" was written by John

Lennon and Paul McCartney and appeared on the Beatles' 1967 album *Sgt. Pepper's Lonely Hearts Club Band*.

"Stella!": Lorelai screaming "Stella!" is a take on a climactic scene in *A Streetcar Named Desire* (see above), in which Stanley screams for Stella to come back to him.

Marcel Marceau (1923–2007): French mime known for his character Bip the Clown. He referred to mime as the art of silence.

Lucy Ricardo: The title character in the classic sitcom *I Love Lucy*, played by Lucille Ball. In 1957's "Lucy Raises Chickens" episode, Lucy at one point mimics a mother chicken in an effort to get the baby chicks she's raising to bond with her.

InStyle: A monthly women's fashion magazine founded in 1994.

Glamour: Women's magazine founded in 1939. In 2019, it became a digital-only magazine.

Cosmo: Short for *Cosmopolitan*, a quarterly fashion and entertainment magazine targeting women, first published in 1886.

Wild Kingdom, **Marlin Perkins**: *Mutual of Omaha's Wild Kingdom* is a documentary television series that originally aired from 1963 to 1988, with various revivals and iterations airing in the years since. Perkins (1905–1986) was a zoologist who hosted the series from its debut until 1985, when he retired for health reasons.

A Streetcar Named Desire, **Vivien Leigh, Jessica Tandy**: Leigh and Tandy are actresses who played the role of Stella in *A Streetcar Named Desire* (see above). Leigh (1913–1967) played the role in the 1951 film version and is perhaps best known for playing Scarlett O'Hara in the 1939 film version of Margaret Mitchell's *Gone With the Wind*. Tandy (1909–1994) originated the role in the 1948 Broadway production, for which she won a Tony. She appeared in such films as *Cocoon*, *Fried Green Tomatoes*, and won an Academy Award for *Driving Miss Daisy*.

Michael Douglas: Actor and producer known for such films as *Wall Street*, *Fatal Attraction*, and *Romancing the Stone*. Linked to many women over the years, in the early 1990s Douglas was rumored to have a sex addiction, which he denied.

Joan and Melissa Rivers: Joan Rivers (1933–2014) was a famous acerbic comedian, actress, and television host. Her daughter, Melissa, is also an actress and host. The pair gained popularity beginning in the 1990s for their witty red carpet celebrity interviews.

Harry Houdini (1874–1926): Popular escape artist and illusionist known for his harrowing escape acts.

Miguel de Cervantes (1547–1616): Spanish writer best known for the novel *Don Quixote.*

"Beautiful Dreamers": A 2001 song by Grant Lee Phillips.

EPISODE 1.15: CHRISTOPHER RETURNS
Written by Daniel Palladino. Directed by Michael Katleman. Aired March 1, 2001.
The return of Rory's father shakes things up at the Gilmore household.

Rincon: Located between Ventura and Santa Barbara counties in southern California, Rincon Point, known as "Queen of the Coast," is one of the country's prime surfing destinations.

Pinky Tuscadero: Carol "Pinky" Tuscadero is the fictional former girlfriend of Fonzie on the sitcom *Happy Days.* She was played by actress Roz Kelly.

Alfalfa: Fictional character from the *Our Gang/Little Rascals* short comedy films produced from the 1920s to the 1940s and in various incarnations since, including a popular 1994 film. The role was notably played by Carl Switzer.

Bonnie Bell Lip Smackers: Bonnie Bell is a cosmetic company aimed at teenagers that was founded in 1927. In the 1970s, they expanded into a line of lip balms called Lip Smackers, which became the company's signature product.

George Clooney: Actor known for the TV series *ER* and films such as *Syriana, The Perfect Storm,* and *O Brother, Where Art Thou?*

Brad Pitt: Actor known for such films as *Troy, Mr. & Mrs. Smith,* and *Fight Club.*

Billy Crudup: Actor known for such works as *Almost Famous, Big Fish,* and *The Morning Show.*

Oxford English Dictionary: Principal historic dictionary of the English language first published in 1884.

Monolith, *2001: A Space Odyssey*: A monolith is a mysterious black slab discovered throughout the Solar System in Arthur C. Clarke's *Space Odyssey* series of science-fiction novels and films. *2001: A Space Odyssey* is the 1968 epic film produced and directed by Stanley Kubrick inspired by Clarke's works. It follows a group of scientists and astronauts who travel to Jupiter to investigate a monolith.

"Smoke on the Water": Signature song of the English rock band Deep Purple, from their 1972 album *Machine Head*. Its lyrics are based on an actual fire at the Montreux Casino in Switzerland.

"Jumpin' Jack Flash": Song by the English rock band The Rolling Stones, released as a single in 1968.

Chuck Berry, "My Ding-a-Ling": Berry (1926–2017) was a pioneering rock and roll singer and musician known for such songs as "Roll Over Beethoven" and "Johnny B. Goode." "My Ding-a-Ling" is a novelty song written and originally recorded by Dave Bartholomew, but Berry's rendition was released in 1972 and became his only number-one single on the Billboard Hot 100 charts.

Lucy, Schroeder, "Suppertime," *You're a Good Man Charlie Brown*: Lucy and Schroeder are characters from the enduring comic strip *Peanuts*, created by Charles M. Schulz. Lucy was often depicted leaning against the small piano played by Schroeder. *You're a Good Man, Charlie Brown* is a 1967 musical based on the *Peanuts* characters, and "Suppertime" is a song from the play.

George W. Bush: Eldest son of President George H. W. Bush, George W. Bush served as president of the United States from 2001 to 2009.

Armageddon: The location for the battle at the end of time from the Bible's Book of Revelations. It is often interpreted less as an actual place and more as a symbolic end-of-time battle between good and evil.

Citizen Kane: Classic 1941 drama film directed and produced by and starring Orson Welles about the life and legacy of fictional media baron Charles Foster Kane.

Mazatlán: Tourist destination city in Mexico that has been a popular spring break spot for young people, Lorelai's inference in this scene being that Christopher's tattoo was possibly a drunken spring break type of decision.

Whoville: The fictional town from Dr. Seuss's *How the Grinch Stole Christmas* (see earlier entry).

Chernobyl, Hindenburg: Two well-known disasters. The Chernobyl disaster was the 1986 explosion at the Chernobyl Nuclear Power Plant in the Ukraine. It is the worst nuclear disaster in history. The Hindenburg disaster happened in New Jersey in 1937. The Hindenburg was a German commercial passenger-carrying airship. Filled with hydrogen, it caught fire while trying to dock and resulted in multiple fatalities. Radio journalist Herbert Morrison's eyewitness newsreel recording of the crash is the source of the phrase "Oh, the humanity!"

Fred Mertz, Golden Gloves: Fred Mertz was the fictional neighbor and landlord on the 1950s sitcom *I Love Lucy*. The character was said to have been a former boxer and, in the episode "Changing the Boys' Wardrobe," he was seen wearing a sweatshirt that read Golden Gloves 1909. The Golden Gloves was an amateur boxing championship.

I Love Lucy: While several references to this classic 1950s sitcom have already been made, this is the first mention of it by name. It was a pioneer in the sitcom genre, starring Lucille Ball and Desi Arnaz, a real-life husband and wife who played Lucy and Ricky Ricardo, a middle-class couple living in New York City. It aired on CBS from 1951 to 1957.

Charles Manson (1934–2017): Cult leader who led the infamous Manson Family in the 1960s and early 1970s. In 1971, he was convicted of first-degree murder and conspiracy to commit murder after a group of cult members committed a series of at least nine murders.

The Offspring: Punk rock band formed in 1984 that gained popularity in the 1990s with hits like "Come Out and Play" and "Pretty Fly (for a White Guy)."

Metallica: Heavy metal band formed in 1981. Among their biggest records are 1986's *Master of Puppets* and 1988's *. . . And Justice for All*.

Jose Cuervo: Best-selling brand of tequila. Its roots date back to the 1750s, when Don José Antonio de Cuervo established a family farm in Mexico where they grew the blue agave plant, which is fermented and distilled to create tequila.

Fiddler on the Roof: A 1964 musical with music by Jerry Bock, lyrics by Sheldon Harnick, and book by Joseph Stein, about a Russian milkman who attempts to maintain his Jewish cultural traditions despite outside influences. Part of the play concerns the potential marriages of his daughters, in a village where mates are often paired up by a matchmaker.

Tony Randall (1920–2004): Actor best known for playing Felix Unger on the 1970–1975 sitcom *The Odd Couple*. At the age of seventy-five, he married a twenty-five-year-old woman and fathered two children.

Episode 1.16: Star-Crossed Lovers and Other Strangers
Teleplay by John Stephens and Linda Loiselle Guzik. Story by Joan Binder Weiss. Directed by Lesli Linka Glatter. Aired March 8, 2001.
Dean's preparations for his and Rory's three-month anniversary don't go as planned. Luke's old girlfriend, Rachel, returns to Stars Hollow.

Tito Puente (1923–2000): Musician and bandleader known for mambo and Latin jazz music.

"Heavenly": A 2000 song by Grant Lee Phillips.

"Bam!": Catchphrase of celebrity chef and TV personality Emeril Lagasse, who hosted the popular Food Network shows *Essence of Emeril* and *Emeril Live* in the mid-1990s and early 2000s. He would shout "bam!" when adding something spicy to the dish he was preparing.

Iron Chef: Japanese cooking competition show that aired originally in the 1990s and has led to multiple spinoff series.

"Cleopatra, Queen of Denial": Cleopatra (70/69 BC–30 BC) was queen and last active ruler of Egypt from 51 to 30 BC. This phrase is a spin on "Cleopatra, Queen of the Nile," a common epithet for Cleopatra. It was also the name of a 1993 country music song by artist Pam Tillis, which rose to number 11 on the Billboard Hot Country Singles chart.

Cabbage Patch: A dance in which a person moves their clenched fists in front of their body in a horizontal, circular motion.

"Hell hath no fury": "Hell hath no fury like a woman scorned" is a spin on a line that originated in the play *The Mourning Bride* by English playwright William Congreve.

Belle Watling: Fictional sex worker and brothel madam in Margaret Mitchell's novel *Gone With the Wind*. The character was portrayed by Ona Munson in the 1939 film version.

Elizabeth Barrett Browning (1806–1861): Popular English Victorian poet.

Mr. Coffee: The reference to "Mrs. Coffee" is a play on this enduring brand of coffee machines introduced in 1970.

Johnny Depp: Actor who rose to fame in the 1980s, known for such works as *Edward Scissorhands*, *Ed Wood*, and the *Pirates of the Caribbean* film series.

Lady and the Tramp: A 1955 Disney animated film about a pampered Cocker Spaniel who falls for a homeless street mutt. In a famous scene, the two share a plate of spaghetti and end up slurping different ends of the same long noodle until their mouths unexpectedly meet.

Kathy Bates, *Misery*: Bates is a beloved actress known for such works as *Fried Green Tomatoes*, *Delores Claiborne*, *Matlock*, and her Academy Award–winning role in 1990's *Misery*. It is an adaptation of the 1987 Stephen King novel of the same name. Bates plays Annie Wilkes, an obsessed fan of an author who kidnaps and torments the man.

Tuesdays with Morrie: The reference to Morrie points to the 1997 memoir by author Mitch Albom titled *Tuesdays with Morrie: An Old Man, A Young Man and Life's Greatest Lesson*. It details Albom's visits with his former sociology professor, Morrie Schwartz, who was dying from amyotrophic lateral sclerosis. It was adapted into a 1999 TV movie starring Jack Lemmon and Hank Azaria.

Glenfiddich: Single malt Scotch whiskey distillery in Moray, Scotland, founded in 1886.

Ken: A fashion doll created in 1961 as the male counterpart to Barbie.

Whac-A-Mole: An arcade game created in 1975 in which plastic moles randomly appear from holes in a waist-high cabinet. Players earn points by whacking each mole with a soft mallet.

Bambi: A 1942 animated Disney film based loosely on the 1926 Felix Salten novel *Bambi, A Life in the Woods*. It concerns the life and love of a young white-tailed deer.

Daughters of the American Revolution: Founded in 1890 and abbreviated as DAR, it is a lineage-based organization for women who are directly descended from patriots of the American Revolutionary War.

The New Yorker: Magazine first published in 1925, featuring news, commentary, criticism, literature, cartoons, poetry, and more.

Kreskin (1935–2024): Famous mentalist who gained popularity in the 1970s. From 1972 to 1975, he hosted *The Amazing World of Kreskin* and appeared on a variety of late-night talk shows.

Christine: A 1983 horror film adapted from the Stephen King novel of the same name about a car possessed by supernatural forces.

Beirut: The capital city of Lebanon. Rory is referring to the city in the context of the Lebanese Civil War, which took place from 1975 to 1990.

"Mockingbirds": A song by Grant Lee Phillips's band Grant Lee Buffalo.

Episode 1.17: The Breakup, Part II
Written by Amy Sherman-Palladino. Directed by Nick Marck. Aired March 15, 2001.
Rebounding from her fight with Dean, Rory makes an unexpected connection at a party. Lorelai reconnects with Max.

Nancy Drew: Fictional teenage sleuth created by publisher Edward Stratemeyer, who has appeared in a variety of books, movies, and TV shows beginning in 1930. She first appeared in the *Nancy Drew Mystery Stories* series of books, which were ghostwritten by a variety of authors.

"Sleep with the fishes": A phrase popularized in 1972's *The Godfather* film, meaning to be dead and disposed of in a body of water.

Who's Afraid of Virginia Woolf?: A 1962 play by Edward Albee about the marriage of a middle-aged couple named George and Martha and younger couple Nick and Honey. The title is a play on the song "Who's Afraid of the Big Bad Wolf?" from Disney's *Three Little Pigs*, inserting the name of English author Virginia Woolf, author of such classics as *Mrs Dalloway* and *To the Lighthouse*.

Love Story: A 1970 drama film based on the Erich Segal novel of the same name starring Ali MacGraw and Ryan O'Neal as a couple who fall in love, get married, and later deal with the wife's terminal illness.

The Champ: A 1931 film starring Wallace Beery as a washed-up, alcoholic boxer attempting to get his life together for the sake of his son. Jon Voight starred in a 1979 remake.

An Affair to Remember: A 1957 film starring Cary Grant and Deborah Kerr as a man and woman who begin an affair despite being involved with other people.

Ishtar: A 1987 adventure comedy film starring Warren Beatty and Dustin Hoffman as a duo of talentless songwriters who stumble into a Cold War standoff in Morocco. It was universally panned upon release and became a notorious box-office bomb but has since developed a loyal cult following.

Old Yeller: A 1957 Disney film based on the 1956 Fred Gipson novel of the same name about a Texas boy and his stray dog.

"Jump back," Kevin Bacon, *Footloose*, Chris Penn: With "jump back," Lorelai is quoting a famous line from the 1984 film *Footloose*, in which an urban teen moves to a small town that has outlawed dancing. The line is Bacon's character's response to hearing about the law. In addition to this film, Bacon is known for such works as *A Few Good Men*, *Apollo 13*, and *Mystic River*. Chris Penn (1965–2006) appeared in such films as *Reservoir Dogs* and *Rush Hour* before dying from heart disease at age forty.

G.I. Jane: A 1997 action film starring Demi Moore as a fictional woman who undergoes training similar to that of the US Navy SEALS. Moore famously sported a buzz cut for the role.

Sesame Street: Iconic children's educational program that has aired on PBS since 1969 and introduced the world to such culturally iconic characters as Big Bird, Elmo, and many others.

It's a Small World: A boat ride located at various Disney theme parks, first appearing in 1966. It features over 300 animatronic dolls representing cultures from around the world. The song "It's a Small World (After All)" is from the ride.

The Bell Jar: A 1963 semi-autobiographical novel by Sylvia Plath detailing a woman's descent into mental illness.

Hearst Castle: Historic estate in San Simeon, California, conceived by publishing tycoon William Randolph Hearst and built between 1919 and 1947. Today, it is open to the public as a museum and is designated a National Historic Landmark.

Robin Leach (1941–2018): British-American entertainment reporter who hosted the TV series *Lifestyles of the Rich and Famous* from 1984 to 1995, which profiled the lavish homes of celebrities.

Sodom and Gomorrah: Two cities from the Bible that God destroyed for the wicked behavior of their residents.

"No glove, no love": Slang phrase meaning no sex without a condom.

Madame Curie: Marie Curie (1867–1934) was a Polish physicist and chemist who pioneered work in radioactivity. She was the first woman to win a Nobel Prize and the first person to win twice.

Jennifer Lopez: Singer, actress, and dancer known for roles in films such as *Selena* and *The Wedding Planner* and for dance-pop hits like "If You Had My Love" and "Waiting for Tonight."

Avon Lady: Avon is a multinational cosmetics and skincare company founded in 1886. It is a multi-level marketing company whose door-to-door salespeople are often referred to as "Avon ladies."

Episode 1.18: The Third Lorelai

Written by Amy Sherman-Palladino. Directed by Michael Katleman. Aired March 22, 2001.
Lorelai's paternal grandmother visits from England.

"Dig it man," "peace out, Humphrey": Hippy slang phrases from the 1960s. The reference to Humphrey is most likely a nod to Hubert Humphrey, a Democratic politician who served as vice president of the United States from 1965 to 1969. During his time as a senator, he was lead author of the Civil Rights Act of 1965 and introduced the first initiative to create the Peace Corps.

Kennedy clan: A prominent family in American politics. At least one member of the family has served in federal office since 1947, including John F. Kennedy, who served as US president from 1961 until his assassination in 1963.

Camelot: While Camelot is the castle and court of King Arthur, legendary folk hero and king of Britain, it was also used to describe the presidency of John F. Kennedy. His widow, Jacqueline Kennedy, used the term when saying there would never be another Camelot again after the assassination of the president.

David Mamet: Pulitzer Prize–winning author and playwright known for such works as *Glengarry Glen Ross* and *Speed-the-Plow*.

Grumpy McFarland: This is likely a play on the name Spanky McFarland, a character from the *Our Gang/Little Rascals* short comedy films.

Queen Elizabeth I (1533–1603): Queen of England and Ireland from 1558 until her death in 1603. She was the daughter of Henry VIII and his second wife, Anne Boleyn.

Cabin in the woods: This is a reference to Ted Kaczynski, a US domestic terrorist known as "The Unabomber," who lived as a recluse in a cabin in the woods. In the mid-1990s, he mailed or hand delivered a series of bombs that killed three and injured several others. That year, he also published the essay "Industrial Society and Its Future," which authorities referred to as the Unabomber Manifesto. He was arrested in 1996 and sentenced to life in prison without parole.

Marx Brothers: Successful vaudeville comedy act active from 1905 to 1949, consisting of brothers who went by the stage names Chico, Harpo, Groucho, Gummo, and Zeppo.

Miss Manners: The pen name of columnist and etiquette authority Judith Martin.

Hanibal Lecter: Fictional cannibalistic serial killer created by novelist Thomas Harris, first appearing in the 1981 novel *Red Dragon*, which was adapted into the 1986 film *Manhunter*. The character had a larger role in the 1988 novel *The Silence of the Lambs*. Its 1991 film adaptation is perhaps the character's best-known incarnation. Anthony Hopkins portrayed Lecter and won an Academy Award for the role.

"Louis, I think this is the beginning of a beautiful friendship": A classic line from the 1942 film *Casablanca*, spoken between Humprey Bogart's character, American expatriate Rick Blaine, and Claude Rains's character, the corrupt police captain Louis Renault.

Friedrich Nietzsche, Dawson Leery: Nietzsche (1844–1900) was an influential German scholar, philosopher, and cultural critic. Dawson Leery is the fictional protagonist of the teen drama series *Dawson's Creek*, which ran on The WB network from 1998 to 2003 and starred James Van Der Beek in the title role.

Pink Ladies, Sandy: The Pink Ladies were the fictional girl clique from the stage play and popular 1978 film adaptation *Grease*. Sandy is the female lead, who begins as a sweet, goody-two-shoes type and is transformed with the help of the Pink Ladies into a greaser girl who wins the affections of gang leader Danny.

Tower of London: Rory's phrase "sent to the Tower" is a reference to the Tower of London, formally known as His Majesty's Royal Palace and Fortress of the Tower of London, a historic castle built in 1066. While today a popular tourist destination, for many years it was used as a prison, where the phrase "being sent to the tower" came to mean imprisonment.

Spanish Inquisition: A judicial institution ostensibly established in 1478 to combat heresy in Spain, but served to consolidate power in the monarchy through violent means. Thousands died during the inquisition, which ended in 1834.

"Neither a borrower nor a lender be": A famous line from William Shakespeare's *Hamlet*, in which the character Polonius advises his son on money matters.

"It's the Life": A song by the band Grant Lee Buffalo.

"Money," *Cabaret*, Liza Minelli, Joel Grey: This scene is referring to the 1972 film version of the stage musical *Cabaret*, in which Liza Minelli starred as Sally Bowles and Joel Grey as the master of ceremonies. "Money" is a song from the show. The play and film revolve around the nightlife at the seedy Kit Kat Club, where Minelli's character performs. In addition to this role, Minelli is an iconic singer, actress, entertainer and the daughter of Judy Garland. Grey is a multi-award-winning singer, actor, and dancer.

The Elephant Man: Joseph Merrick (1862–1890) was an Englishman known for his severe deformities who was exhibited as part of a freak show under the name The Elephant Man. In 1986, pop singer Michael Jackson was reported to have attempted to purchase Merrick's remains to add to his collection of rare and unusual memorabilia. He denied it as tabloid fodder.

The Cranberries: Irish rock band formed in 1989, led by singer Dolores O'Riordan, who joined the band the following year. Among their biggest hits were "Zombie," "Dreams," and "Linger," any of which could be the annoying song Lorelai is referencing. But "Zombie," with its repeated lyric "in your head," does fit with her line of dialogue.

Gaslight: A 1944 psychological thriller directed by George Cukor and starring George Boyer and Ingrid Bergman. It follows Bergman's character, who is being manipulated by Boyer's character into believing that she is going insane.

Whore of Babylon: A symbolic female figure from the Bible's Book of Revelation, seen as comparable to the pagan nations opposing Christianity.

"Let them eat cake": A phrase often attributed to Marie Antoinette, who served as queen of France from 1774 to 1792, in response to being told that the peasants had no bread to eat. There is no evidence, however, that she ever said it.

Fergie: The nickname of Sarah, Duchess of York, born Sarah Ferguson, who became British royalty after marrying Prince Andrew in 1986. She was known to have a rather casual, loud demeanor, which was often at odds with the more staid Royal Family. The couple divorced in 1996.

EPISODE 1.19: EMILY IN WONDERLAND

Written by John Stephens and Linda Loiselle Guzik. Directed by Perry Lang. Aired April 26, 2001.

Rory shows Emily around Stars Hollow and awakens some painful memories from the past.

Hansel and Gretel: Lorelai is referencing this German fairy tale about a brother and sister who stumble upon a house made of bread and cake and end up running afoul of its owner, a cannibalistic witch.

Biedermeier: Referring to an era in Europe between 1815 and 1848, during which the middle class began to take a higher interest in the arts. Furniture designed during the period is known for its high-quality craftsmanship.

Lost Weekend: A period of eighteen months between 1973 and 1975 in which musician John Lennon was separated from his wife, Yoko Ono. Lennon marked it as a time of self-introspection, intense creativity, and outrageous behavior, including embarking on an affair with his assistant, May Pang.

Boo Radley: Fictional character in Harper Lee's 1960 novel *To Kill a Mockingbird*, Arthur "Boo" Radley was the town recluse who lived down the street from the novel's protagonist, Scout Finch.

The Grapes of Wrath: Classic, Pulitzer Prize–winning 1939 John Steinbeck novel set during the Great Depression, following the Joads, a poor family of farmers who leave the Oklahoma Dust Bowl to set out for California.

***Charlie's Angels*, Kate Jackson, Shelly Hack, Cheryl Ladd, Farrah Fawcett, Jaclyn Smith, Tanya Roberts**: *Charlie's Angels* is a crime-drama TV series that aired on ABC from 1976 to 1981. It centered around a revolving cast of three female private detectives who took orders from their unseen boss, Charlie. Jackson, Fawcett, and Smith were the original Angels. Hack, Ladd, and Roberts joined the cast in subsequent seasons as other cast members departed.

The Williams sisters: Two professional tennis players, sisters Venus and Serena. Venus is a seven-time Grand Slam title winner, and Serena a twenty-three time winner.

Statue of Liberty: The "go build us another statue!" line is a reference to the Statue of Liberty, the colossal statue of a draped woman holding a torch above her head, which was gifted to the United States by France in 1886.

Martha Washington (1731–1802): Wife of President George Washington and the inaugural First Lady of the United States from 1789 to 1797.

Working Girl: A 1988 romantic comedy film starring Melanie Griffith as an ambitious secretary who takes over her boss's role after the latter has an injury, and attempts to make her way in the corporate world. One part of the movie shows Griffith's character opting for comfortable walking shoes for her commute into Manhattan, keeping her heels in her briefcase.

Joy Division: English post-punk band formed in 1976. The band's vocalist, Ian Curtis, died by suicide in 1980. The band's surviving members regrouped as New Order.

Nick Cave: Australian musician whose music is known for its emotional intensity.

Robert Smith: English rock musician, singer, and songwriter who co-founded the band The Cure.

Johnny Cash, San Quentin: Cash (1932–2003) was an influential country music singer-songwriter nicknamed the Man in Black, whose many hits include "I Walk the Line," "Ring of Fire," and "Get Rhythm." San Quentin is a state prison in California. In the late 1950s, Cash began performing concerts at prisons, including San Quentin. In 1969, he released a live album of one such concert, *Johnny Cash at San Quentin*.

Charlie Parker (1920–1955): Influential jazz musician.

Balthazar's: A French restaurant in New York City, opened in 1997, that has been a popular place for celebrity sightings.

Lou Reed (1942–2013): Musician and songwriter who was a member of the band The Velvet Underground in addition to having a successful and influential solo career.

98 Degrees, Backstreet Boys: Along with the previously discussed NSYNC, these are boy bands popular in the late 1990s and early 2000s.

Gallup: An analytics company founded in 1935, known for its public opinion polls.

Vulcan: A fictional extraterrestrial humanoid species from the *Star Trek* franchise, known for such characteristics as telepathy.

Pinocchio: Lorelai's line "her nose didn't grow" is a nod to Pinocchio, the main character in the 1883 children's novel *The Adventures of Pinocchio* by Carlo Collodi, and the popular Disney animated film version. The character is a wooden puppet who dreams of becoming a real boy, and whose nose grows when he tells a lie.

Prince (1958–2016): Genre-mixing singer, musician, and actor known for such hits as "Purple Rain," "When Doves Cry," "Strawberry Beret," "I Would Die 4 U," and "1999."

CosmoGirl: A teen-targeted spinoff magazine of *Cosmopolitan*, published from 1999 to 2008.

Hello Kitty: Fictional anthropomorphized white cat created by Yuko Shimizu in 1974. The character has become a popular brand franchise consisting of apparel, video games, an animated series, and more.

Steven Tyler: Singer-songwriter best known as the frontman of the rock band Aerosmith.

Saving Private Ryan: Epic war film released in 1998, directed by Steven Spielberg and written by Robert Rodat. Set during World War II, it stars Tom Hanks as a captain leading a mission to locate a missing private. An early sequence of the film depicts soldiers landing on Omaha Beach on D-Day and is said to be among the most brutal depictions of war ever put on film.

"Blah blah blah Ginger": Lorelai is referring to a comic from the popular *The Far Side* strip by Gary Larson, which ran from 1980 to 1995. The panel shows a man scolding his dog, Ginger. The first panel reads "What we say to dogs," and depicts the man telling Ginger to stay out of the garbage. The second panel reads "What they hear," and is just the word "blah" repeating with the occasional "Ginger" inserted.

Episode 1.20: P.S. I Lo . . .

Written by Elaine Arata and Joan Binder Weiss. Directed by Lev L. Spiro. Aired May 3, 2001.

Between dealing with her breakup with Dean and her mother's rekindled romance with Max, an angry Rory escapes to her grandparents' house.

Anna Nicole Smith (1967–2007): Actress and model who started her career as a *Playboy* centerfold before moving into fashion modeling and acting. From 2002 to 2004, she starred in a reality sitcom based on her life on the E! network. She died of an accidental drug overdose in 2007.

Mary Kay Letourneau (1962–2020): Teacher who began a relationship with her twelve-year-old student in the mid-1990s. She pleaded guilty to felony second-degree rape of a child in 1997. Letourneau married her former student upon her release from prison, after they had already had two children. They separated in 2019. She died from colon cancer the following year.

Emma Goldman (1869–1940): Activist and writer who played a pivotal role in anarchist political philosophy.

Patton: A 1970 epic war film starring George C. Scott, based on the life of World War II US General George S. Patton, a hard-driving and aggressive military leader.

Up With People: Nonprofit organization founded in 1968 that stages enthusiastic song and dance performances touching on issues like equality and positive thinking.

Meryl Streep, *Out of Africa***, Isak Dinesen**: Streep is a versatile award-winning actress known for such works as *Kramer vs. Kramer*, *Sophie's Choice*, *Death Becomes Her*, and *The Devil Wears Prada*. She also starred in 1985's Academy Award–winning *Out of Africa*, an epic romance film based on the 1937 memoir of the same name by Dinesen (1885–1962), whose real name was Karen Blixen. The book details her eighteen years living in Kenya. Streep, known for acting in accents as roles require, studied recordings of Blixen reading her works in order to adopt her accent.

Seven Brides for Seven Brothers: A 1954 musical film based on the short story "The Sobbin' Women" by Stephen Vincent Benét, which revolves around a group of ill-mannered, grizzled woodsmen.

"I'm Too Sexy": Lorelai paraphrases lyrics from this 1991 hit by British pop duo Right Said Fred.

The Art of Fiction: A book of literary criticism by David Lodge, published in 1992, featuring essays that first appeared as weekly columns in *The Independent*, a British newspaper. Each chapter focuses on an aspect of the art of fiction.

Henry James (1843–1916): Author considered to be among the greatest novelists in the English language, whose notable works include *The Portrait of a Lady*, *The Turn of the Screw*, and *The Wings of the Dove*.

Fabio: Italian model and actor widely known for appearing on the covers of romance novels in the 1990s.

GQ: Short for *Gentleman's Quarterly*, *GQ* is a men's fashion magazine founded in 1931.

Goofus and Gallant: Children's comic strip created by Garry Cleveland Myers, appearing in the *Highlights for Children* monthly magazine beginning in 1940. The strips detail the opposing behaviors of the two title characters, with Gallant behaving well and Goofus behaving badly.

Air Supply: Australian soft rock duo consisting of Russell Hitchcock and Graham Russell, whose hits include "All Out of Love," "Even the Nights Are Better," and "Making Love Out of Nothing at All."

The Amityville Horror: Horror franchise that began as a 1977 book by Jay Anson, based on claims by a family who said they were terrorized by paranormal phenomena in the home they purchased in suburban Amityville, New York, which had been the site of a gruesome multiple murder years before. The book spawned a series of films, including 1979's successful *The Amityville Horror*.

Howard Cosell (1918–1995): Prominent sports journalist and broadcaster who worked for ABC Sports from 1953 until 1985.

Taylor Hanson: Singer, songwriter, and musician known as a member of the pop band Hanson, along with his brothers Isaac and Zac. The trio rose to fame in their teens with the 1997 hit "MMMBop."

Bee Gees: Popular musical group founded in 1958 by brothers Barry, Robin, and Maurice Gibb, who achieved considerable commercial success during the disco era of the 1970s. Their hits include "Stayin' Alive," "Night Fever," and "How Deep Is Your Love."

EPISODE 1.21: LOVE, DAISIES AND TROUBADOURS

Written by Daniel Palladino. Directed by Amy Sherman-Palladino. Aired May 10, 2001.

Lorelai's relationship with Max takes a new turn—as does Luke's relationship with Rachel. Rory attempts to reconnect with Dean.

Mr. Muckle: While a tricky one, Lorelai is most likely referencing the character Mr. Muckle from the 1934 W. C. Fields comedy film *It's a Gift*. Fields plays a put-upon grocer who, in one humorous scene, must deal with Mr. Muckle, played by Charles Sellon, a customer whose blindness leads to much destruction around the store.

Blue Man Group: A performance art company formed in 1987 that features three men who perform with their skin painted blue. They gained widespread popularity when opening at the Luxor Theater in Las Vegas in 2000.

Margot Kidder (1948–2018): Actress best known for playing Lois Lane in the original *Superman* films in the 1970s and 1980s. She was diagnosed with bipolar disorder in 1988 and, in 1996, suffered a widely publicized manic episode during which she disappeared for four days.

Webster's Dictionary: English language dictionary edited in the early nineteenth century by Noah Webster. Webster's first dictionary, titled *A Compendious Dictionary of the English Language*, dates back to 1806.

Stretch Cunningham: Fictional practical-joking character from the sitcom *All in the Family*, played by James Cromwell. The character was a friend and coworker of the show's protagonist, Archie Bunker.

Dick Tracy: Comic strip created by Chester Gould that first appeared in 1931. The title character is a police detective. The strip inspired a 1990 live-action film starring Warren Beatty in the title role.

Wheel of Fortune: Lane is referencing this popular game show when she says "turning letters." Created by Merv Griffin, it debuted in 1975 and, for much of its run, was hosted by Pat Sajak until he retired in 2024 and Ryan Seacrest took over. Gameplay resembles that of Hangman and involves contestants spinning a giant wheel for prize money while attempting to solve a puzzle by guessing letters on a game board. Co-host Vanna White, a former model and beauty pageant contestant, turns the letters on the puzzle board as contestants make their guesses.

The Matrix: A 1999 science-fiction action film starring Keanu Reeves about a dystopian future in which humanity is trapped inside a simulated reality. The film—and the subsequent franchise it spawned—is known for its unique fight sequences.

The Seven Dwarfs: Lane's reference to Mopey and Dopey is a play on this group of fictional characters from the 1812 Brothers Grimm fairy tale *Snow White*, popularized in the 1937 Walt Disney animated film *Snow White and the Seven Dwarfs*, where they were named things like Bashful, Sneezy, Grumpy, and Dopey. (There was no Mopey.)

Peter Frampton: English-American musician who began his career with the bands The Herd and Humble Pie before embarking on a solo career which included his breakthrough record, 1976's *Frampton Comes Alive!* His hits include "Baby, I Love Your Way" and "Show Me the Way." With a career of multiple ups and downs, Frampton attempted multiple comebacks in the 1980s and 1990s, including 1995's release of *Frampton Comes Alive! II*. Despite heavy promotion, it sold poorly.

Blur: An English "Britpop" band formed in 1988, fronted by Damon Albarn.

"Honey Don't Think": A song by the band Grant Lee Buffalo.

PJ Harvey: English singer-songwriter whose hit albums include *To Bring You My Love* and *Stories from the City, Stories from the Sea*.

Judy Garland, Courtney Love: Garland (1922–1969) was an iconic actress and singer known for such films as *The Wizard of Oz*, *Meet Me in St. Louis*, and *A Star Is Born*. The pressures of her early stardom affected her physical and mental health and, throughout adulthood, she struggled with substance use disorder. She died from an accidental barbiturate overdose in 1969. In 2001, a biographical TV movie titled *Life with Judy Garland: Me and My Shadows*, aired on ABC. It was based on the memoir of Garland's daughter, actress Lorna Luft. Love is a singer and musician who rose to fame in the 1990s grunge era, fronting the rock band Hole, and who has also had publicized issues with substance use disorder. She was married to Nirvana frontman Kurt Cobain from 1992 until his death in 1994.

"Sadness Soot": A 2001 song by Grant Lee Phillips.

Lee Harvey Oswald, John Muir, The Unabomber, Henry David Thoreau: This is a list of people who have been described (for better or for worse) as loners. Oswald (1939–1963) was a US Marine veteran who assassinated

President John F. Kennedy in 1963. Muir (1838–1913) was a naturalist who advocated for the preservation of wilderness in the United States. The Unabomber refers to US domestic terrorist Ted Kaczynski (see earlier entry). Thoreau (1817–1862) was a philosopher and author known for writing *Walden*, a reflection upon simple, natural living.

Winchester Mystery House: Victorian and gothic-style mansion and tourist attraction in San Jose, California, that was once home to Sarah Winchester, widow of firearms magnate William Wirt Winchester. Its ongoing construction projects revolved around Winchester's supposed belief that she would die when the house was complete. The superstition led to a seemingly endless variety of additions.

Girl Scouts, Brownies: The Girl Scouts is a youth organization for girls founded in 1912 that involves activities like camping, community service, and annual cookie sales. The Brownies is a division of the Girl Scouts for younger kids.

Hare Krishna: A Gaudiya Vaishnava Hindu religious organization founded by A. C. Bhaktivedanta Swami Prabhupada in 1966.

Soul Train: Musical-variety television series that ran from 1970 to 2006, primarily featuring performances by R&B and soul artists.

Adolph Eichmann (1906–1962): German-Austrian official and member of the Nazi party who was among the major organizers of the Holocaust.

"Everybody Needs a Little Sanctuary": A song by Grant Lee Buffalo.

Season Two: 2001–2002

EPISODE 2.1: SADIE, SADIE

Written and directed by Amy Sherman-Palladino. Aired October 9, 2001.
Emily is upset when she hears of Lorelai's engagement from Sookie. Rory brings Dean to her grandparents' house for dinner.

Balkans: A region in southeastern Europe with a turbulent history as the site of several wars, such as the decade-long Yugoslav War and the Kosovo War, which lasted from 1998 to 1999.

Jeopardy!, **Alex Trebek**: *Jeopardy!* is a quiz-format game show created by Merv Griffin that debuted in 1964. Players compete by being given the answer to a trivia question and having to provide the correct question. Alex Trebek (1940–2020) hosted the show from 1984 until his death in 2020.

All in the Family: Sitcom that aired on CBS from 1971 to 1979, starring Carroll O'Conner as the narrow-minded, outspoken Archie Bunker and Jean Stapleton as his endearing wife, Edith. Sally Struthers, who plays Babette on *Gilmore Girls*, co-starred as their daughter, Gloria.

Sally Field, *Not Without My Daughter*: Field is an actress known for such works as *Norma Rae*, *Places in the Heart*, and *Steel Magnolias*. The film Lane refers to in the scene is *Not Without My Daughter*, a 1991 drama based on the 1987 book of the same name. Field plays an American citizen attempting to escape her abusive ex-husband in Iran.

Ivana Trump (1949–2022): Model and businesswoman who rose to fame in the 1980s primarily because she was married to Donald Trump from 1977 to 1990. She later sold lines of beauty products and fashion and wrote an advice column for the tabloid magazine *Globe*.

InStyle Weddings: A special offshoot of the *InStyle* fashion magazine targeting brides-to-be.

Ranger Bob: While there are some options for fictional Ranger Bob characters, a likely suspect is the television character played by Timothy Trombitas throughout the 1980s and 1990s on the children's program *Ranger Bob's Buckaroo Club*.

J. Edgar Hoover (1895–1972): Attorney who served as the first director of the Federal Bureau of Investigation from 1935 until his death in 1972.

Cornell University study on rats: Michel refers to a famous 1935 scientific study from Cornell University, led by Dr. Clive McCay, in which rats were placed on a calorie-restrictive diet that extended their lifespan.

Fame: A 1980 teen drama film about the lives of a group of students attending the High School of Performing Arts in New York City. The film's theme song, "Fame," was performed by Irene Cara and written by Michael Gore and Dean Pitchford. It includes the lyrics "I'm going to live forever."

"Sadie, Sadie," *Funny Girl*: "Sadie, Sadie" is a song from the 1964 Broadway play and 1968 musical film adaptation *Funny Girl*. The film was directed by William Wyler and written by Isobel Lennart. It is loosely based on the life and career of comedienne Fanny Brice, played by Barbra Streisand in both the original Broadway production and film.

Bobby Flay: Celebrity chef and restaurateur who has hosted a variety of shows on the Food Network and Cooking Channel, including *Food Nation* and *Boy Meets Grill*.

Stephanie Seymour, Guns N' Roses: Seymour is a model and actress known for features in the *Sports Illustrated Swimsuit Issue* and *Vogue*. Guns N' Roses is a hard rock band formed in 1985 whose hits include "Welcome to the Jungle" and "Sweet Child o' Mine." Seymour appeared in the group's music video for their song "November Rain," which was released as a single in early 1992. In it, she is seen wearing a very short wedding dress.

Cujo: A 1981 Stephen King horror novel about a rabid Saint Bernard. It was adapted into a film in 1983.

Gregg Allman (1947–2017): Singer and musician known for performing as part of the Allman Brothers Band, whose hits included "Midnight Rider" and "Ramblin' Man." He was married to Cher (see earlier entry) from 1975 to 1978. Their son, Elijah Blue Allman, was born in 1976.

Zelda Fitzgerald (1900–1948): Novelist and socialite who became an icon of the Jazz Age in the 1920s during her marriage to author F. Scott Fitzgerald. She was dubbed the first American flapper.

"Silly Rabbit": This exchange between Lorelai and Rory is a spin on the tagline of Trix, a brand of fruit-flavored breakfast cereal introduced in 1954, known for its advertising campaign featuring a rabbit who attempts to steal the cereal. Its tagline, "Silly Rabbit, Trix are for kids," has been used for decades.

Tears and Laughter: The Joan and Melissa Rivers Story*, *The Tonight Show: *Tears and Laughter* is a 1994 made-for-television movie chronicling the lives of the famous mother and daughter, who play themselves in the film. *The Tonight Show* is a late-night TV talk show that has aired on NBC since 1954. Rivers rose to prominence during the 1960s for her guest appearances on the show, which at the time was hosted by her mentor, Johnny Carson. The pair had a public falling out in the mid-1980s when Rivers was given her own late-night show, which made her the first woman to host such a series. The feud led to Rivers being banned from appearing on *The Tonight Show*. She didn't appear again until 2014, when Jimmy Fallon began hosting the show.

Stephen Hawking (1942–2018): Renowned English physicist, cosmologist, and author who served as the Lucasian Professor of Mathematics, a prestigious position with the University of Cambridge, from 1979 to 2009. He wrote the bestselling book *A Brief History of Time: From the Big Bang to Black Holes*, published in 1988.

***La traviata*, La Scala**: *La traviata* is an opera by Giuseppe Verdi set to an Italian libretto by Francesco Maria Piave, which premiered in 1853. The title translates as *The Fallen Woman*. La Scala is an historic opera house in Milan, Italy, which opened in 1778.

EPISODE 2.2: HAMMERS AND VEILS

Written by Amy Sherman-Palladino. Directed by Michael Katleman. Aired October 9, 2001.

Worried her college applications will be lacking in extracurricular charity work, Rory volunteers to build houses, upsetting Dean in the process. Lorelai contemplates wedding veil choices.

Diana, Princess of Wales (1961–1997): Born Diana Spencer, Princess Diana became a member of the British Royal Family when she married Charles III, then Prince of Wales, in 1981. At the ceremony, she wore an ivory silk taffeta and antique lace gown featuring a record-breaking twenty-five-foot-long train and a 459-foot-long tulle veil.

Vladimir Putin: Russian politician who has served as president of Russia since 2012. He also served in the role from 2000 to 2008. Rory's reference to an arms race stems from Putin's 2001 warning to the United States that the Bush administration's proposed missile defense system could trigger an arms race.

"Happy Happy, Joy Joy": A line and song from the animated series *The Ren & Stimpy Show*, which aired on Nickelodeon from 1991 to 1996. It chronicled the misadventures of a chihuahua and a Manx cat.

Grace Kelly (1929–1982): Actress known for such films as *The Country Girl, Dial M for Murder*, and *Rear Window*. She married Prince Rainier III in 1956, becoming Princess of Monaco.

A. J. Benza: Gossip columnist and television personality who has hosted such shows as *Mysteries and Scandals* and *A. J. After Dark*.

Thelma and Louise: A 1991 film starring Susan Sarandon and Geena Davis as two women who embark on a road trip.

Jell-O shots: A type of mixed drink made by combining Jell-O gelatin dessert with an alcohol (typically vodka) to be consumed as a shot. The alcohol is mixed with the gelatin powder in place of water.

Light as a feather, stiff as a board: A game often played at children's slumber parties in which one person lies flat on their back, and the rest of the players attempt to lift them up using only their fingertips.

Xuxa: A Brazilian TV host and actress who hosted programming for children.

Speed Racer: A 1960s Japanese manga series about a young race car driver, written and illustrated by Tatsuo Yoshida, which was also adapted into an animated series.

Bette Midler: Singer and actress whose hits include "Wind Beneath My Wings" and "The Rose." Her film credits include *Beaches, Hocus Pocus*, and *The First Wives Club*.

Gettysburg Address: Famous speech delivered by President Abraham Lincoln in 1863, during the Civil War, at the formal dedication of the Soldiers' National Cemetery in Gettysburg, Pennsylvania, in which he called for a "new birth of freedom." Beginning with the oft-quoted phrase "Four score and seven years ago," the speech was both brief and powerful.

Timmy in the well: This phrase has come to represent a general scenario from the TV series *Lassie*, which ran from 1954 to 1973, about a loyal Collie and her human companions, one of whom was a young boy named Timmy, who often got himself into predicaments requiring rescue by Lassie. The phrase about rescuing Timmy from a well has become a bit of a TV trope, although the character never actually fell into a well on the show.

VIVA Glam: A campaign launched in 1994 by MAC Cosmetics that features a yearly line of special lipsticks and lip glosses, the proceeds from which are used to fund and raise awareness for HIV/AIDS programs.

A Connecticut Yankee in King Arthur's Court: Lane paraphrases the title of this classic Mark Twain novel, first published in 1889, in which a Connecticut man is transported to England during the reign of King Arthur after a blow to the head.

Who's on first?: A famous routine by comedy team Abbott and Costello. In the sketch, Abbott attempts to identify players on a baseball team for Costello, the catch being that the names of the players sound like the answers to the questions Costello is asking. The name of the player on first base is indeed Who, so the answer to the question "Who's on first?" is "Who's on first."

Bob Vila: A home improvement television personality who hosted *This Old House* from 1979 to 1989 and *Bob Vila's Home Again* from 1990 to 2005.

Barbarella: A 1968 science-fiction film directed by Roger Vadim, based on the French comic series by Jean-Claude Forest. Jane Fonda stars as the titular space traveler who sets out to find a scientist with a weapon that has the power to destroy humanity.

Mother Teresa (1910–1997): Catholic saint, nun, and founder of Missionaries of Charity.

"I will not be ignored": Lorelai paraphrases a famous scene from the 1987 thriller *Fatal Attraction*, in which Glen Close stars as a woman who begins stalking the man with whom she had a brief affair, played by Michael Douglas.

Fidel Castro (1926–2016): Revolutionary and politician who served as leader of Cuba from 1959 to 2008. The country became a one-party

Communist state under his rule. Over a million Cubans fled the country for the United States under Castro's rule as political refugees.

Bingo: Popular game of chance in which players match numbers printed in varying arrangements on cards. The card is printed with the letters B-I-N-G-O across the top, with columns of numbers below each letter. A caller calls out numbers (e.g., B9, I28, N32, etc.) and the first player to match a number across each row or complete a full column wins that round's prize.

"Hey, Mr. DJ, put a record on . . .": Rory is quoting a line from the song "Music" by Madonna, who wrote the song with Mirwais Ahmadzaï. It was the lead single and title track of her 2000 album *Music* and rose to the top spot on the Billboard Hot 100 charts.

The Damned: English punk rock band formed in 1976.

"Tie a Yellow Ribbon Round the Ole Oak Tree": Song by Tony Orlando and Dawn, written by Irwin Levine and L. Russell Brown. In the 1970s, a yellow ribbon emerged as a symbol of remembrance of an absent loved one—serving in the military or in jail—who would be welcomed home upon their return.

Heinz: Food processing company founded in Pennsylvania in 1869, best known for their popular brand of ketchup. The brand's ad campaigns often played up the ketchup's thick, rich consistency as being slow to pour from its glass bottle but its taste being worth the wait.

Elizabeth Taylor (1932–2011): Legendary actress known for such films as *National Velvet*, *Cleopatra*, and *Who's Afraid of Virginia Woolf?* Her personal life was ripe for tabloid fodder, and she was married eight times to seven men.

EPISODE 2.3: RED LIGHT ON THE WEDDING NIGHT
Written by Daniel Palladino. Directed by Gail Mancuso. Aired October 16, 2001. At her bachelorette party, Lorelai realizes she has misgivings about her engagement to Max.

Guy Fawkes Day: Fawkes (1570–1606) was a member of a group of English Catholics involved in the Gunpowder Plot of 1605, a failed attempt to kill Protestant King James I and replace him with a Catholic head of state. Fawkes was arrested while guarding the explosives the group intended to use, thereby thwarting the assassination attempt. People began celebrating that the king survived and the day—November 5—was commemorated as Guy Fawkes Day, celebrated with bonfires and fireworks.

Sinclair Lewis (1885–1951): Novelist and playwright who became the first American to win the Nobel Prize in Literature. His works include *Main Street* and *Babbitt*. Rory's chosen quote about love comes from his 1927 novel *Elmer Gantry*.

Lord Byron (1788–1824): British poet and prominent figure of the Romantic movement. The quote Rory chose is from *Childe Harold's Pilgrimage*, Byron's long narrative poem that was published in parts between 1812 and 1818.

Benito Mussolini (1883–1945): Italian dictator who founded the National Fascist Party. The quote comes from *Writings and Discourses of Mussolini*, a twelve-volume work that was published between 1934 and 1940.

V-J Day: Victory over Japan Day marks the day in which Japan surrendered in World War II. The day is commemorated in the United States on September 2—the day in 1945 when the surrender document was signed and the war officially ended.

Mensa: The largest and oldest high-IQ society in the world, open to people who score in the ninety-eighth percentile or higher on IQ tests. It was founded in 1946.

Monty Python and the Holy Grail: A 1975 British comedy based on the Arthurian legend, written and performed by the Monty Python comedy troupe, that parodies the legend of King Arthur's search for the Holy Grail.

Monty Python's Life of Brian: A 1979 British comedy from the Monty Python comedy troupe about a young Judean man—born on the same day as and beside Jesus—who gets mistaken for the Messiah.

Billy Jack: Fictional Green Beret Vietnam veteran character, portrayed by Tom Laughlin, first introduced in the 1967 outlaw biker film *The Born Losers*, which is the film being watched in the episode.

Electra Woman and Dyna Girl: A live-action superhero children's TV series that aired for sixteen episodes in 1976 as part of *The Krofft Supershow*. Diedre Hall played the caped hero Electra Woman, and Judy Strangis played her teen sidekick, Dyna Girl.

"Taking back Poland": This is a reference to the start of World War II, which was sparked by the Nazi Germany invasion of Poland in 1939.

Them!: A 1954 science-fiction nuclear monster film about an invasion of giant ants.

Hartford Courant, New York Times: *The Hartford Courant* is the largest daily newspaper in Connecticut, founded in 1764. *The New York Times* is that city's daily newspaper, founded in 1851. Max's other daily read, *The Wall Street Journal*, was addressed in an earlier entry.

A.I. Artificial Intelligence: A 2001 science-fiction film directed by Steven Spielberg, about a childlike android played by Haley Joel Osment who has the ability to love.

Adolf Hitler (1889–1945): Austrian-born Nazi German dictator from 1933 until his death by suicide. His invasion of Poland in 1939 started World War II.

401(k): An employee-sponsored retirement savings plan.

Jan Brady: Lorelai's reference to "poor Jan" is a nod to this fictional middle sister from the sitcom *The Brady Bunch*, which aired on ABC from 1969 to 1974. The character, played by Eve Plumb, was the quintessential awkward "middle child," often jealous of her big sister Marcia.

Queen Victoria: While here it is the name of the drag club, Queen Victoria (1819–1901) was queen of the United Kingdom from 1837 until her death.

Lucifer: The name of the Devil in Christian theology.

Joan Crawford (190?–1977): Legendary actress known for such films as *Mildred Pierce* and *Whatever Happened to Baby Jane?*—as well as for her acrimonious relationship with two of her older children that formed the basis of the book and film *Mommie Dearest*.

Tony Manero: Character portrayed by John Travolta in the 1977 film *Saturday Night Fever*, a man who spent his time dancing and drinking at the local disco bar.

Mae West (1893–1980): Actress and singer known for her sexual innuendo and double entendres.

Shirley Temple drink: A non-alcoholic mixed drink named after the famed child star, traditionally made with ginger ale or Sprite and a splash of grenadine.

"Seeing pink elephants": A euphemism for hallucinations brought upon by drinking too much. The term dates back to the early twentieth century, including a reference in Jack London's 1913 novel *John Barleycorn*.

Richard Burton, Mike Todd: Both married to actress Elizabeth Taylor (see earlier entry), Burton (1925–1984) was an actor known for his work in Shakespeare's *Hamlet* and several films, and Todd (1907–1958) was a producer known for the 1956 film *Around the World in 80 Days*. Todd was married to Taylor from 1957 until his death in a plane crash the following year. Burton was married to Taylor twice: from 1964 to 1974 and again from 1975 to 1976. They first met when filming *Cleopatra* in 1962 and went on to star together in eleven films. Their relationship became ripe for media attention, and the pair were dubbed "Liz and Dick" by the media.

Bono: Irish musician and activist known as the frontman for the rock band U2.

Bryan Ferry: English musician known as the frontman for the band Roxy Music.

Bob Dylan: Influential singer-songwriter who rose to prominence in the 1960s with songs like "The Times They Are a-Changin'" and "Blowin' in the Wind." A prolific and poetic songwriter, he was awarded the Nobel Prize for Literature in 2016.

Alanis Morissette: Canadian singer-songwriter who rose to fame in the mid-1990s with the release of her landmark album *Jagged Little Pill*, which sold thirty-three million copies and won four Grammys.

Dave Matthews: Singer-songwriter best known as the frontman of The Dave Matthews Band.

Buena Vista Social Club: A Cuban music ensemble formed in 1996.

Enya: Best-selling Irish singer and composer whose eclectic music blends genres such as Celtic, world, classical, and Irish folk.

Yogi Berra (1925–2015): Professional baseball player who primarily played for the New York Yankees from 1946 to 1963. He was also known for his malapropisms and paradoxical statements.

Janet Jackson: Singer, actress, and dancer whose many hits include "Nasty," "Miss You Much," and "Rhythm Nation."

Celine Dion: Canadian pop singer known for power ballads, whose hits include "The Power of Love," "It's All Coming Back to Me Now," and "My Heart Will Go On," the theme from 1997's *Titanic*.

Colette (1873–1954): French author whose works include the 1944 novel *Gigi*, which became a popular film and stage production.

EPISODE 2.4: THE ROAD TRIP TO HARVARD

Written by Daniel Palladino. Directed by Jamie Babbit. Aired October 23, 2001. Looking to avoid her pending nuptials, Lorelai takes Rory on a spontaneous road trip that lands them at Harvard.

AC/DC, *Highway to Hell*: AC/DC is an Australian rock band formed in 1973. *Highway to Hell* is their sixth album, released in 1979.

Hootie & the Blowfish: Rock band formed in South Carolina in 1986. Their debut, 1994's *Cracked Rear View*, was a massive hit, with singles like "Hold My Hand," "Let Her Cry," and "Only Wanna Be With You."

Behind the Music: A documentary television series airing on VH1 from 1997 to 2014. Each episode profiles the life and career of a popular musical artist or group.

Nicholas Cage, *Captain Corelli's Mandolin*: Cage is an actor known for such films as *Moonstruck, Raising Arizona,* and *Leaving Las Vegas. Captain Corelli's Mandolin* is a 2001 war film based on the 1994 novel of the same name by Louis de Bernières. In it, Cage plays Captain Antonio Corelli and, at one point, utters the line spoken by Rory. The film was panned by critics.

Cheshire Cat, *Alice in Wonderland*: *Alice's Adventures in Wonderland* is a classic 1865 children's novel by Lewis Carroll in which a young girl falls through a rabbit hole and ends up in a fantasy world full of strange and beguiling characters, including the Cheshire Cat, an anthropomorphic cat known for his mischievous grin who enjoys misdirecting the lost Alice. The story was adapted into a beloved 1951 Disney animated film.

Liberace (1919–1987): Flamboyant pianist, singer, and actor who was, at his peak, the highest-paid entertainer in the world.

Certs: A brand of breath mint introduced in 1956 and discontinued in 2018.

"Anarchy in the U.K.": The first single by the U.K. punk rock band the Sex Pistols, released in 1976.

U2: Irish rock band formed in 1976, known for such hits as "With or Without You," "I Still Haven't Found What I'm Looking For," and "Sunday Bloody Sunday."

"Gypsies, Tramps & Thieves": A 1971 single by Cher that became her first number-one record as a solo artist.

David Lynch: Filmmaker known for employing surrealist, dreamlike qualities into his works. His films include *Eraserhead* and *Mulholland Drive*, as well as the television series *Twin Peaks*.

Space pen: A pen patented in 1965 that uses pressurized ink cartridges enabling it to write in zero gravity, underwater, and upside down. Its technology was used in the US and Soviet space programs.

Salem Witch Trials: A series of hearings and prosecutions against people accused of witchcraft in Salem, Massachusetts, in 1692 and 1693. Thirty people were found guilty, and nineteen people hanged.

John Adams (1735–1826): American Founding Father and second president of the United States, who served in the role from 1797 to 1801. Lorelai confuses this Adams with the Samuel Adams brand of beer.

W. E. B. Du Bois (1868–1963): Sociologist, activist, and author who was the first African American to earn a doctorate and was one of the founders of the National Association for the Advancement of Colored People. Notable works include *The Souls of Black Folk* and *Black Reconstruction in America*.

Yo-Yo Ma: Famous, multi-award-winning cellist.

Fred Gwynne, Herman Munster: Gwynne (1926–1993) was an actor known for such works as *Car 54, Where Are You?* and *My Cousin Vinny*. His best-known role, however, was playing Herman Munster, the fictional Frankenstein monster patriarch on the CBS sitcom *The Munsters*.

Who Moved My Cheese?: A 1998 motivational business fable by Spencer Johnson that describes various reactions to change.

Happy Days: A sitcom that aired on ABC from 1974 to 1984, focusing on the lives of the Cunninghams, a Midwestern family in the 1950s and early 1960s.

"Valley Girls": A 1982 song by Frank Zappa, featuring his daughter Moon, which satirized teen culture in the San Fernando Valley in Los Angeles, California.

Linkin Park: Alternative rock band formed in 1996 whose hits include "One Step Closer," "Crawling," and "In the End."

Rizzo: Fictional character from the stage play and movie adaptation of *Grease*, about the romance between a greaser guy and a goody-two-shoes girl. In a scene from the film that takes place in the bathroom of a drive-in theater, another character, Marty, tells Rizzo, portrayed by Stockard Channing, that she caught someone attempting to put aspirin in her Coke at the school dance.

Seneca the Younger (4 BC–AD 65): Stoic philosopher of ancient Rome who is the topic of the lecture Rory crashes.

Marcus Aurelius, *Meditations*: Aurelius (121–180) was a Roman emperor and Stoic philosopher noted for *Meditations*, his series of personal writings and ideas on philosophy.

"Forget it, Jake. It's Chinatown.": *Chinatown* is a 1974 neo-noir mystery film directed by Roman Polanski, starring Jack Nicholson and Faye Dunaway. Rory quotes a classic line from the end of the film.

Katherine Hepburn (1907–2003): Actress known for such works as *Morning Glory*, *Guess Who's Coming to Dinner*, *The Lion in Winter*, and *On Golden Pond*—all of which earned her Academy Awards. Lorelai refers to Hepburn's relationship with actor Spencer Tracy, her co-star in nine films. Tracy remained married but separated from his wife during their years-long relationship, which has become the stuff of Hollywood legend.

"Close enough for jazz": A slang phrase used primarily by musicians to refer to an instrument that isn't perfectly tuned. It basically means "good enough."

"I kissed the tarmac": Pope John Paul II had a habit of kissing the ground as a sign of respect whenever he first arrived in a country.

Elvis Costello: English singer-songwriter whose best-known songs include "Alison," "I Can't Stand Up for Falling Down," and "(What's So Funny 'Bout) Peace, Love and Understanding."

The Doors: Rock band formed in 1965, led by Jim Morrison, with whom Nico (see earlier entry) had a relationship.

Iggy Pop: Rock musician who led the band the Stooges. He is known as the "Godfather of Punk."

David Bowie (1947–2016): Influential English singer-songwriter known for reinvention and experimental stage presentations.

Lewis and Clark Expedition: Meriwether Lewis and William Clark were American explorers who led an expedition across the then-newly acquired western portion of the country following the Louisiana Purchase in the early 1800s.

EPISODE 2.5: NICK & NORA/SID & NANCY

Written by Amy Sherman-Palladino. Directed by Michael Katleman. Aired October 30, 2001.

Rory looks forward to the start of the school year until she receives an unexpected assignment from Paris for the school newspaper. Luke adjusts to the arrival of his nephew, Jess.

Charles Mingus, *The Black Saint and the Sinner Lady*: Mingus (1922–1979) was a renowned bandleader and jazz upright bass musician. His 1963 record *The Black Saint and the Sinner Lady* is a single continuous composition divided into four tracks.

The Sonics, *Here Are the Sonics*: Garage rock band formed in Washington in 1960. *Here Are the Sonics* is their debut album, released in 1965.

MC5, *Kick Out the Jams*: MC5 was a rock band formed in Michigan in 1963 who have been listed among the greatest hard rock artists of all time. *Kick Out the Jams* is their debut album, released in 1969. While initially panned upon release, the album has gone on to be considered an important forerunner in punk music.

Fairport Convention, *Liege & Lief*: Fairport Convention is an English folk rock band formed in 1967 who started out playing mostly Bob Dylan and Joni Mitchell covers. *Liege & Lief* is their fourth album, released in 1969.

Odessa: The sixth album by the Bee Gees (see earlier entry), a double LP released in 1969.

Mojo: A U.K. music magazine launched in 1993. Lane is referring to *The Mojo Collection: The Greatest Albums of All Time*, which was a special edition book published in 2001.

Whistler, Chaucer, Detroit, and Greenhill: Pseudonyms for David Bullock, Scott Fraser, Eddie Lively, Phil White, and John Carrick. They released one album in 1968: *The Unwritten Works of Geoffrey, Etc.*, a psychedelic folk-rock album produced by a young T Bone Burnett.

Grups: Short for "grown ups," taken from an episode of the TV series *Star Trek*, in which the show's characters discover a planet inhabited by children who use the term to refer to adults.

Frosted Flakes: A brand of breakfast cereal consisting of sugar-coated corn flakes, introduced in 1952. The brand's advertising campaign features a cartoon tiger named Tony whose catchphrase, which Jess mimics, is "They're g-r-r-eat!"

Der Wienerschnitzel: Fast food chain specializing in hot dogs, opened in 1961.

The Shawshank Redemption: A 1994 prison drama film written and directed by Frank Darabont, based on a 1982 Stephen King novella. It tells the story of a man sentenced to life in Shawshank State Penitentiary for murdering his wife and her lover.

Fredo Corleone: Character in the 1969 Mario Puzo novel *The Godfather*, portrayed by actor John Cazale in the 1972 film adaptation, which chronicles the lives of the fictional Corleone Mafia family in New York. Fredo is portrayed as a weaker member of the family and therefore carries little power or influence.

Riff: Fictional character in the stage play *West Side Story* (see earlier entry), who leads the Jets gang.

Federico Fellini (1920–1993): Italian filmmaker known for blending fantasy and baroque imagery. His works include *La Strada*, *La Dolce Vita*, and *Juliet of the Spirits*.

"Solidarity, sister!": A feminist phrase popular in the 1960s and 1970s.

"Dodo on the Regis Show": This is a dig at the search for a new cohost on the daytime talk show *Live! with Regis and Kathie Lee*. (See earlier entry on Regis Philbin.) Co-host Kathie Lee Gifford departed the show in 2000, leading to a series of guest hosts before actress Kelly Ripa was chosen as a permanent replacement in 2001.

Tool: Rock band formed in Los Angeles in 1990.

Twenty Questions: A parlor game in which one person selects a person or object, keeping it a secret, and players can ask up to twenty questions in order to guess what it is.

John and Jackie: A reference to US President John F. Kennedy (1970–1963) and his wife, Jacqueline (1929–1994).

Pulitzer Prize: Prestigious annual award given by Columbia University to honor achievements in journalism, arts, and letters. They were first awarded in 1917.

Hooked on Phonics: A brand of educational materials designed to teach reading through letter-sound correlations. It was introduced in 1987.

Dr. Laura Schlessinger: Author and talk radio host who hosts *The Dr. Laura Program*, where she dispenses advice.

The Breakfast Club: A 1985 film by John Hughes about a group of teens from different high school cliques who are forced to spend a Saturday together in detention. One of the characters, the antagonistic, rule-breaking Bender, would be the most Jess-like of the five.

Nick and Nora Charles: Fictional married couple introduced in the 1934 Dashiell Hammett novel *The Thin Man*, who solved mysteries while exchanging witty repartee. The characters were adapted into a variety of radio, film, TV, and stage projects.

Sid and Nancy: A 1986 biographical film directed by Alex Cox that portrays the destructive relationship between rock musician Sid Vicious, member of the band the Sex Pistols, and his girlfriend, Nancy Spungen.

Barbara Walters (1929–2022): Broadcast journalist and television personality known for in-depth interviews. She appeared on a variety of TV programs throughout her career, including *Today*, *20/20*, and *The View*.

Pledge of Allegiance: A patriotic verse pledging allegiance to the flag of the United States, often said aloud by students in school classrooms. The first version appeared in 1892; the current version appeared in 1954.

Color Me Mine: A chain of studios founded in 1996 where people can create their own pottery pieces.

Tupperware: A brand of preparation, storage, and serving containers for the home and kitchen, founded by Earl Tupper in 1946. The products were often sold through party-style in-home presentations.

The Artful Dodger, *Oliver Twist*: *Oliver Twist* is the second novel by Charles Dickens, originally published in serial form between 1837 and 1839. It is the journey of the titular orphan who escapes to London and eventually reconnects with his family. Along the way, he comes across a group of child street criminals, one of whom is Jack Dawkins, a pickpocket known as The Artful Dodger.

EPISODE 2.6: PRESENTING LORELAI GILMORE

Written by Sheila R. Lawrence. Directed by Chris Long. Aired November 6, 2001. Rory agrees to Emily's invitation to be presented to society at a debutante ball.

Liesl, Brigitta, Gretl: Characters from the 1959 stage musical and 1965 film adaptation of *The Sound of Music*, based on the 1949 memoir *The Story of the Trapp Family Singers* by Maria von Trapp. It is the retelling of her experiences as governess to seven children, three of whom had these names.

George and Martha: Characters from *Who's Afraid of Virginia Woolf?* (See earlier entry.)

Mark Twain House: Historic home in Hartford, Connecticut, that was home to the famous author and his family from 1874 to 1891 and where he wrote many of his most famous works. It operates as a museum dedicated to showcasing Twain's life and work.

Harriet Beecher Stowe (1811–1896): Abolitionist and author who wrote *Uncle Tom's Cabin*.

The Lion King: Stage musical based on the 1994 animated Disney film of the same name. It features actors in animal costumes and giant puppets.

Terrance McNally (1938–2020): Playwright and screenwriter labeled "the bard of the American theater." Notable works include *Master Class*, *Ragtime*, *Kiss of the Spider Woman*, and *Love! Valour! Compassion!*

CNN: Acronym for Cable News Network, a multinational news organization founded by Ted Turner and Reese Schonfeld in 1980. It was the first cable network in the United States to provide twenty-four hour news coverage.

Debutante ball: A debutante, or deb for short, is an aristocratic young woman who has reached maturity and is "presented" to society in a formal gathering, commonly called a debutante ball.

Spinal Tap: Fictional heavy metal band created by comedians and musicians who first appeared in the 1979 comedy pilot *The T.V. Show* then later starred in the 1984 mockumentary *This Is Spinal Tap*. Their history included a series of drummers, all of whom supposedly died under mysterious circumstances.

Lily Tomlin, John Travolta: Tomlin is an actress and comedian known for such works of stage and screen as *Rowan & Martin's Laugh-In*, *The Search for Signs of Intelligent Life in the Universe*, *9 to 5*, and *Grace and Frankie*. Travolta is an actor whose notable works include *Grease*, *Saturday Night Fever*, *Urban Cowboy*, and *Pulp Fiction*. The pair starred together in the 1978 drama film *Moment by Moment*, which was universally panned by critics.

"Some mice, a dog, a pumpkin . . .": A nod to the animated Disney version of *Cinderella*, in which the fairy godmother turns a pumpkin into a coach and a dog and mice into attendants to get Cinderella to the ball.

Boston Tea Party: A 1773 political protest against the Tea Act, which allowed for the sale of tea from China in the American colonies without paying taxes. In response, a group known as the Sons of Liberty destroyed an entire shipment of tea.

Boston Strangler: The name given to the serial killer who murdered thirteen women in Boston in the 1960s. The crimes were attributed to Albert DeSalvo.

Doris Duke (1912–1993): Billionaire tobacco heiress and socialite who was often called "the richest girl in the world." She suffered a severe stroke at age eighty and died shortly after. She had named her Irish butler, Bernard Lafferty, the executor of her $1.2 billion estate six months before her death, which led to speculation that he was involved in the incident, but no charges were ever filed.

Gloria Vanderbilt (1924–2019): Fashion designer, heiress, and socialite who was involved in a notorious child custody battle between her mother and aunt in her youth, and who later launched a line of fashion and beauty products in the 1970s.

Cary Grant (1904–1986): Classic Hollywood leading man known for such works as *His Girl Friday*, *The Philadelphia Story*, and *North by Northwest*. He was married for a time to Barbara Hutton (see earlier entry), who is among the famous debutantes discussed by Christopher and Lorelai.

976 numbers: Premium phone numbers on a local level (akin to 900 numbers nationally) that emerged in the 1970s and were often used as lines for adult entertainment.

Endless Love: A poorly received 1981 drama film by Franco Zeffirelli, based on the 1979 Scott Spenser novel of the same name, starring Brooke Shields. Despite the film's poor performance, its theme song, performed by Diana Ross and Lionel Richie, was a massive hit.

Kate Spade New York: Fashion house founded in 1993 by Kate and Andy Spade.

Little Debbie: While not what Lorelai is referencing in the scene, Little Debbie is actually a brand of snack cakes launched in 1960 and named after the founders' granddaughter.

Rock and Roll Hall of Fame: A museum and hall of fame in Cleveland, Ohio, that documents the history of rock music. Artists are inducted into the Rock and Roll Hall of Fame each year.

Neil Young: Singer-songwriter known for such critically acclaimed albums as *After the Goldrush* and *Harvest*. In addition to his successful solo work, he was a member of Buffalo Springfield and Crosby, Stills, Nash & Young. His induction into the Rock and Roll Hall of Fame was in 1995.

BattleBots: A robot combat television series that originally aired on Comedy Central.

Jiggy: As defined in the Oxford English Dictionary (see earlier entry), *jiggy* means "Excitedly energetic or uninhibited, often in a sexual manner; to get jiggy: to engage in sexual activity." The word gained popularity from the 1997 Will Smith single "Gettin' Jiggy wit It."

George Lucas: Filmmaker best known for creating the *Star Wars* and *Indiana Jones* franchises. The THX sound system was developed at his company, Lucasfilm, to ensure that the soundtrack to his film *Return of the Jedi* would be accurately reproduced in theaters.

Michael Jackson: Lorelai's mention of a glittery glove and a freaky face are references to "King of Pop" Michael Jackson (1958–2009). In addition to his many hits, including "Bad," "Thriller," and "Beat It," he was also known for the changing appearance of his face and for the silver rhinestone glove he wore in the 1980s.

"Nobody puts Baby in a corner": Famous line from the 1987 film *Dirty Dancing*, starring Patrick Swayze, Jennifer Grey, and Kelly Bishop. Grey stars as Baby, a young woman who falls for the dance instructor (Swayze) at a vacation resort. Swayze says the line during the film's climax.

The Brady Bunch: Sitcom created by Sherwood Schwartz that aired on ABC from 1969 to 1974, about a couple who wed and blend their families, each bringing three children from previous marriages into the household. The iconic series has spawned several revival shows and feature films.

"Rapture": A 1981 song by the rock band Blondie that blends new wave and disco with a distinctive rap section by vocalist Debbie Harry.

Children of the American Revolution: Youth organization founded in 1895 by Harriett Lothrop, a member of the Daughters of the American Revolution.

Chanel: Luxury fashion house founded by Coco Chanel in Paris, France, in 1910. Among its most notable products is its No. 5 perfume.

Final Net: Brand of hairspray made by Clairol.

Cirque du Soleil: Canadian entertainment company and the world's largest contemporary circus production, founded in 1984.

Shakey's: A pizza restaurant chain that was the first such style of chain in the United States. It was founded in 1954.

Trident: A brand of sugar-free chewing gum introduced in 1960. For years, the brand was advertised by saying "four out of five dentists surveyed recommend sugarless gum for their patients who chew gum."

Jeeves: While the term has become the quintessential name for a fancy manservant, Jeeves was originally a fictional character from a series of comedic stories and novels by author P. G. Wodehouse beginning in 1915. The character was a valet to a wealthy Londoner.

"Jubilee": A song by Grant Lee Buffalo.

"Oh, Sherrie," Journey: Journey is a rock band formed in San Francisco in 1973. Their hits include "Open Arms" and "Don't Stop Believin.'" "Oh, Sherrie" was actually the first single by the band's lead singer, Steve Perry, when he embarked on a solo career in 1984.

Glass slipper: Another reference to *Cinderella*, who wore glass slippers to the ball and left one behind during her hasty departure.

Shecky Green (1926–2023): Comedian and actor who rose to fame performing in Las Vegas nightclubs.

EPISODE 2.7: LIKE MOTHER, LIKE DAUGHTER

Written by Joan Binder Weiss. Directed by Dennis Erdman. Aired November 13, 2001.

Rory is encouraged to make more friends at Chilton and becomes involved with an exclusive high school clique. Lorelai is recruited to assist with the school's booster club.

Bay City Rollers: Scottish pop band who rose to fame in the 1970s with hits like "Bye, Bye, Baby," "Keep on Dancing," and "Saturday Night."

Barry Manilow: Singer-songwriter whose hits include "Mandy," "Could It Be Magic," and "Copacabana (At the Copa)."

Bryan Adams: Canadian singer-songwriter whose hits include "Cuts Like a Knife," "Straight From the Heart," "Summer of '69," and "(Everything I Do) I Do It for You."

Mount Pilot: A fictional neighboring town to Mayberry, the setting of the classic sitcom *The Andy Griffith Show*. Its name, and the inspiration for Mayberry, is derived from the actual town of Pilot Mountain, North Carolina.

"Looks Like We Made It": Song by Barry Manilow from his 1976 album *This One's for You*.

Spice Girls: English girl group who rose to fame in the 1990s with hits like "Wannabe," "Say You'll Be There," and "2 Become 1."

Dido: English singer-songwriter whose hits include "Here With Me," "Thank You," and "White Flag."

Olivia Newton-John (1948–2022): British and Australian singer and actress whose screen credits include *Grease*, *Xanadu*, and *Sordid Lives*. Her hit songs include "Hopelessly Devoted to You," "I Honestly Love You," and "Physical."

"Macarena": Song by the Spanish pop duo Los del Río originally released in 1993. The song was remixed by producers the Bayside Boys and, in 1996, became an international phenomenon accompanied by a popular dance craze.

Edna St. Vincent Millay (1892–1950): Pulitzer Prize–winning poet and noted feminist whose major works include "Ballad of the Harp-Weaver."

William Faulkner (1897–1962): Celebrated writer known for such works as *The Sound and the Fury* and *As I Lay Dying*.

Gore Vidal (1925–2012): Noted author and essayist whose works include *The City and the Pillar*, *Myra Breckinridge*, and *Lincoln*.

Eudora Welty (1909–2001): Author and photographer known for writing about the American South, whose works include *The Optimist's Daughter*.

Fat Albert: Obese cartoon character from the series *Fat Albert and the Cosby Kids*, created by Bill Cosby. It ran from 1972 to 1985. Fat Albert's catchphrase was "Hey, hey, hey!"

***Matrix* coat**: In the 1999 film *The Matrix* (see earlier entry), the character played by Keanu Reeves wore a long black leather coat.

"Toto, we're not in Kansas anymore": A paraphrased line spoken by Dorothy Gale to her dog, Toto, in the 1939 film *The Wizard of Oz*, after the pair are transported by tornado from Kansas to the magical land of Oz.

Coming Home: A 1978 film directed by Hal Ashby, starring Jane Fonda, Bruce Dern, and Jon Voight. It centers around a woman who begins a relationship with a paraplegic war veteran while her husband is deployed in Vietnam.

Cosa Nostra: Another name for the Sicilian Mafia.

Sandra Day O'Conner (1930–2023): Associate Justice of the Supreme Court of the United States from 1981 to 2006.

Poppin' Fresh: Better known as the Pillsbury Doughboy, the advertising mascot of the Pillsbury brand of canned biscuits, rolls, and cookies. The character, who wears a scarf and a chef's hat, giggles when poked in the belly. He was first introduced in 1965.

Saks Fifth Avenue: Luxury department store chain founded by Andrew Saks in 1867.

Kate Moss: English supermodel who rose to fame in the early 1990s.

Leonardo DiCaprio: Academy Award–winning actor and producer known for such films as *Titanic*, *The Wolf of Wall Street*, and *The Revenant*.

Monkey habitat: This remark is likely a reference to England's Monkey World, an ape and monkey sanctuary set up in 1987 by Jim Cronin. It has been the focus of multiple TV projects and interviews, including the documentary series *Monkey Business*, which ran from 1998 to 2006.

"Snow-White and Rose-Red": German fairy tale about two young sisters who encounter a friendly bear and an ungrateful dwarf.

Mariah Carey: Best-selling pop singer known for such hits as "Emotions," "Fantasy," and the holiday favorite "All I Want for Christmas Is You." She suffered a public mental health breakdown in 2001, posting unusual messages on her website and behaving erratically. She did in fact post a message to her fans claiming she was fine and staring at a beautiful rainbow.

Gary Mule Deer: Comedian and musician known for appearances on such shows as *The Tonight Show Starring Johnny Carson*, *Late Show with David Letterman*, *Hee Haw*, and others.

Leaning Tower of Pisa: Bell tower in Pisa, Italy, known for its visible lean resulting from an unstable foundation. It was built between 1173 and 1372.

Nancy Reagan (1921–2016): Wife of Ronald Reagan and First Lady of the United States from 1981 to 1989.

Soc: Short for Socials, a reference to the gang of wealthy teenagers from the film *The Outsiders* (see earlier entry).

Disney movie: Walt Disney Pictures is a film production company known largely for family-friendly entertainment.

Anne Sexton (1928–1974): Pulitzer Prize–winning poet known for confessional verse.

"Sing Out, Louise": Famous line from the 1959 Broadway musical *Gypsy*.

Divine Secrets of the Ya-Ya Sisterhood: A 1996 Rebecca Wells novel, adapted into a 2002 Sandra Bullock film, about a group of girls who take a blood oath to one another.

Cuban Cigar: Cigars manufactured in Cuba, known to be among the world's finest. A US ban on Cuban cigars dates back to a 1962 trade embargo.

EPISODE 2.8: THE INS AND OUTS OF INNS

Written by Daniel Palladino. Directed by Michael Katleman. Aired November 20, 2001.

Lorelai and Sookie make plans to open their own business as the owner of the Independence Inn visits Stars Hollow. Rory agrees to sit for an oil portrait for Richard.

"Danger, Will Robinson": Catchphrase from the science-fiction television series *Lost in Space*, which aired on CBS from 1965 to 1968. The phrase stems from a robot character warning Robinson of impending threats.

Billy Idol: English punk rock singer known for such hits as "White Wedding" and "Dancing with Myself," as well as for his trademark platinum blond, spiky hair and snarling expression.

Vincent Van Gogh (1853–1890): Influential Dutch painter who suffered from psychotic episodes and delusions.

Monticello: Plantation outside Charlottesville, Virginia, owned by Thomas Jefferson (see earlier entry). It was built in 1772.

"Chickie run down at the salt flats": A chickie run refers to two people driving toward one another—or toward an object—and the first to swerve away becomes the "chickie" (or "chicken"). Such an event is depicted in the 1955 film *Rebel Without a Cause*. An homage to that film's scene can be found in 1984's *Footloose*, set in Utah and the likely source of the salt flats reference.

Paul Revere (1735–1818): Boston silversmith and American Revolution patriot who made a midnight ride to alert the colonial militia of the pending arrival of the British forces ahead of the battles of Lexington and Concord.

The Money Pit: In slang terms, a money pit is a property that requires an excessive amount of money to maintain it. It is also the name of a 1986 comedy film starring Tom Hanks and Shelley Long as a couple struggling to renovate their newly purchased home.

Donald Trump: Businessman, media personality, and politician who served as president of the United States from 2017 to 2021 and was elected to the office again in 2024.

Ruth's Chris Steakhouse: Chain of upscale steakhouses. It was originally called Chris Steakhouse and was founded in New Orleans in 1927 by Chris Matulich. The business was purchased in 1965 by divorced single mother Ruth Fertel, who kept the original name while adding her own to it.

"Forever and Ever": The wordplay between Fran and Lorelai about forever and ever being a very long time is taken from the song "Forever and Ever," written by Michael D. Abbott and Sarah Weeks and performed by the characters Christopher Robin and Winnie the Pooh in the 1997 animated film *Pooh's Grand Adventure: The Search for Christopher Robin*.

California Gold Country: Region in northern California famous for its gold mines that attracted immigrants known as the '49ers during the California Gold Rush of 1849.

Keith Richards: English musician known for his tenure with the Rolling Stones.

Boy Scouts: The Boy Scouts of America is one of the largest youth organizations in the world, founded in 1910.

John Birch Society: Right-wing political advocacy group founded in 1958, named after an Air Force intelligence officer and Baptist missionary.

"Beam me up, Scotty": Catchphrase from *Star Trek* (see earlier entry), referring to the command given by Captain Kirk to Montgomery "Scotty" Scott. It is actually a misquote. While variations were stated on the show, the exact phrase was never spoken.

Siegfried & Roy: German-American duo of magicians and entertainers consisting of Siegfried Fischbacher (1939–2021) and Roy Horn (1944–2020). They were known for performing in Las Vegas and using white lions and white tigers in their act. In 2003, Horn was critically injured by a tiger during a show.

Phasers on stun: This is another *Star Trek* reference, phasers being the standard weapon of the show's characters, and stun being a setting for the device.

The Wild West: The Wild West is a reference to the undeveloped American frontier during the period of the country's expansion from the seventeenth to the early twentieth century. Lorelai refers to a Western comedy movie and vaudeville performance trope in which witnesses to a town's gunslinger battle would dive into water troughs to escape injury.

Glitter: A 2001 film starring Mariah Carey as an aspiring singer. It was panned by critics and was a box office bomb.

Sulu: Yet another reference from *Star Trek*. Lieutenant Hikaro Sulu is a character portrayed by George Takei.

Tar and feather: A form of public humiliation and torture in which the victim is stripped, covered in tar, and doused with feathers.

"Nothin' Is for Sure": A 2000 song by Grant Lee Phillips.

Blue Book laws: Blue laws are laws that restrict specific activities on certain days, usually Sunday.

To Kill a Mockingbird: A Pulitzer Prize–winning 1960 novel by Harper Lee, set in the fictional small town of Maycomb, Alabama, narrated by six-year-old Scout Finch. It was adapted into an Academy Award–winning film in 1962.

Holden Caulfield: The antihero protagonist in J. D. Salinger's 1951 novel *The Catcher in the Rye*. Caulfield has come to epitomize teenage rebellion and angst.

Rembrandt: Rembrandt Harmenszoon van Rijn (1606–1669) was a Dutch painter considered among the greatest in the history of Western art.

EPISODE 2.9: RUN AWAY LITTLE BOY

Written by John Stephens. Directed by Danny Leiner. Aired November 27, 2001. Dean isn't pleased when Rory is paired with Tristan in a school production. Lorelai goes on her first date since calling off her wedding.

Bringing Up Baby: A 1938 comedy film directed by Howard Hawks, and starring Katharine Hepburn and Cary Grant, about a paleontologist, an heiress, and a leopard.

Saint Peter: In the Bible, one of the twelve apostles of Jesus Christ said to guard the gates to Heaven.

Macbeth: Tragedy by William Shakespeare about a Scottish general who receives a prophecy by a group of witches that he will become king and goes to murderous lengths to make it happen.

Richard III: Play by William Shakespeare about Richard of Gloucester's determination to gain the crown of England.

Mafiosi: A member of the Mafia, the criminal organization dating back to Sicily in the mid-nineteenth century.

The Sonny & Cher Comedy Hour: Comedy-variety show hosted by husband-and-wife pop singers Sonny Bono and Cher, airing on CBS from 1971 to 1974.

Chang and Eng: Chang and Eng Bunker (1811–1874) were conjoined twin brothers from Siam who were widely exhibited as curiosities. Their fame gave rise to the term "Siamese twins."

Sock hops and clambakes: Sock hops were informal dance events for teenagers that gained popularity in the 1940s and 1950s. A clambake event is a gathering where seafood is steamed in a pit.

Butch Cassidy and the Sundance Kid: A 1969 Western film based loosely on fact about a pair of outlaws on the run following a string of train robberies. Paris uses a play on the term Sundance in the scene.

On the Town: A 1944 Broadway musical with music by Leonard Bernstein and book and lyrics by Betty Comden and Adolph Green, as well as a 1949 film, about three American sailors on shore leave in New York City during World War II. The three characters wear identical sailor suits.

Billy Graham (1918–2018): Evangelist and southern Baptist minister who operated a variety of media and publishing outlets.

Pamela Anderson, Tommy Lee: Anderson is a model and actress known for such works as *Baywatch* and for appearing in *Playboy*. She was married to Lee, a musician who co-founded the heavy metal band Mötley Crüe, from 1995 to 1998. During their marriage, personal home videos of the couple were stolen and sold as a sex tape.

The Twilight Zone: Media franchise that began as an anthology television series created by Rod Serling, in which characters find themselves dealing with strange and unusual events. It began in 1958 and has continued through a variety of films, series, books, theme park attractions, and more.

Automat: A type of restaurant where food and drinks are served through vending machines.

"Hey Hey, We're the Monkees": A line from "(Theme From) The Monkees," the theme song to *The Monkees*, a musical sitcom that ran from 1966 to 1968. It starred and focused on the adventures of four young men trying to make it as a rock and roll band.

John Houseman (1902–1988): Actor and producer known for collaborations with Orson Welles and Raymond Chandler and for such works as *The Paper Chase*. He wrote a series of memoirs, which were distilled into *Unfinished Business: Memoirs, 1902–1988*, published in 1988.

"Hail Hail, the Gang's All Here": Tristan paraphrases this 1917 song written by D. A. Esrom and Arthur Sullivan for the comic opera *The Pirates of Penzance*.

Friar Tuck: While there are friar characters in *Romeo & Juliet*, Friar Tuck is actually a member of the Merry Men, the heroic band of outlaws in the Robin Hood folklore.

Destiny's Child: Pop group whose most notable lineup consisted of Beyoncé Knowles, Kelly Rowland, and Michelle Williams. Their hits included "Say My Name" and "Bug a Boo." They disbanded in 2006 with Knowles going onto a successful solo career.

***Romeo + Juliet*, Claire Danes**: *Romeo + Juliet* is a modernized film adaptation of the William Shakespeare tragedy starring Leonardo DiCaprio (see earlier entry) and Claire Danes in the title roles. Danes's other notable roles include the television series *My So-Called Life* and *Homeland* and the films *Little Women* and *The Hours*.

Joseph Stalin (1878–1953): Political dictator who led the Soviet Union from 1924 until his death in 1953.

Vanna White: TV personality and game show hostess who has co-hosted *Wheel of Fortune* since 1982. Her role is to turn the letters on the game board as contestants attempt to solve the puzzle by guessing consonants and vowels.

***Inside the Actors Studio*, James Lipton**: *Inside the Actors Studio* is a TV talk show that premiered in 1994 in which original host James Lipton (1926–2020) interviewed actors in a conversational format for an audience of drama students. Lipton retired from the show in 2018.

Mystic Pizza: A 1988 film starring Julia Roberts, Annabeth Gish, and Lili Taylor as three friends who work at a pizza parlor in a small seaside Connecticut town.

Cocoon: A 1985 film about a group of elderly people rejuvenated by aliens.

No Doubt: Rock band formed in 1986 and fronted by singer Gwen Stefani. Their hits include "Don't Speak" and "Just a Girl." They opened for U2 (see earlier entry) on tour in 2001.

Absolutely Fabulous: Known as *Ab Fab* for short, *Absolutely Fabulous* is a British TV sitcom starring Jennifer Saunders and Joanna Lumley that aired between 1992 and 2012.

The River Wild: Lorelai references this 1994 thriller film starring Meryl Streep and Kevin Bacon (see earlier entries), about a family whose rafting vacation is thwarted by a pair of fugitives.

Priest in a Madonna video: This is most likely a reference to the music video of the Madonna (see earlier entry) song "Like a Prayer," released in

1989. While a priest isn't actually depicted in the video, it did feature scenes set in a church, and its content led to protests by religious groups.

"Bye George, I think he's got it": A paraphrased line from the 1964 musical film *My Fair Lady*, adapted from the 1956 Broadway play, which was itself based on the 1913 play *Pygmalion*. It focuses on a young, working class lady who takes speech lessons from a professor in order to pass as an upper-class lady.

The Beave: Character in the 1958–1963 sitcom *Leave It to Beaver*, about the misadventures of a young boy, nicknamed the Beaver, and his family and friends.

The Powerpuff Girls: An animated children's television series about a trio of superhero girls with powers that debuted on the Cartoon Network in 1998.

"The horse is dead": A reference to the expression "beat a dead horse," meaning that an effort is futile.

Bar Mitzvah: Coming-of-age ceremony in Judaism undertaken when a boy turns thirteen.

Doogie Howser, M.D.: A medical sitcom that aired on ABC from 1989 to 1993, starring Neil Patrick Harris as a genius teenage physician.

Jerry Lee Lewis (1935–2022): Pianist and singer-songwriter known as a pioneer of rock and roll, whose hits include "Great Balls of Fire" and "Whole Lotta Shakin' Goin' On."

Chuck E. Cheese: Restaurant chain founded in 1977, specializing in pizza and arcade games for children.

"Slow and steady wins the race": The moral of the tale of the Tortoise and the Hare, about the race between a slow-moving turtle and a speedy rabbit. The overconfident hare lets his arrogance be his downfall, losing the race to the slower but reliable tortoise.

EPISODE 2.10: THE BRACEBRIDGE DINNER

Written by Daniel Palladino. Directed by Chris Long. Aired December 11, 2001. The cancellation of a planned gathering results in all of Lorelai and Rory's friends and family converging on the Independence Inn for the holidays.

Mrs. Potato Head: A toy introduced in 1953 as a companion to the popular Mr. Potato Head, which was released a year earlier. The toys are plastic potato "heads" to which various plastic parts can be attached—eyes, lips, ears, hats, feet, etc.

***The Godfather* trilogy, Francis Ford Coppola, Sophia Coppola**: *The Godfather Part III* is a 1990 epic crime film produced and directed by Francis Ford Coppola, the third and final in the *Godfather* trilogy, preceded by *The Godfather* and *The Godfather Part II*. Coppola cast his daughter, Sophia, in a role in the film after the original actress, Winona Rider, dropped out. Her performance was panned by critics, and it was suggested that casting her hurt both her father's and her own career.

Michaelangelo: Michelangelo di Lodovico Buonarroti Simoni (1475–1564) was an Italian sculptor, painter, and architect known for such works as *David* and the ceiling of the Sistine Chapel.

Ernest movies: Lorelai's reference to the fictional film *Ernest Builds a Snowman* is a nod to the series of comedy films in which actor Jim Varney portrayed the character of Ernest P. Worrell, a rubber-faced, dim-witted Southern man who wore a denim vest and baseball cap. The character first appeared in TV commercials in the early 1980s before springboarding into the Saturday morning sketch comedy series *Hey Vern, It's Ernest* and slapstick comedy films like *Ernest Goes to Camp*, *Ernest Goes to Jail*, and *Ernest Saves Christmas* from the mid-1980s through the 1990s.

Mexican jumping bean: Seed pods native to Mexico that have been inhabited by the larva of a small moth. As the larvae curl and uncurl, they hit the wall of the pod, giving the appearance that it is jumping.

The Thomas Crown Affair: A 1999 heist film in which a woman (Rene Russo) investigates an art heist orchestrated by billionaire Thomas Crown (Pierce Brosnan). It is a remake of a 1968 film by the same name starring Steve McQueen and Faye Dunaway.

Anne Heche (1969–2022): Actress known for *Another World*, *Donnie Brasco*, *Wag the Dog*, and *Six Days, Seven Nights*, as well as for her three-year relationship with Ellen DeGeneres in the late 1990s. Heche experienced highly publicized mental health issues in which she claimed God was speaking directly to her. During one event, she drove to Fresno, California, and, wearing only a bra and shorts, wandered down a rural road, where she wound up at the home of a man who alerted authorities. Heche told authorities that she was God and was going to take everyone back to Heaven in a spaceship.

Slip 'N Slide: Toy introduced in 1961 consisting of a plastic sheet that becomes slippery when wet, allowing the user to slide along it.

Jack Nicholson: Actor known for *The Shining* (see earlier entry), *One Flew Over the Cuckoo's Nest*, *Terms of Endearment*, *As Good as It Gets*, and many other films.

Pixies: Alternative rock band formed in 1986 that achieved success before breaking up in 1993. They did ultimately reunite in 2004.

Tammy Faye Bakker (1942–2007): Televangelist and entertainer known for the Christian TV show *The PTL Club*, which she co-founded with her husband Jim Bakker, who was eventually jailed for counts of fraud and conspiracy. Bakker was also known for her flamboyantly glamorous persona, including her penchant for wearing heavy makeup.

Woody Allen, Soon-Yi Previn: Allen is a filmmaker whose works include *Annie Hall*, *Manhattan*, and *Crimes and Misdemeanors*. Previn married Allen in 1997. She is the adopted daughter of actress Mia Farrow, who was romantically involved with Allen from 1980 to 1992. In 1992, Farrow accused Allen of sexually abusing their adopted daughter, Dylan.

Def Comedy Jam: An HBO comedy series that aired from 1992 to 1997.

Iliad: Ancient Greek epic poem by Homer set during the Trojan War.

Monopoly: A fast-dealing property trading board game introduced in 1935.

Stella McCartney: English fashion designer and daughter of musician Paul McCartney.

Washington Irving (1783–1859): Author and essayist whose works include the stories "Rip Van Winkle" and "The Legend of Sleepy Hollow."

Madrigal: A form of vocal music from the Renaissance and early Baroque periods.

The Joy Luck Club: Lorelai uses a play on words that is a nod to this 1989 novel by Amy Tan about a group of Chinese immigrant families in California who start a mahjong club. It was adapted into a 1993 film.

Ben-Hur: A 1959 epic religious film starring Charlton Heston as the title character, an aristocratic Jewish man who incurs the wrath of a childhood friend, now a Roman tribune. One famous sequence involves a chariot race.

Doctor Dolittle: Character from a series of children's books debuting in 1920 who can speak to animals in their own language. There have been numerous adaptations of the character, including a series of films starring Eddie Murphy.

Björk: Icelandic singer-songwriter known for her distinctive voice.

Architectural Digest: Design and architectural magazine founded in 1920.

Chuck Mangione: Musician known for playing the flugelhorn and trumpet.

Abbott & Costello: Comedy duo consisting of comedians Bud Abbott and Lou Costello, popular in the 1940s and 1950s. They are known for a series of films such as *Abbott and Costello Meet Frankenstein* and *Abbott and Costello Meet the Mummy*, as well as the legendary comedy skit "Who's on first?" (see earlier entry).

"Believe": Lorelai references this chart-topping 1998 hit song by Cher (see earlier entry) when the group is discussing her during dinner. They also make mention of her ex-husband Sonny Bono without naming him.

Prague Symphony: Popular name referencing Symphony No. 38 by Mozart (see earlier entry), written in the 1780s during the composer's first visit to the city.

"Hotel California": A 1977 song by the rock band The Eagles, written by Don Felder, Don Henley, and Glenn Frey.

Days of Our Lives: Lorelai's line is a modification of the opening lines of this TV soap opera that debuted in 1965. The show's opening title sequence shows sand trickling through an hourglass, accompanied by the spoken words, "Like sands through the hourglass, so are the days of our lives."

Episode 2.11: Secrets and Loans

Written by Linda Loiselle Guzik. Directed by Nicole Holofcener. Aired January 22, 2002.
Lorelai struggles to find financing when the house is in need of major repairs.

Ethel Mertz: Character from the 1950s sitcom *I Love Lucy*, who was neighbor to and best friends with the titular Lucy.

The Rocky Horror Picture Show: A 1975 musical/comedy/horror film about a young couple who find themselves stranded in a castle full of costumed characters having a party. Lorelai references several characters from the film, which has become known for its midnight showings encouraging audience participation.

Miller Time: A reference to the slogan of the Miller brand of beer, which was introduced in 1903.

Twister: A multiplayer game consisting of a large plastic mat with colored circles on it. A spinner tells players on which color dot they must place their hand or foot and balance without falling.

Purple Rain: A 1984 rock musical drama film starring Prince. It was accompanied by a popular soundtrack album that has sold more than twenty-five million copies.

"Jolly Banker": Lorelai's line is a nod to this Depression-era song by folk singer-songwriter Woody Guthrie.

Coyote Ugly: A 2000 movie based on an actual chain of drinking establishments known for its bartenders dancing atop the bar.

Silkwood: A 1983 biographical drama film starring Meryl Streep, Kurt Russell, and Cher, about the life of Karen Silkwood, a whistle-blower and labor union activist who investigated wrongdoings at the plutonium plant where she worked.

The two Coreys: A reference to actors and friends Corey Haim (1971–2010) and Corey Feldman, who were frequently paired together in films in the 1980s, including *The Lost Boys* and *License to Drive*.

Tara: Fictional plantation that was the setting of the novel and film *Gone With the Wind*.

Robert Benchley, The Algonquin: Benchley (1889–1945) was a columnist, writer, and actor who was part of the Algonquin Round Table, a group of influential writers who would meet at New York's Algonquin Hotel for lunch from 1919 until 1929. The hotel opened in 1902.

The Energizer Bunny: Mascot of the Energizer brand of batteries; a pink bunny wearing sunglasses and flip-flops that beats a bass drum emblazoned with the Energizer logo. The character first appeared in ads in the late 1980s. Thanks to its Energizer battery, it "just keeps going and going and going . . ."

Ping Pong: A game akin to a table-top version of tennis, first played in nineteenth century England.

Tony Soprano: Fictional character and protagonist from the HBO mafia crime series *The Sopranos*, portrayed by James Gandolfini.

Clarence Thomas: Associate Justice of the Supreme Court of the United States. Thomas has been known for his long stretches of silence, asking no questions during oral arguments.

"Alice, pow! Right to the moon!": Catchphrase from the 1950s TV sitcom *The Honeymooners*, about short-tempered bus driver Ralph Kramden (Jackie Gleason) and his sharp-tongued wife, Alice (Audrey Meadows)—the phrase being a common empty threat Ralph would shout to Alice.

Bridge: A group-based card game played between two teams of two players.

Monday Night Football: National Football League game telecasts airing on Monday nights beginning in 1970.

Chicago Bulls: Professional basketball team based in Chicago, Illinois, founded in 1966.

Shaquille O'Neal: Known commonly as Shaq, a former professional basketball player and sports analyst who rose to fame in the 1990s. He played for such teams as the Orlando Magic and the Los Angeles Lakers.

"Be True to Your School": A 1963 song by the Beach Boys.

John Waters: Filmmaker who rose to fame in the 1970s with transgressive cult films such as *Female Trouble* and *Pink Flamingos*. Additional credits include *Hairspray*, *Cry-Baby*, and *Serial Mom*.

Madness: English ska and pop band formed in 1976, whose songs include "Our House" and "One Step Beyond" (the song Lane chose for the cheer).

Episode 2.12: Richard in Stars Hollow

Written by Frank Lombardi. Directed by Steve Gomer. Aired January 29, 2002.
Driven crazy by his constant presence, Emily begs Lorelai to spend the day with the newly retired Richard in Stars Hollow.

The Judds: Famous family of entertainers consisting of mother Naomi and daughters Wynonna and Ashley. Naomi and Wynonna emerged as a popular country music duo in the 1980s with hits like "Why Not Me" and "Love Can Build a Bridge" before Naomi retired for health reasons in the early 1990s and Wynonna began a successful solo career. Ashley is an actress known for such films as *Kiss the Girls* and *Double Jeopardy*. Naomi died by suicide in 2022, shortly before The Judds were to embark on a reunion concert tour.

Knock-knock jokes: Audience-participation joke in which one person says, "Knock knock," and another responds, "Who's there?" The back-and-forth continues to the punchline.

Rock star belt: A belt typically studded with metal or other hardware, often associated with rock and punk music.

Gustave Flaubert (1821–1880): French novelist known for *Madame Bovary*.

Winston Churchill (1874–1965): British statesman who served as Prime Minister of the United Kingdom from 1940 to 1945.

Tabitha Stephens: Fictional character from the TV sitcom *Bewitched*, which aired from 1964 to 1972 and focused on a witch who marries an ordinary man and becomes a suburban housewife, while still routinely casting spells, often by twitching her nose. Tabitha is the young daughter of the couple who also exhibits witch powers. The character was the focus of a one-season spinoff series airing in 1977–1978.

Andrés Oppenheimer: The Oppenheimer award Paris references is likely named after journalist and author Andrés Oppenheimer, who won the Pulitzer Prize in 1987 as a member of *The Miami Herald* team who uncovered the Iran-Contra scandal.

Three Days of the Condor: A 1975 political thriller film directed by Sydney Pollack, starring Robert Redford as a CIA researcher who comes back from lunch to discover his colleagues murdered.

Shoah: A 1985 French documentary film about the Holocaust that clocks in at nearly nine and a half hours in length.

The Jerk: A 1979 comedy film directed by Carl Reiner and featuring Steve Martin in his first starring role in a feature film.

Kevin Costner, *Bull Durham*, *Dances with Wolves*, *The Postman*, Tom Petty: Costner is an actor known for such works as *The Bodyguard*, *Yellowstone*, *Field of Dreams*, and the films Lorelai mentions in the scene. *Bull Durham* is a 1988 romantic comedy baseball film. *Dances with Wolves* is a 1990 epic Western that Costner directed as well as starred in and produced. It won the Academy Award for Best Picture and Best Director. *The Postman* is a 1997 adventure film produced and directed by, and starring, Costner, set in a post-apocalyptic America. Rock star Tom Petty (1950–2017) has an extended cameo in the film as the mayor of a city Costner's character visits. Upon meeting him, Costner's character says, "I know you. You're famous."

But it is never confirmed if Petty is actually meant to be playing himself. Petty is best known as frontman for the band Tom Petty and the Heartbreakers, whose hits included "American Girl," "Don't Come Around Here No More," and "You Don't Know How It Feels."

Harold and Maude, Taxi: *Harold and Maude* is a 1971 comedy-drama film about the friendship and eventual romantic relationship between a young man (Bud Cort) and an elderly woman (Ruth Gordon). See earlier entries for more on Gordon and her film *Rosemary's Baby*. Taxi is a TV sitcom that ran from 1978 to 1982, about a group of New York City cab drivers. Gordon won an Emmy Award for her 1979 appearance in the episode "Sugar Mama," in which she plays a woman who attempts to solicit the services of the show's protagonist, played by Judd Hirsch, as a male escort.

Cool as Ice, Hudson Hawk, Breakin' 2: Electric Boogaloo: *Cool as Ice* is a 1991 musical teen drama film starring rapper Vanilla Ice in his film debut. *Hudson Hawk* is a 1991 action-comedy film starring Bruce Willis, which employed cartoon-style slapstick despite being a live-action movie. *Breakin' 2: Electric Boogaloo* is a 1984 dance-musical film centered around the break-dancing trend of the era. The films were all notorious flops.

Showgirls: The film Rory takes from the young boys is this 1995 erotic drama film starring Elizabeth Berkley as a woman with dreams of becoming a professional dancer. It was a commercial and critical failure.

Lifetime, Nancy McKeon: Lifetime is a cable TV channel launched in 1984 that originally targeted female viewers and was known for its sappy made-for-TV movies. Nancy McKeon is an actress best known for playing the character Jo Polniaczek on the 1980s sitcom *The Facts of Life*. When that series ended in 1988, she went on to star in several TV movies.

Anita Bryant (1940–2024): Singer and anti-gay activist who served as a brand ambassador for the Florida Citrus Commission from 1969 to 1980.

Slinky: A helical spring toy introduced in 1945.

Angela Lansbury (1925–2022): Beloved actress whose most notable works include a Tony Award–winning run in *Mame* in 1966 and a twelve-season stint as amateur sleuth Jessica Fletcher on the TV series *Murder, She Wrote*.

"Dr. Feelgood": A 1989 song by the heavy metal band Mötley Crüe, about a drug dealer.

Frank Capra (1897–1991): Prominent filmmaker in the 1930s and 1940s, known for such films as *It's a Wonderful Life, It Happened One Night,* and

Mr. Smith Goes to Washington. Paris's comment is a likely nod to *It's a Wonderful Life*, which is set in the idyllic, Stars Hollow–like small town of Bedford Falls.

Deathrock: A subgenre of music blending punk, gothic, and glam rock.

Reese Witherspoon: Actress known for such works as *Cruel Intentions*, *Walk the Line*, and the TV series *The Morning Show*. Lorelai's joke is a nod to one of Witherspoon's best-known roles, that of sorority girl turned Harvard Law School graduate Elle Woods in the 2001 comedy film *Legally Blonde*.

Shamu: An orca captured in 1965 and sold to the SeaWorld theme park, where she became a star attraction. After her death in 1971, the name Shamu carried on at various SeaWorld parks in the decades following.

Captain Kirk and Spock: Characters from the *Star Trek* franchise. Captain James T. Kirk was portrayed by William Shatner in the original series and Spock by Leonard Nimoy.

Patricia Krenwinkel: Convicted murderer and member of the Manson family cult.

Pat Buchanan, Jerry Falwell, Kathie Lee Gifford: Buchanan is a conservative author and politician. Fallwell (1933–2007) was a conservative Baptist minister and televangelist who co-founded the Moral Majority. Gifford is a TV host and businesswoman who co-hosted *Live! with Regis and Kathie Lee* from 1985 to 2000 and the fourth hour of *Today* with Hoda Kotb from 2008 to 2019. She is known to express Christian values and, in the 1990s, came under fire when it was revealed that sweatshop labor was being used to manufacture a line of clothing branded under her name.

Dumbo: A 1941 animated Disney fantasy film about an elephant who is ridiculed for his oversized ears.

Babe: A 1995 comedy-drama film about a farm pig who wants to do the work of a sheepdog.

EPISODE 2.13: A-TISKET, A-TASKET
Written by Amy Sherman-Palladino. Directed by Robert Berlinger. Aired February 5, 2002.
The Stars Hollow picnic basket auction leads to a bidding war between Dean and Jess for Rory's affection, as well as a surprise for Sookie.

William Holden, *Sunset Boulevard, Sabrina, Stalag 17*: Holden (1918–1981) was an Academy Award–winning actor known for, among other things, the films mentioned in the scene. *Sunset Boulevard* is a 1950 comedy film noir in which Holden plays a struggling screenwriter who gets drawn into the deranged world of former silent film star Norma Desmond (Gloria Swanson). *Sabrina* is a 1954 romantic comedy-drama film with Audrey Hepburn in the title role. *Stalag 17* is a 1953 war film about a group of American airmen confined in a German prisoner-of-war camp during World War II.

Andy Hardy: Fictional character portrayed by Mickey Rooney in a series of films in the 1930s and 1940s. The Hardy family lived in an idealized fictional Midwestern town full of wholesome characters, with plot points often involving Andy getting into minor trouble but eventually doing the right thing.

From Here to Eternity: A 1953 romantic war film based on the 1951 novel of the same name by James Jones, about a group of Army soldiers and the women in their lives.

Running of the bulls: An event in which people run in front of a group of bulls that have been let loose in a sanctioned-off section of a town. The most famous bull-run takes place in Pamplona in Spain.

Ling Ling (1985–2008): Panda who lived in the Ueno Zoo in Tokyo, Japan, and became an important symbol of the zoo and of the friendship between Japan and China.

Ghostbusters: A 1984 supernatural comedy film starring Bill Murray and Dan Aykroyd, about a group of New York City ghost hunters. Its success spawned a still-popular franchise.

Lenny Bruce (1925–1966): Stand-up comedian and satirist known for his critical style of comedy.

Edgar Bergan, Charlie McCarthy: Bergan (1903–1978) was a popular vaudeville comedian and ventriloquist best known for his act with famed dummy companion Charlie McCarthy, who was attired in a top hat, tuxedo, and monocle.

Shipping off to Nam: A reference to soldiers who were deployed to fight in the Vietnam War, which took place between 1955 and 1975.

John Cleese: English comedian and actor who co-founded the Monty Python comedy troupe.

Dungeons & Dragons: Fantasy tabletop role-playing game first published in 1974.

The Dating Game: TV game show that first aired in 1965 and has been repackaged in various iterations in the ensuing decades. The basic premise sees a woman questioning three bachelors, all hidden from her view. At the end of her questions, she would pick one for a date.

***The Fountainhead,* Ayn Rand**: Rand (1905–1982) was a Russian-American writer and philosopher often associated with the libertarian movement. *The Fountainhead* is her 1943 novel about an innovative architect battling against conventional standards.

Ernest Hemingway (1899–1961): Nobel Prize–winning author and journalist known for such works as *A Farewell to Arms* and *The Sun Also Rises*.

***The Children's Hour, Julia,* Jane Fonda, Lillian Hellman, Hellmann's mayonnaise**: *The Children's Hour* is a 1934 play by Hellman set at an all-girl boarding school. In addition to her success as a writer, Hellman (1905–1984) was also known for her communist views and political activism. *Julia* is a 1977 drama film based on a section of Hellman's 1973 book *Pentimento*, in which she describes her friendship with the titular Julia, her lifelong friend, who fought against the Nazis in the years leading up to World War II. Fonda played Hellman in the film. Fonda, an Academy Award–winning actress, is also known for such works as *9 to 5*, *Barefoot in the Park*, and *Grace and Frankie*, as well as for political activism and a string of 1980s aerobics videos. Hellmann's is a brand of food products, most notably mayonnaise.

Swiss neutrality: Lorelai's reference to not taking sides as being Swiss refers to Switzerland's foreign policy principle of not getting involved in armed conflicts between other states.

Sylvester Stallone: Actor best known for playing boxer Rocky Balboa in the *Rocky* film series, as well as films such as *Rambo*, *Cliffhanger*, and *Tango and Cash*.

The Boy in the Plastic Bubble: A 1976 made-for-TV drama film starring John Travolta as a boy with a compromised immune system, forcing him to live his life in an incubator-like "bubble."

Episode 2.14: It Should've Been Lorelai

Written by Daniel Palladino. Directed by Lesli Linka Glatter. Aired February 12, 2002.

Christopher arrives for a visit with his new girlfriend in tow.

"Music has charms to soothe a savage breast": Famous line from William Congreve's 1697 play *The Mourning Bride*.

"Leave the gun, take the cannoli": A famous line from 1972's *The Godfather*.

The Outer Limits: Science-fiction anthology TV series that aired on ABC from 1963 to 1965.

"Duck, Harvey": A nod to the 1950 comedy-drama film *Harvey*, starring James Stewart as a man whose best friend is a six-foot-tall invisible white rabbit named Harvey.

Dr. Dre: Rapper who co-founded Death Row Records, known for such songs as "Let It Ride." He has been accused of multiple incidents of violence against women and other crimes.

Reader's Digest: General interest family magazine that debuted in 1922. Among its other offerings have been condensed versions of novels and music anthology albums.

Cooperstown: Village in New York that is home to the National Baseball Hall of Fame and Museum.

Two Fat Ladies: British traveling cooking program starring Jennifer Paterson and Clarissa Dickson Wright that aired from 1996 to 1999.

Jack Kevorkian (1928–2011): Doctor who rose to fame in the 1990s for championing physician-assisted suicide. He was convicted of second-degree murder in 1999, serving eight years.

"Jimmy Bob" slow: "Jimmy Bob" is a dig at a stereotypical Southerner who talks slower than people from other regions.

Willie Nelson: Legendary country music singer-songwriter known for such songs as "On the Road Again."

Harold Pinter (1930–2008): Nobel Prize–winning British playwright known for such works as "The Birthday Party," "The Homecoming," and "Betrayal."

Belle and Sebastian: Scottish indie pop band formed in 1996.

Yankees: Professional baseball team based in New York, established in 1903.

Death with Dignity Act: A 1997 act (which Paris mistakenly calls the Death Without Dignity Act), which allows terminally ill people to end their lives through the voluntary self-administration of lethal medications, expressly prescribed by a physician for that purpose.

Alain Ducasse: A famous French chef and restaurateur.

"Awe shucks, Pa": A paraphrased line echoing that of young Opie to his father on *The Andy Griffith Show*, a 1960–1968 sitcom set in a small, rural town. Griffith played mild-mannered sheriff Andy Taylor, and Ron Howard played Opie.

Martin Sheen: Emmy Award–winning actor known for such works as *Apocalypse Now*, *Wall Street*, *The West Wing*, and *Grace and Frankie*, as well as for his political activism and protests.

White Castle: Restaurant chain founded in 1921 that serves hamburger sliders.

Home & Garden Channel: HGTV is a cable TV channel launched in 1994, focusing largely on home improvement and real estate programming.

Soup to nuts: Idiom meaning "from beginning to end," such as in a full-course dinner.

Bruce Springsteen: Rock singer-songwriter, nicknamed The Boss, known for such hits as "Born in the U.S.A." and "Human Touch."

Rabbit boiling on the stove: Reference to the film *Fatal Attraction*. (See "I will not be ignored" reference.) In a classic scene, Glenn Close's character boils a pet rabbit on the stove.

"We Are Family": A 1979 song by Sister Sledge.

Ricki Lake: TV talk show hosted by the actress that aired from 1993 to 2004, known for sensationalist topics.

Pee Wee Herman: Child-like comedy character created and portrayed by actor Paul Reubens, who starred as the character in the TV series *Pee Wee's Playhouse* (1986–1991) and films such as *Pee Wee's Big Adventure*. Chairy and Captain Carl were characters on *Playhouse*.

Matthew Broderick, *Ferris Bueller's Day Off*, *The Producers*: Broderick is an actor whose best-known works include *Ferris Bueller's Day Off*, a 1986 teen comedy about a charismatic high school slacker's attempt to successfully skip school, and *The Producers*, a Broadway play by Mel Brooks about two scheming producers. Broderick and Nathan Lane appeared in the original Broadway run, which debuted in 2001. It is adapted from the 1967 Brooks film of the same name.

The Barrymores: Famous British-American acting family with roots dating back to the nineteenth century British stage. Notable members include Lionel, Ethel, John, and Drew Barrymore.

Episode 2.15: Lost and Found

Written by Amy Sherman-Palladino. Directed by Gail Mancuso. Aired February 26, 2002.

Luke and Jess are feeling cramped in their small apartment. Rory convinces Lorelai to hire Jess for some household projects and frantically searches for a missing gift from Dean.

Ida Morganstern: Fictional character portrayed by Nancy Walker on the CBS sitcom *Rhoda*, which aired from 1974–1979. Ida was Rhoda's mother, a character that first appeared on *The Mary Tyler Moore Show*.

Rockefeller family: American industrial and political family known for being very wealthy.

Vanity Fair: A pop culture and fashion magazine founded in 1983.

Mel Brooks, *The 2000 Year Old Man*, *Young Frankenstein*, *Silent Movie*: Brooks is an actor, comedian, and filmmaker known for comedy spoof films and specials like the works mentioned in the scene. *The 2000 Year Old Man* is a comedy sketch created by Brooks and Carl Reiner. *Young Frankenstein* is a 1974 film parodying classic horror films, and *Silent Movie* is a 1976 film parodying slapstick comedies.

"Calgon, take me away": Catchphrase for the Calgon brand of bath powders, popularized in TV commercials for the product in the 1970s and 1980s, the gist being that a luxurious bath with Calgon powder will help take away the stressors of life.

The Huns: Nomadic people who lived in Central Asia and Eastern Europe between the fourth and sixth centuries AD, known for devastating raids.

"Patience, grasshopper": A phrase from the 1970s action-adventure Western series *Kung Fu*, in which the character Master Po would advise his student, Kwai Chang Caine, to be patient.

The Shaggs: Rock band formed in New Hampshire in 1965, whose music—largely bizarre songs performed on untuned guitars—has been described as both the worst of all time and brilliant.

Coca-Cola with Lemon: While Coca-Cola is a soda brand so ubiquitous it hasn't warranted inclusion so far, the brand launched a flavor infused with lemon in 2001 to compete with competitor Pepsi's Pepsi Twist flavor.

"Just walk against the wind": Metaphorical phrase meaning to pursue a difficult goal, derived from a popular activity performed by mimes.

Inherit the Wind: Play by Jerome Lawrence and Robert Edwin Lee that fictionalizes the 1925 Scopes "Monkey" trial, in which a teacher broke a Tennessee state law by teaching Darwin's theory of evolution in class.

Letters to a Young Poet: A collection of letters by poet Rainer Maria Rilke (1875–1926) to Franz Xaver Kappus (1883–1966), a nineteen-year-old officer cadet at the Theresian Military Academy in Wiener Neustadt, written between 1903 and 1908.

The Lord of the Rings: A trilogy of epic fantasy films based on the novels of the same name by J. R. R. Tolkien. Based on the airdate of the episode, Dean is talking specifically about the first film in the series, *The Lord of the Rings: The Fellowship of the Ring*, which was released in 2001.

Autumn in New York: A 2000 drama film starring Richard Gere and Winona Ryder about a womanizer who falls for a terminally ill woman.

I Like Ike: Advertising slogan during the 1952 presidential campaign of Dwight D. Eisenhower.

Euell Gibbons (1911–1975): Author, outdoorsman, and health food advocate who was known for eating wild foods and for appearing in commercials for Grape-Nuts breakfast cereal in the 1970s. In one of the ads, he asks viewers if they've ever eaten a pine tree, because "many parts are edible."

Wayne Gretzky: Canadian former ice hockey player who spent twenty seasons in the National Hockey League from 1979 to 1999.

Donna Karan: Prominent fashion designer who created Donna Karan New York and DKNY clothing labels.

Miami Sound Machine: Latin pop band formed in 1975 and featuring the vocals of Gloria Estefan. Hits include "Conga" and "Rhythm Is Gonna Get You."

Mets: Professional baseball team located in Queens, New York.

Attica: Maximum security state prison located in Attica, New York, opened in 1931.

Franny and Zooey: A 1961 book by author J. D. Salinger including the short story "Franny" and the novella *Zooey*.

Mary Poppins: A 1964 hybrid live-action/animated musical film about a magical English nanny, starring Julie Andrews and Dick Van Dyke.

"I've been pinned": When a young woman would receive the fraternity pin of her boyfriend, signifying fidelity.

Bye Bye Birdie: A 1960 musical and 1963 film adaptation about fictional teen idol Conrad Birdie, who gets drafted into the United States Army.

Mission: Impossible: Multimedia franchise based on a fictional secret espionage agency. It began as a TV series that aired for seven seasons beginning in 1966. Various revivals have followed, including a successful film series starring Tom Cruise.

EPISODE 2.16: THERE'S THE RUB

Written by Sheila R. Lawrence. Directed by Amy Sherman-Palladino. Aired April 9, 2002.

Lorelai and Emily visit a spa. Rory's quiet night at home is thwarted by unexpected visitors.

George Washington (1732–1799): Founding Father and first president of the United States, serving from 1789 to 1797.

Risky Business: A 1983 teen comedy written and directed by Paul Brickman, starring Tom Cruise as a teenager who stays home alone while his parents are on vacation, with hijinks ensuing.

Driving Miss Daisy: A 1989 comedy-drama film directed by Bruce Beresford and written by Alfred Uhry, based on his 1987 play. It concerns a wealthy elderly woman (Jessica Tandy) and her chauffeur (Morgan Freeman).

The Moonies: Informal name for members of the Unification Church, a religious movement derived from Christianity, founded in 1954 by Sun Myung Moon in Seoul, South Korea. It has faced controversy from people who felt their family members were brainwashed into joining.

Luca Brasi: Fictional character in the novel and film *The Godfather* (see earlier entry). Luca is a personal enforcer. He was portrayed by Lenny Montana in the film.

Ted Nugent: Singer-songwriter, guitarist, and conservative political activist.

J. D. Salinger (1919–2010): Author best known for the novel *A Catcher in the Rye*.

Mr. Peanut: Mascot character for the Planters brand of nuts, depicted as an anthropomorphic peanut who wears a top hat and monocle and carries a cane. The character debuted in 1916.

Casino: A 1995 epic crime drama film directed by Martin Scorsese, starring Robert De Niro as a gambling expert asked to oversee operations at a Las Vegas casino and hotel.

The Beat Generation: Literary subculture movement started by a group of authors whose work explored and influenced post–World War II culture, including Allen Ginsburg, William S. Burroughs, and Jack Kerouac, among others.

National Enquirer: Supermarket tabloid magazine founded in 1926.

Charles Bukowski (1920–1994): Poet, novelist, and short story author known for writing about the lives of poor Americans.

Frankenstein: Character from an 1818 novel of the same name by Mary Shelley, about a scientist, Dr. Frankenstein, who creates a large sapient creature. The creature is commonly referred to as Frankenstein and has become a popular monster character.

West Side Story: Originally a Tony Award–winning 1957 stage musical with a book by Arthur Laurents, music by Leonard Bernstein, and lyrics by Stephen Sondheim. Set in New York City's Upper West Side, it follows the rivalry of opposing teenage street gangs the Jets and the Sharks, and was inspired by William Shakespeare's *Romeo & Juliet*. It was adapted into an Academy Award–winning 1961 film. Another remake followed in 2021.

Chairman of the Board: Nickname of singer Frank Sinatra (see earlier entry).

Chicken Ranch: Illegal Texas brothel that operated from 1905 until 1973, notably dramatized in the Broadway musical and film adaptation *The Best Little Whorehouse in Texas*.

EPISODE 2.17: DEAD UNCLES AND VEGETABLES

Written by Daniel Palladino. Directed by Jamie Babbit. Aired April 16, 2002.
Luke plans his uncle's funeral. A new farmers market opens in town, sending Taylor into a tizzy.

"Wake Me Up Before You Go-Go": A 1984 song by Wham!

Jerry Lewis (1926–2017): Actor, comedian, and humanitarian known for his comedy films and for his annual Labor Day telethon supporting the Muscular Dystrophy Association.

Mrs. Folger, Juan Valdez: The reference to Mrs. Folger is likely a nod to Mrs. Olson, aka the Folgers Coffee Woman, from a series of Folgers coffee commercials in the 1960s and 1970s. She was portrayed by actress Virginia Christine. Juan Valdez is a fictional Colombian coffee farmer appearing in advertisements for the National Federation of Coffee Growers of Colombia since 1958.

Jehovah's Witness: Lorelai's line is a nod to this restorationist Christian denomination known for going door-to-door to preach and distribute literature.

Jeannie, Major Healey: Characters from the fantasy sitcom *I Dream of Jeannie*, which ran on NBC from 1965 to 1970. Barbara Eden starred as a beautiful genie and Larry Hagman as the astronaut with whom she falls in love.

Revolutionary War: Conflict between American Patriot forces and the British Army, fought between 1775 and 1783, ending with Great Britain formally recognizing the independence of the United States of America.

Feng shui: A form of Chinese geomancy that involves using energy forces to harmonize with one's surrounding environment.

David and Lisa: A 1962 drama film directed by Frank Perry, about a man who has a fear of being touched.

Steven Spielberg: Successful filmmaker known for such works as the *Indiana Jones* films, *E.T. The Extra-Terrestrial*, *The Color Purple*, and many others.

Cracker Jack: Snack food brand consisting of caramel popcorn and peanuts that are packaged in a box with a small trinket toy inside.

Richard Nixon (1913–1994): The thirty-seventh president of the United States from 1969 to 1974, when he resigned as a result of the Watergate scandal. A 1976 book by Bob Woodward and Carl Bernstein, titled *The Final Days*, discussed the disgraced president's last days in office.

Adam and Eve on a raft and wreck 'em: Popular diner dish consisting of scrambled eggs served on toast, Adam and Eve being the first man and woman according to the Bible.

Van Halen: Rock band formed in 1973, known for such hits as "Jump"—and for their big hair.

Wimpy: Lorelai referring to a burger as a "wimpy" is a nod to J. Wellington Wimpy, a hamburger-loving character from the *Popeye* comic strip responsible for the catchphrase, "I'll gladly pay you Tuesday for a hamburger today." The character inspired a fast-food hamburger chain of the same name that was founded in 1934.

Library of Alexandria: Massive ancient library in Alexandria, Egypt, that was destroyed multiple times by fire.

Colossus of Rhodes: Ancient Greek statue of the sun god Helios erected in 280 BC, considered one of the Seven Wonders of the Ancient World. It was destroyed when an Arab force conquered the city of Rhodes.

Pop Rocks: Type of candy embedded with pressurized carbon dioxide gas bubbles that create a small popping reaction when dissolved. It faced controversy over the years when rumors and myths circulated that eating Pop Rocks while consuming soda was dangerous.

Neiman Marcus: Department store chain founded in 1907.

Patricia Hearst, SLA: Hearst is an actress and granddaughter of publishing magnate William Randolph Hearst who became known in the 1970s when she was kidnapped by the Symbionese Liberation Army (SLA), a militant far-left organization active between 1973 and 1975 and considered a terrorist organization by the FBI. She became wanted for committing serious crimes with the SLA, including bank robbery, before eventually being arrested, tried, and convicted of the bank robbery despite a defense that included brainwashing. Her sentence was commuted, and she was later pardoned.

Hippie: A person associated with 1960s and 1970s counterculture.

Mac and Tosh: A pair of extremely polite animated gophers in Warner Bros.' *Looney Tunes* and *Merrie Melodies* cartoons.

Charlie Rose: PBS talk show hosted by journalist Charlie Rose, which aired from 1991 to 2017.

Lady Godiva: Anglo-Saxon noblewoman and wife of Leofric, Earl of Mercia, known for a legend that says she rode naked through the streets of Coventry, covered only by her long hair, to gain remission of repressive taxation imposed by her husband.

World War II: Global conflict fought between the Allies and Axis powers between 1939 and 1945.

Toto: The dog owned by Dorothy Gale in L. Frank Baum's *The Wonderful Wizard of Oz*.

William Tecumseh Sherman (1820–1891): General in the Union Army during the American Civil War. The first edition of his memoirs was published in 1875.

Johnny Unitas (1933–2002): Football player who played in the National Football League from 1956 to 1973, primarily with the Baltimore Colts.

Lou Gehrig, Joe DiMaggio, Willie Mays: Famous professional baseball players.

King Tut: Tutankhamun (1341 BC–1323 BC) was an ancient Egyptian pharaoh during the late Eighteenth Dynasty who was buried with thousands of artifacts.

Yellow Pages: Telephone directory for businesses, originally printed on yellow paper, first issued in 1886.

Romanovs: The reigning imperial house of Russia from 1613 to 1917. Nicholas II, the last Emperor of Russia, and his immediate family were executed in 1918.

"One if by land": Line from *Paul Revere's Ride*, a poem by Henry Wadsworth Longfellow.

EPISODE 2.18: BACK IN THE SADDLE AGAIN

Written by Linda Loiselle Guzik. Directed by Kevin Dowling. Aired April 23, 2002.

Rory enlists Richard to assist with a school business project.

Waiting for Godot: Play by Samuel Beckett in which two characters engage in conversation while waiting for a man named Godot, who never arrives.

Paul Cézanne (1839–1906): French Post-Impressionist painter.

Geneva Convention: International laws for humanitarian treatment during war.

Gomer Pyle: Fictional character from the sitcom *The Andy Griffith Show*, portrayed by Jim Nabors, who was a naive and gentle auto mechanic. The character was the focus of the spinoff series *Gomer Pyle, U.S.M.C.*

Bhagavad Gita: The Hindu scripture.

Napoleon, Elba: Napoleon Bonaparte (1769–1821) was a French military and political leader who became Emperor of France in the early 1800s before being forced to abdicate and exiled to the remote island of Elba.

Candide: French novella by Voltaire, first published in 1759.

Mrs. Parker and the Vicious Circle: Rory offers a play on words of this 1994 biographical drama film starring Jennifer Jason Leigh as writer Dorothy Parker, a member of the Algonquin Round Table.

Devo, "Whip It": Devo is a new-wave band formed in Ohio in 1973. They rose to popularity with the song "Whip It," released in 1980.

Pointing to the outfield: A reference to a famous act by Babe Ruth, who pointed to the outfield before hitting a home run during the 1932 World Series.

The Pigeon Sisters: Fictional characters from the Neil Simon play (and film and TV adaptations of) *The Odd Couple*, the ditzy, flirtatious upstairs neighbors of the play's protagonists.

LoJack: A system invented in 1986 for locating stolen and missing cars.

Bobby Fischer (1943–2008): Chess prodigy who won a record eight US Championships, the first of which at age fourteen.

Mötley Crüe: Heavy metal band formed in 1981. A collaborative autobiography of the band, called *The Dirt: Confessions of the World's Most Notorious Rock Band*, was published in 2001.

Ozzy Osbourne (1948–2025): English singer-songwriter and reality TV star known for fronting the heavy metal band Black Sabbath. A story surfaced from his 1980s tour with Mötley Crüe that he snorted a row of ants as though they were cocaine.

David Letterman: Late-night TV host, comedian, and writer who hosted *Late Night with David Letterman* on NBC and *Late Show with David*

Letterman on CBS between 1982 and 2015. In the late 1980s, he was stalked by a woman named Peggy Ray, who stole his car and repeatedly broke into his house.

Ivan Boesky (1937–2024): Stock trader who gained notoriety for his involvement in an insider training scandal in the 1980s. He became a government informant after getting caught, was fined $100 million, and served time in prison.

The Untouchables: This 1987 crime drama film about Prohibition agent Eliot Ness is the source of Brad's reference to a baseball bat. A scene in the film depicts Al Capone, played by Robert De Niro, beating to death one of his henchmen with a bat.

Teen, Young Miss, Seventeen, Spin, Rolling Stone, Jane: These are all magazines, most targeting teens and women, while *Spin* and *Rolling Stone* are music-themed publications.

"When you assume . . .": A reference to the phrase "You know what happens when you assume. You make an ASS out of U and ME."

Posh Spice, David Beckham: Posh Spice is the nickname of Spice Girls (see earlier entry) member, singer, fashion designer, and TV personality Victoria Beckham. In 1999, she married professional soccer player David Beckham.

Buster Keaton (1895–1966): Actor and comedian who appeared in silent films in the 1920s, best known for performing physical comedy stunts with a deadpan expression.

Who's the Boss?: Sitcom that ran from 1984 to 1992, starring Tony Danza as Tony Micelli, the live-in housekeeper to wealthy advertising executive Angela Bower, played by Judith Light. In the show's later seasons, Tony begins attending college. One episode found him taking an advertising class taught by Angela.

EPISODE 2.19: TEACH ME TONIGHT

Written by Amy Sherman-Palladino. Directed by Steven Robman. Aired April 30, 2002.

After learning that Jess is flunking out of school, Luke asks Rory to be his tutor, which has unexpected ramifications.

Cocktail: A 1988 comedy-drama film starring Tom Cruise as a business student who takes up bartending to make ends meet.

Eve Harrington: Fictional title character from the 1950 film *All About Eve*, portrayed by Anne Baxter. The film centers around Margo Channing, an aging Broadway star portrayed by Bette Davis, and Eve, the young fan who schemes to take her place.

Lon Chaney Jr. (1906–1974): Actor known for the film *The Wolfman*, often called "The Man with a Thousand Faces" due to his ability to change his appearance to suit a role.

The Yearling: A 1946 family Western film based on the 1938 novel of the same name by Marjorie Kinnan Rawlings, starring Gregory Peck. It is the story of a young boy who adopts a trouble-making young deer.

The Wizard of Oz: A 1939 musical film based on the L. Frank Baum children's novel *The Wonderful Wizard of Oz*, about a young girl transported from rural Kansas to the magical land of Oz, where she encounters a variety of unusual characters.

The Sting: A 1973 caper film starring Robert Redford and Paul Newman as two grifters who attempt to con a mob boss.

Rocky: A 1976 sports drama film starring Sylvester Stallone as a small-time boxer who gets a shot at a championship title.

Crimes and Misdemeanors: A 1989 comedy-drama film by Woody Allen, who also stars as a documentary filmmaker.

The Singing Detective: A six-part BBC serial drama airing in 1986 about a mystery writer suffering writer's block whose illness sends him into the fantasy world of his novel.

Arthur: A 1981 comedy starring Dudley Moore as a drunken millionaire about to enter into an arranged marriage when he falls for another woman.

Sophie's Choice: A 1982 drama film based on William Styron's 1979 novel of the same name, starring Meryl Streep as a Polish immigrant with a dark secret in her past.

Cabin Boy: A 1994 fantasy-comedy film starring Chris Elliott as a snobbish man who gets stuck on a boat out to sea and ends up on a journey of self-discovery.

Desperately Seeking Susan: A 1985 film starring Rosanna Arquette as a bored New York City housewife and Madonna, in her feature film debut, as a bohemian drifter.

Angie Dickinson: Actress known for such films as *Gun the Man Down* and *Rio Bravo* and the TV series *Police Woman*.

Albert Einstein (1879–1955): Nobel Prize–winning German theoretical physicist who developed the theory of relativity.

Fletch: A 1985 neo-noir comedy-thriller film starring Chevy Chase as a reporter who investigates a murder scheme.

Urban Cowboy: A 1980 romantic Western film about the love-hate relationship between a couple portrayed by John Travolta and Debra Winger.

Woodstock: Legendary music festival held in New York in 1969 that became synonymous with the 1960s counterculture movement. More than 460,000 people attended.

Arctic Flight, Killer Shark, Where Are Your Children?, Sudden Danger, Suspense: These are all low-budget films produced in the 1940s and 1950s by Monogram Pictures, a company known for its B movies.

Snow Dogs: A 2002 comedy film starring Cuba Gooding Jr., as a dentist who travels to the Alaskan wilderness with a pack of sled dogs in search of an inheritance.

Pauline Kael (1919–2001): Film critic who wrote for *The New Yorker* from 1968 to 1991.

J.Lo: Nickname of singer and actress Jennifer Lopez (see earlier entry).

Akira Kurasawa, *Seven Samurai*: Kurasawa (1910–1998) was a Japanese filmmaker. *Seven Samurai* was one of his best-known works, a 1954 epic samurai film about a village of farmers who seek to hire samurai to stop bandits from stealing their crops.

***The Facts of Life*, Asaad Kelada**: *The Facts of Life* is a sitcom that ran on NBC from 1979 to 1988, starring Charlotte Rae as Mrs. Garrett, the housemother (and later dietician) at an all-girl boarding school. Later seasons saw Mrs. Garrett and her primary charges—Blair, Tootie, Natalie, and Jo—living together and operating first a bakery then a gift shop. Asaad Kelada is an Egyptian-American director of a variety of sitcoms, including many episodes of *The Facts of Life*.

Blue film: A "blue" film refers to a film that is pornographic in content.

Babe: Pig in the City: Kirk's reference to *Babe 2* is a nod to this film, a sequel to 1995's *Babe* (see earlier entry), which sees the titular pig on an adventure in the fictional city of Metropolis.

Egg cream: A soda fountain drink made from milk, carbonated water, and a flavored syrup such as chocolate.

Whatever Happened to Baby Jane?: A 1962 psychological thriller film starring Bette Davis and Joan Crawford as an aging former child star and the paraplegic sister she torments.

Schoolhouse Rock!: A series of animated educational musical shorts that originally ran between 1973 and 1985, focusing on such topics as grammar, civics, science, and history.

Marshall Plan: A 1948 American initiative to provide foreign aid to Western Europe following World War II.

Please Kill Me: The Uncensored Oral History of Punk: A 1996 book by Legs McNeil and Gillian McCain featuring interviews with a variety of punk musicians.

The Clash, "The Guns of Brixton": The Clash is an influential English punk rock band formed in 1976. "The Guns of Brixton" is a 1979 song by the band, written and sung by bassist Paul Simonon, from their album *London Calling*.

Coldplay: Best-selling British rock band formed in 1996 who are well known for their live performances. The band is led by vocalist Chris Martin.

Othello: Tragedy by William Shakespeare written circa 1603 about a military commander who is manipulated into thinking his wife is having an affair.

Kurt Cobain (1967–1994): Rock musician known for fronting the grunge band Nirvana. He died by suicide at age twenty-seven. He was married to singer Courtney Love (see earlier entry) from 1992 until his death.

Paula Zahn: Journalist and newscaster who has served as an anchor with ABC News, CBS News, Fox News, and CNN.

"As you wish": While a common phrase, it has also come to be closely associated with the 1987 fantasy comedy film *The Princess Bride*, about a farmhand, Westley, who sets out to rescue his true love, Princess Buttercup, from marriage to an awful man. In the film, Buttercup has a tendency to order Westley around, to which he always replies, "As you wish."

***Terms of Endearment*, Shirley MacLaine**: *Terms of Endearment* is a 1983 tragicomedy film adapted from Larry McMurtry's 1975 novel of the same name, covering the thirty-year relationship between a mother and daughter. In a classic scene, the mother (played by MacLaine) screams at a nurse to administer pain relief to her terminally ill daughter. In addition to this film, MacLaine, an Academy Award winner for *Endearment*, is also known for such films as *The Apartment* and *Steel Magnolias*. She has also authored books on spirituality and reincarnation.

Stan Freberg (1926–2015): Actor, comedian, and musician known for parody songs and satire.

Ash: Northern Irish rock band formed in 1992.

Sinéad O'Connor (1966–2023): Irish singer-songwriter and activist known for the song "Nothing Compares 2 U" and for sporting a shaved head. She was a controversial figure, once ripping up a photo of the Pope during a live appearance on *Saturday Night Live* in 1992 as a form of protest against abuse in the Catholic church.

Marianne Faithful (1946–2025): English rock singer-songwriter who rose to fame in the 1960s with songs like "As Tears Go By." Personal problems overshadowed her music in the 1970s, including a heroin addiction.

Emily the Strange: The sticker Lane puts on Rory's cast is one of this fictional character from comics, graphic novels, and merchandise, created by Rob Reger.

EPISODE 2.20: HELP WANTED
Written by Allan Heinberg. Directed by Chris Long. Aired May 7, 2002.
Lorelai helps Richard search for a secretary at his new business. Lane is excited when a new music shop opens in Stars Hollow.

The Little Locksmith: A 1943 memoir by Katharine Butler Hathaway detailing the effects of spinal tuberculosis on her life.

Automatons: Self-operating machines programmed to follow predetermined instructions.

Don Rickles (1926–2017): Stand-up comedian and actor known for his insult comedy.

Large Marge: Lorelai paraphrases this character, a fictional ghostly truck driver from the 1985 film *Pee-Wee's Big Adventure*.

Government cheese: Processed commodity cheese provided by the US government, mainly during the Reagan administration, to welfare recipients, the elderly receiving Social Security benefits, and other groups.

Don't throw the baby out with the bathwater: Lorelai paraphrases this common expression in which something good is eliminated when trying to get rid of something bad.

Wu-Tang Clan: Hip hop music collective formed in New York in 1992, credited for revitalizing East Coast hip hop.

Nanook of the North: A 1922 silent film documentary that follows the struggles of an Inuk man named Nanook and his family as they travel, trade, and search for food in the Canadian Arctic.

Carnac the Magnificent: Lorelai's line about holding an envelope up to one's head is a nod to this fictional character portrayed by comedian Johnny Carson on *The Tonight Show Starring Johnny Carson*. Carnac was a turban-wearing "mystic from the East" who would hold to his head a sealed envelope with an unseen question and psychically provide the answer.

The Wind Done Gone: A 2001 historical novel by Alice Randall that presents an alternate version of the story in Margaret Mitchell's *Gone With the Wind* from the point of view of slaves from the era. While not necessarily the source of Lorelai's reference, it was popular during the time frame.

Hit parade: A ranked list of popular songs at a given point in time.

Dawn Powell (1896–1965): Novelist and playwright known for *A Time to Be Born* and *The Locusts Have No King*.

Sal Mineo, Chachi: Mineo (1939–1976) was an actor known for such works as *Rebel Without a Cause*. Chachi was a fictional character portrayed by Scott Baio in the TV sitcoms *Happy Days* and its spinoff *Joanie Loves Chachi*.

Eurostat: Office that provides statistical information to the institutions of the European Union.

Mickey Hargitay (1926–2006): Bodybuilder and actor who was the 1955 Mr. Universe.

Keith Moon, Neil Peart, Rick Allen: All famous drummers. Moon (1946–1978) was a member of The Who, Peart (1952–2020) a member of Rush, and Allen of Def Leppard. Allen's arm was amputated in 1985.

*M*A*S*H*: Standing for Mobile Army Surgical Hospital, *M*A*S*H* is a TV sitcom that aired from 1972 to 1983 and followed a group of doctors and nurses staffing such a unit during the Korean War. Its final episode remains among the most watched in television history. The tiny fellow Richard refers to is the character Corporal Walter "Radar" O'Reilly (Gary Burghoff), who had a keen sense of perception.

Breadcrumbs: Lorelia's mention of bringing breadcrumbs is from the fairy tale Hansel and Gretel (see earlier entry). In the tale, Hansel leaves a trail of breadcrumbs behind him and his sister in hopes of following them back for a safe return home.

EPISODE 2.21: LORELAI'S GRADUATION DAY
Written by Daniel Palladino. Directed by Jamie Babbit. Aired May 14, 2002.
Lorelai attends her graduation from community college. Rory pays a surprise visit to Jess.

Tonto: Fictional Native American sidekick to the Lone Ranger, a popular radio and television character introduced in 1933.

Jumping frog, "The Lottery": The jumping frog remark is a reference to the 1865 Mark Twain short story "The Celebrated Jumping Frog of Calaveras County," the plot of which you can infer by Lorelai's comment. Rory's lottery response is a nod to "The Lottery," a 1948 short story by Shirley Jackson in which a town's custom of a lottery drawing has dire results for the winner.

Michael Landon (1936–1991): Actor known for *Bonanza*, *Little House on the Prairie*, and *Highway to Heaven*. He also wrote, produced, directed, and starred in a semi-autobiographical TV movie in 1976 called *The Loneliest Runner*, about the troubled upbringing of an aspiring Olympic runner.

"Ramble On," John Bonham: "Ramble On" is a 1969 song by the rock band Led Zeppelin, written by Jimmy Page and Robert Plant. Bonham (1948–1980) was the band's drummer.

"I can't believe I ate the whole thing!": Famous line from a 1970s Alka-Seltzer commercial, uttered by a husband who is experiencing indigestion after eating too much of his wife's cooking.

The Beatles at Shea Stadium, George Harrison, Ringo Starr: Famous, record-setting 1965 concert by the Beatles (see earlier entry) held at Shea

Stadium, a stadium located in Queens, New York, which opened in 1964. The sell-out concert drew over 55,000 people and is considered to be the height of "Beatlemania." Lorelai references two band members, George Harrison (1943–2001) and Ringo Starr.

John Nash (1928–2015): Nobel Prize–winning mathematician who spent time in various psychiatric hospitals being treated for schizophrenia. His life was the subject of the book and film *A Beautiful Mind*.

Jessica Hahn: Model and actress who accused televangelist Jim Bakker of rape when working as his secretary in the early 1980s. She later posed for *Playboy* and was a frequent guest on *The Howard Stern Show*.

Mick Jagger: English singer-songwriter known for fronting The Rolling Stones—and also known for his many relationships with women. He has eight children with five women.

David Lee Roth: Rock singer known for his time as lead vocalist for the band Van Halen. In 1993, he was arrested in New York City's Washington Square Park for buying marijuana from an undercover cop.

Jean-Georges Vongerichten: Famous French-American chef and restaurateur.

Zagat's, Concorde: Zagat's is a company that collected and sorted restaurant ratings and published them in guidebook formats. The Concorde is a Franco-British supersonic luxury airliner.

Sting: English musician known for fronting the new-wave band The Police and for his successful solo career.

Screech: Samuel "Screech" Powers was a fictional character from the Saturday morning teen sitcom *Saved by the Bell*, portrayed by Dustin Diamond.

Boone's Farm, bota bag: Boone's Farm is a brand of flavored malt beverage popular with young people and college students because of its low cost. A bota bag is a Spanish canteen.

What Color Is Your Parachute?: Self-help book aimed at job seekers by Richard Nelson Bolles, first published in 1970.

The Graduate: A 1967 film starring Dustin Hoffman as a recent college graduate seduced by an older woman.

Hummel: Brand of porcelain figurine based on the drawings of Sister Maria Innocentia Hummel, a German nun.

The Big Apple: Nickname for New York City, coined in the 1920s.

High Fidelity: A 2000 film starring John Cusack as a music enthusiast and record store manager.

Slint: Indie rock band formed in Louisville, Kentucky, in 1982.

The Go-Go's, Belinda Carlisle: The Go-Go's are an all-female punk rock band formed in 1978, whose hits include "We Got the Beat" and "Our Lips Are Sealed." Carlisle is the band's lead singer who also embarked on a successful solo career with hits like "Heaven Is a Place on Earth" and "I Get Weak."

Boonesville: Slang for a remote, rural town.

Annie Hall: A 1977 romantic comedy-drama film by Woody Allen (see earlier entry), who costars in the film alongside Diane Keaton. In a scene from the film, Allen's character is attempting to try cocaine, only to sneeze and have it go everywhere.

Shaun Cassidy: Singer and actor who was a popular teen idol in the 1970s with a series of hit records and TV roles before moving into producing and writing in his later years.

Ermenegildo Zegna: Italian entrepreneur and CEO of the luxury fashion house that bears his name, founded in 1910 by his grandfather.

Baz Luhrmann: Australian director, writer, and producer whose works include *Strictly Ballroom*, *Elvis*, and *Moulin Rouge!*

The Ritz: Nickname for the Ritz-Carlton, a brand of luxury hotels.

Pup 'N' Taco: California fast-food restaurant chain active from 1956 until 1984 when they were bought out by Taco Bell, known for menu items like tacos, hamburgers, and hot dogs.

Marcus Shankenberg: Swedish model and actor known for appearing in Calvin Klein advertisements in the early 1990s.

Bury the lede: Journalism lingo meaning to hide the most important part of a story.

EPISODE 2.22: I CAN'T GET STARTED

Written by Amy Sherman-Palladino and John Stephens. Directed by Amy Sherman-Palladino. Aired May 21, 2002.

Lorelai asks Christopher to accompany her to Sookie and Jackson's wedding. Rory and Paris run for student government.

Ella Fitzgerald (1917–1996): Jazz singer known as the First Lady of Song.

"I Can't Get Started": A 1936 song by Vernon Duke and Ira Gershwin, originally performed by Bob Hope and Eve Arden in the musical *Ziegfeld Follies of 1936*.

Annie Sullivan (1866–1936): Teacher and companion to deaf, blind, and mute Helen Keller. The water pump reference is a nod to a breakthrough that Sullivan achieved when using a water pump to spell out W-A-T-E-R by dripping the liquid into Keller's hand. Keller eventually signified recognition via her first spoken word.

"Hey Jude": A 1968 song by the Beatles written by Paul McCartney (see earlier entry).

"Seasons in the Sun": A 1974 song by Terry Jacks about a dying man's farewell to his loved ones.

"Cat's in the Cradle": A 1974 song by Harry Chapin about a father and son.

"Don't Cry Out Loud": A 1976 song by Melissa Manchester about not showing emotion.

Girl, Interrupted: A 1999 psychological drama film based on the 1993 memoir of the same name by Susanna Kaysen, about a young woman's time in a psychiatric hospital following a suicide attempt.

"Whatchoo talkin' 'bout, Willis?": Catchphrase from the sitcom *Diff'rent Strokes*, which ran on NBC from 1978 to 1985. It was spoken by young Arnold to his older brother, Willis.

Mr. Freeze: Supervillain from the *Batman* comics, created by Dave Wood and Sheldon Moldoff, first appearing in the 1950s. The character is a rogue scientist who, after an experiment gone wrong, needs subzero temperatures to survive.

Garfield: Comic strip character created by Jim Davis, first appearing in 1978. Garfield is a fat, lazy, orange cat who hates Mondays and loves lasagna.

"Ask not what your country can do for you": A famous quote from the 1961 inaugural address by President John F. Kennedy (see earlier entry), meant to inspire civic participation.

Sharon Stone, *Basic Instinct*: Stone is an actress who rose to fame playing a femme fatale in such films as *Basic Instinct*, a 1992 thriller featuring an infamous scene in which Stone's character crosses her legs while wearing a short dress and no underwear.

William Randolph Hearst (1863–1951): Rory's brief mention of Randloph is a nod to this famous businessman, newspaper magnate, and one-time presidential candidate.

Farrelly Brothers: Brothers Peter and Bobby, a famous pair of screenwriting and filmmaking siblings whose works include *Dumb and Dumber* and *There's Something About Mary*.

Yin and Yang: Ancient Chinese concept of harmonizing opposites.

Joel and Ethan Coen: Filmmaking brothers whose works include *The Big Lebowski* and *O Brother, Where Art Thou?*

Matt Damon, Ben Affleck: Actors, filmmakers, and friends who co-wrote and starred in the 1997 film *Good Will Hunting*.

"Little birds help you get dressed": A reference to *Cinderella*.

Rebecca of Sunnybrook Farm: A 1903 children's book by Kate Douglas Wiggin about a little girl sent to live with her aunts.

Hillary Clinton: First Lady of the United States from 1993 to 2001. She was then elected senator and eventually ran for president.

Brigadoon: A 1954 musical film directed by Vicente Minelli, based on the 1949 Broadway musical of the same name, about two American tourists in Scotland who get lost in the woods and discover a miraculous village.

Gloria Allred: Attorney known for taking on cases involving the protection of women.

"I'll Go Home with Bonnie Jean": A song from *Brigadoon* (see earlier entry).

"I have lost. Mr. Nixon has won.": Paris is referring to the 1968 concession speech by presidential candidate Hubert Humphrey (see earlier entry), acknowledging his loss to Richard Nixon (see earlier entry).

Jennifer Aniston: Actress best known for the 1994–2004 sitcom *Friends*. She was married to Brad Pitt (see earlier entry) from 2000 to 2005.

Fourth rung of hell: A reference to the *Inferno*, the first part of Italian writer Dante Alighieri's (see earlier entry) epic poem the *Divine Comedy*. Inferno is about Dante's journey through hell, consisting of nine concentric circles of torment, the fourth rung of which is described as being for the hoarders of wealth.

Greg Louganis: Olympic diver who won gold medals in 1984 and 1988.

Animal Planet: Cable network launched in 1996 focusing on nature documentaries and other animal-related content.

Sleepless in Seattle: A 1993 romantic comedy film starring Tom Hanks and Meg Ryan.

Jodie Foster: Actress known for such films as *Taxi Driver* and *The Silence of the Lambs*. The letter-writing reference refers to John Hinkley Jr., who stalked Foster in the late 1970s by sending her letters and poetry. In 1981, he attempted to assassinate President Ronald Reagan.

Prince William: Member of the British Royal Family and next in line for succession to the British throne.

Season Three: 2002–2003

Episode 3.1: Lazy-Hazy-Crazy Days

Written and directed by Amy Sherman-Palladino. Aired September 24, 2002.
Rory returns from Washington, DC, to deal with conflict between Dean and
Jess. Lorelai learns that Christopher's girlfriend is pregnant.

Connie Chung: Broadcast journalist and news anchor who has appeared on
NBC, CBS, ABC, CNN, and MSNBC.

Leopold and Loeb: Nathan Freudenthal Leopold Jr. (1904–1971) and
Richard Albert Loeb (1905–1936), two college students who kidnapped
and murdered a fourteen-year-old in Chicago in 1924 in an attempt to
demonstrate their "superior intellect" by committing the perfect crime and
facing no consequences. They were arrested and sentenced to life in prison.

Bill Mahr, *Politically Incorrect*: Mahr is a comedian, actor, and political
commentator who hosted the late-night political talk show *Politically
Incorrect* from 1993 to 2002.

Woodward and Bernstein: Bob Woodward and Carl Bernstein are journalists who, while working for the *Washington Post* in the early 1970s, reported
on much of the Watergate scandal.

Harry Thomason: Film and television director and producer whose credits
include producing the sitcom *Designing Women* with his wife, Linda
Bloodworth-Thomason. The Thomasons were also friends with Bill Clinton
and contributed to his 1992 presidential election campaign and held positions during the presidency.

Senator Tom Daschle: Politician who served as US Senator from South
Dakota from 1987 to 2005.

"I did not have sexual relations with that woman": A line from a speech by
President Bill Clinton, claiming that he did not have sex with White House
intern Monica Lewinsky in the late 1990s.

Vincente Minnelli (1903–1986): Director whose films include *Meet Me in St. Louis* and *Gigi*. He was married to actress Judy Garland (see earlier entry) from 1945 to 1951 and is the father of Liza Minnelli.

Mini-Me: A reference to the *Austin Powers* comedy film franchise. The title character's nemesis is Dr. Evil, portrayed by Mike Meyers, who creates a small clone of himself, portrayed by Verne Troyer.

Senator Barbara Boxer: Politician who served as US Senator from California from 1993 to 2017.

American Secretary of the Treasury: Paris refers to Paul H. O'Neill (1935–2020), who served in the role of Secretary of the Treasury from 2001 to 2002. He visited Africa with U2 frontman Bono (see earlier entry) in May 2002 to draw attention to poverty.

Carson Daly: Radio and TV personality who hosted the MTV series *Total Request Live* in the late 1990s and early 2000s.

Dick Cheney: Vice President of the United States from 2001 to 2009.

Freddie Prinze Jr.: Actor whose credits include *I Know What You Did Last Summer* and *Scooby-Doo*.

Colin Powell (1937–2021): Politician who served as US Secretary of State from 2001 to 2005.

NATO: The North Atlantic Treaty Organization, an intergovernmental transitional military alliance between thirty-two member states, established after World War II, who agree to defend each other against outside attacks.

Doug Ose: Politician who served as a member of the US House of Representatives from California from 1999 to 2005.

Archie Bunker: Protagonist of the sitcom *All in the Family* (see earlier entry), portrayed by Carroll O'Connor. The chair that Archie sat in on the show is on display at the Smithsonian.

Smithsonian: Group of museums and research centers in Washington, DC, created by the US government in 1846.

Trent Lott: Politician who represented Mississippi in the US House of Representatives from 1973 to 1989 and the US Senate from 1989 to 2007.

Sunny von Bülow (1932–2008): Heiress and socialite whose husband, Claus, was convicted of trying to murder her by injection overdose in the early 1980s. She lived nearly three decades in a vegetative state.

Glenn Close: Actress whose works include *The Big Chill*, *Fatal Attraction*, and *Dangerous Liaisons*. She portrayed Sunny von Bülow in the 1990 drama film *Reversal of Fortune*.

Oscar Wilde (1854–1900): Irish author and playwright known for *The Picture of Dorian Gray* and *The Importance of Being Earnest*.

Battle of Atlanta: Civil War battle in which General William Tecumseh Sherman (see earlier entry), leading Union forces, successfully defeated Confederate forces, taking the city of Atlanta, Georgia, and ordering many of its buildings, homes, and businesses to be burned.

Nell: A 1994 drama film starring Jodie Foster in the titular role as a woman who comes face to face with people after being raised in total isolation. She communicates through a language she developed.

Ralph Lauren: Luxury fashion company founded in 1967 by its namesake.

Leon Trotsky (1879–1940): Lorelai's line is a pun on the name of this Soviet politician who developed a school of Marxism known as Trotskyism.

Peaches & Herb: Vocal duo consisting of Herb Fame and various women filling the role of "Peaches." Hits include "Shake Your Groove Thing" and "Reunited."

Napoleon complex: Imaginary syndrome named after Napoleon Bonaparte (see earlier entry), suggesting that a man's short stature attributes to an angry, aggressive demeanor.

Bauhaus: English rock band formed in 1978.

Snow White: Fictional character from a German fairy tale and the Disney animated film *Snow White and the Seven Dwarfs*, about a princess who lives with her wicked stepmother. The stepmother's magic mirror proclaims that the beautiful Snow White is "the fairest in all the land."

Blondes have more fun: Rory's line is a reference to a 1950s Clairol hair dye advertising campaign whose tagline was "Is it true . . . blondes have more fun?"

Norman Rockwell (1894–1978): Painter whose work is known for reflecting American culture. He created cover illustrations depicting everyday life for the *Saturday Evening Post* magazine.

Manhattan garbage union: The Uniformed Sanitationmen's Association, known as "New York's Strongest," is a more than 800-member union of sanitation workers in New York City. They went on strike in 1968, resulting in 100,000 tons of trash piling up on the street.

Dan Quayle: Politician who served as the forty-fourth vice president of the United States from 1989 to 1993, under President George H. W. Bush.

"Those Lazy-Hazy-Crazy Days of Summer": Song written by Hans Carste, first recorded by Willy Hargara but made famous by Nat King Cole in 1963.

Wimbledon: Famous tennis tournament held since 1877.

EPISODE 3.2: HAUNTED LEG

Written by Amy Sherman-Palladino. Directed by Chris Long. Aired October 1, 2002.

Emily attempts to reunite Christopher and Lorelai, who finds herself fending off the advances of Kirk. Rory is embroiled in a student government conflict.

Mickey Mouse: Animated cartoon mouse created by Walt Disney in 1928.

Ben: Title character from the 1972 horror film *Ben*, about an army of deadly rodents.

The Legend of Bagger Vance: A 2000 sports film directed by Robert Redford, based on the 1995 novel of the same name by Steven Pressfield, starring Matt Damon and Will Smith as a golfer and his caddy, respectively.

Vince Foster (1945–1993): Lawyer who served as deputy White House council in the early months of the Clinton administration. Unhappy with working in politics, he spiraled into depression. His death from a gunshot wound was ruled a suicide, although several conspiracy theories emerged involving murder, even claiming involvement by the Clintons.

Roman Empire: Era of Roman civilization from 27 BC to 395 AD, when it fell after continuous onslaughts from German tribes.

French Revolution: Period of political and societal change in France from 1789 to 1799.

The Crusades: Series of religious wars supported by the Christian Latin church during the medieval period.

"Putting her on an iceberg": Paris refers to the stereotype of Inuit custom of putting elderly people on ice floes to die once they become a burden.

CliffsNotes: Publication series targeting students, started in Nebraska by Clifton Hillegass in 1958, that boil down classic or complicated works into more digestible notes and study guides.

Edgar Degas (1834–1917): French Impressionist artist known for pastel drawings and oil paintings.

Clemenza: Fictional character from *The Bodyguard* (see earlier entry) who kills someone in a car along a deserted road.

Meyer Lansky (1902–1983): Russian-American gangster known as "the Mob's Accountant," who was instrumental in the development of the National Crime Syndicate.

Margaret Thatcher (1925–2013): Prime Minister of the United Kingdom from 1979 to 1990.

Jimmy Carter (1924–2024): President of the United States from 1977 to 1981, known for his post-presidency philanthropic work. He won the Nobel Peace Prize in 2002. Francie's line compares Carter, whose presidency has been considered below-average, to that of Jed Bartlett, the fictional (but very successful) president portrayed by Martin Sheen (see earlier entry) in the TV series *The West Wing*.

French skating judges: Reference to a 2002 Winter Olympics figure skating scandal that alleged that the pairs' skating competition was fixed in favor of the Russians, who were awarded gold despite many believing the Canadian team was superior. Suspicion fell on French judge Marie-Reine Le Gougne, who admitted to being pressured by the head of the French national skating federation to award higher scores to the Russian team in an effort to get an advantage for the French team in another competition. She denied any actual wrongdoing. After an investigation, both the Russians and the Canadians (who had originally been awarded silver medals) received gold medals.

Goldilocks: Fairy-tale character from *Goldilocks and the Three Bears* about a young blonde-haired girl who enters a home owned by three bears and proceeds to help herself to their food and beds.

Noam Chomsky: Professor and intellectual called "the father of modern linguistics," known for political activism and social criticism. Many of his writings have been critical of the US government.

"Love Is in the Air": A 1977 disco song by John Paul Young, written by George Young and Harry Vanda.

Paul Newman (1925–2008): Actor known for *The Color of Money*, *Cat on a Hot Tin Roof*, and *Cool Hand Luke*, and for creating Newman's Own. The food company, known for its salad dressings, donates all its profits to charity.

VH1, *Before They Were Rock Stars*: VH1 (Video Hits 1) is a cable network launched in 1985 that originally focused on music videos before branching into additional original programming. *Before They Were Rock Stars* is a series that aired on the network from 1999 to 2001 and showcased the lives of rock stars before they became famous.

Helmut Newton (1920–2004): Prolific photographer whose work, known for its erotic overtones, appeared in *Vogue* and other publications.

Gays in the military: A reference to the "Don't Ask, Don't Tell" policy allowing gay people to serve in the military as long as they remained in the closet. A Clinton-era policy that was repealed in 2010.

Elizabeth Arden: A cosmetics and fragrance company founded by its namesake in 1910.

Mask and a horse: A likely reference to the Lone Ranger, a fictional masked former Texas ranger that appeared in radio and television shows beginning in the 1930s.

Shane: A 1953 Western film based on the 1949 novel of the same name by Jack Shaefer. Alan Ladd stars as the titular mysterious gun fighter who rides into a valley, protects its homesteaders with his skills, and rides off again. Upon his departure, one of the young members of the village cries out, "Come back, Shane!"

EPISODE 3.3: APPLICATION ANXIETY

Written by Daniel Palladino. Directed by Gail Mancuso. Aired October 8, 2002. Rory and Lorelai seek help with Rory's application to Harvard. Lane interviews band members. Taylor wants to open a soda fountain.

The Brady Bunch Variety Hour: A variety show spinoff of *The Brady Bunch* (see earlier entry), featuring most of the original cast performing skits and songs. Eve Plumb, who played Jan on the original series, did not participate and was replaced by Geri Reischl, who came to be known as "Fake Jan." It ran for one season beginning in 1976.

TV Guide: Currently a digital media company, *TV Guide* began as a print publication in 1948 and featured television listings, program information, and entertainment news.

Holmes & Yo-Yo: A comedy TV series that ran from 1976 to 1977 about a police detective and his android partner.

Hee Haw Honeys: Spin-off of *Hee Haw* (see earlier entry) that ran from 1978 to 1979 as a musical sitcom in which characters from the original series portrayed a family who operated a truck stop restaurant that featured a bandstand. Various country music acts would appear and perform.

Robert Reed (1932–1992): Actor best known for portraying patriarch Mike Brady on *The Brady Bunch*.

Dead Souls: An 1842 Russian novel by Nikolai Gogol about a mysterious traveler and the people he encounters.

The Accelerators: Rock band formed in North Carolina in 1982 by singer Gerald Duncan.

The Adolescents: Hardcore punk rock band formed in California in 1979.

The Adverts: English punk rock band formed in 1976 that was among the first punk bands to achieve mainstream success in the UK.

Agent Orange: Rock band formed in California in 1979, distinctive for being among the first to blend punk and surf music.

The Angelic Upstarts: Politically charged English punk rock band formed in 1977.

The Agnostic Front: Pioneering hardcore punk rock band formed in New York City in 1980.

The Animals: English rock band formed in 1963 whose hits include "Don't Let Me Be Misunderstood."

A-ha: Norwegian band formed in 1982, known for the song "Take On Me."

The Big Kahuna: An idiomatic phrase playing on the Hawaiian term kahuna, meaning the boss or the leader. The phrase was popularized in 1950s and 1960s beach movies.

Jackson Browne, "Doctor, My Eyes": Singer-songwriter and activist whose hits include "Running on Empty." "Doctor, My Eyes" is a 1972 song by Browne that became a surprise top ten hit.

"Wax on, wax off": Famous quote from the 1984 martial arts film *The Karate Kid*, in which a teenage boy, Daniel, learns karate from his mentor, Mr. Miyagi. Among the first tasks Miyagi assigns Daniel is washing and waxing his car, this phrase being his directions. The mundane task actually becomes a valuable part of Daniel's training.

Johnny Bravo: Animated series airing on the Cartoon Network from 1997 to 2004 about an Elvis-esque womanizer.

SpongeBob SquarePants: Animated series that launched on Nickelodeon in 1999 about an anthropomorphic sea sponge and his zany undersea adventures.

Ramones: Punk rock band formed in New York City in 1974, known for "I Wanna Be Sedated" and "Blitzkrieg Bop."

John-Boy: Fictional character from the TV series *The Waltons* (see earlier entry). John-Boy was the protagonist of the series, portrayed by Richard Thomas.

C-SPAN: Cable-Satellite Public Affairs Network, a cable TV network created in 1979 that televises US federal government proceedings and other public affairs programming. Additional networks in its stable include C-SPAN2, focusing on the US Senate, and C-SPAN3, which airs other government hearings and related programs.

Dot-com bust: The end of the dot-com bubble, a stock market bubble that ballooned in the late 1990s as a result of widespread use of the internet. With the dot-com crash in the early 2000s, many online companies folded.

The Brat Pack: Nickname for a group of young actors in the 1980s who often appeared in teen-oriented, coming-of-age films together, such as *The Breakfast Club* and *St. Elmo's Fire*. Among the "members" were Demi Moore, Rob Lowe, Andrew McCarthy, Molly Ringwald, Ally Sheedy, Emilio Estevez, and others.

Kate Hudson: Actress known for such films as *Almost Famous* and *How to Lose a Guy in 10 Days*.

Yes: English rock band formed in London in 1968, known for such songs as "Owner of a Lonely Heart."

Jethro Tull: British rock band formed in 1967.

The Jam: English rock band formed in 1972 whose hits include "That's Entertainment" and "Town Called Malice."

Nirvana: Alternative rock band formed in Washington in 1987 that disbanded in 1994 following the death of lead singer Kurt Cobain (see earlier entry).

Bananarama: English all-female pop group formed in 1980, whose hits include "Venus" and "Cruel Summer."

Kim Deal, the Breeders: Deal is a singer-songwriter and musician who was a member of the Pixies (see earlier entry) before forming and fronting the Breeders, an alternative rock band, in 1989.

Black Cow: Traditional name for a root beer float, a dessert beverage that blends root beer with vanilla ice cream.

Chocolate Phosphate: Soda fountain drink blending chocolate syrup, acid phosphate, and soda water.

Slaloming: Downhill race involving zigzagging between markers.

Dogtown and Z-Boys: A 2001 documentary about a California skateboarding team in the 1970s.

Ted Williams (1918–2002): Professional baseball player for the Boston Red Sox whose children had his remains cryogenically frozen when he died.

Star-Sixty-Nine: A call return service for landline phones in which a person could automatically dial the number of the last-received call by dialing *69.

"Suffragette City": A 1972 song by David Bowie.

Danny Gans (1956–2009): Singer and comedian known for his voice impersonations.

"Farmer John": A 1959 song by Don and Dewey.

The Butcher Lazar Wolf: A character from *Fiddler on the Roof* (see earlier entry).

"Ische ga bibble": Yiddish phrase meaning "I should worry," and the inspiration for the stage name of comedian and cornet player Ish Kabibble.

Dr. Seuss (1904–1991): Children's book author known for such classics as *The Cat in the Hat* and *How the Grinch Stole Christmas*.

David Hockney: Influential British pop artist. In 2018, one of his paintings sold at auction for $90 million.

Franz Kline (1910–1962): Abstract Expressionist painter during the 1940s and 1950s.

Richard Diebenkorn (1922–1993): Abstract Expressionist painter and printmaker.

Zoltan Kemeny (1907–1965): Sculptor, painter, designer, and fashion editor.

Ivan Turgenev (1818–1883): Russian novelist known for *Fathers and Sons*.

Nikolai Gogol (1809–1852): Russian novelist known for *Dead Souls* (see earlier entry).

PalmPilot: A brand of handheld digital assistant device released in 1996. It was an early precursor to the smartphone.

Middle English: A form of the English language spoken from 1150 to 1500.

Sir John Falstaff, *Henry IV Part 1* **and** *Part 2,* *The Merry Wives of Windsor,* *Henry V*: Falstaff is a fictional character who appeared in *Henry IV Part 1* and *Part 2* and *The Merry Wives of Windsor*, all three of which are plays by William Shakespeare, as is *Henry V*.

Frédéric Chopin (1810–1849): Polish composer and pianist of the Romantic period.

Ignacy Jan Padarewski (1860–1941): Polish pianist and composer who became a spokesman for Polish independence and served as prime minister in 1919, signing the Treaty of Versailles, which ended World War I.

Mesozoic Era, Paleozoic Era: The Mesozoic Era is the era of Earth's geological history, lasting from about 252 to 66 million years ago, comprising the Triassic, Jurassic, and Cretaceous Periods, all of which are mentioned in the scene. This is when dinosaurs roamed the earth. The Paleozoic Era is the era that immediately predated the Mesozoic Era.

Robertson Davies, *The Manticore* (1913–1995): Davies was a Canadian writer whose notable works include *The Deptford Trilogy*, of which *The Manticore* is the second novel, published in 1972.

Franco-Prussian War: European conflict lasting from 1870 to 1871 between the Second French Empire and the North German Confederation. Germany won.

"Istanbul (Not Constantinople)": Lorelai quotes this 1953 novelty song written by Jimmy Kennedy and Nat Simon and originally performed by The Four Lads. A 1990 cover by They Might Be Giants, however, is the best known version.

Henri Matisse (1869–1954): French artist known for his intense use of color and fluid.

Fauvism: An artistic style that emerged in France in the early twentieth century by a group of artists known as *les Fauves* (the wild beasts).

Sid Vicious: Carol's line about being holed up in Chelsea references this rock star. (See earlier entry for *Sid and Nancy*.)

Hindu deities: Brahma is the Creator God, Shiva the Destroyer, and Vishnu the Preserver.

Dead Kennedys, Jello Biafra: Dead Kennedys is a punk rock band formed in San Francisco in 1978. Biafra was their lead singer and songwriter. They disbanded in 1986. Years later, band members brought legal charges against Biafra over songwriting credits and unpaid royalties. They reformed without him in 2001.

The Courtship of Eddie's Father: Sitcom that ran from 1969 to 1972 about a widower and his young son, Eddie, who was portrayed by Brandon Cruz. Cruz became a musician and was the vocalist for the reformed Dead Kennedys from 2001 to 2003.

Steve Urkel: Fictional character from the sitcom *Family Matters*, which aired from 1989 to 1998. Jaleel White was hired to portray Urkel, the quintessential sitcom nerd, for a guest appearance. He proved so popular, Urkel became a regular fixture and eventually the primary focus of the series.

Malcolm in the Middle: Sitcom airing on Fox from 2000 to 2006, starring Frankie Muniz as the titular character—the middle child of a dysfunctional, lower-class family.

Butthole Surfers: Rock band formed in Texas in 1981. Despite a loyal fanbase, they didn't achieve more mainstream success until their seventh album, released in 1996.

The Kinks: English rock band formed in 1963.

Et Cetera: A French-Canadian band active during the 1970s.

"Smile": A song by Grant Lee Phillips.

EPISODE 3.4: ONE'S GOT CLASS AND THE OTHER ONE DYES

Written by Daniel Palladino. Directed by Steven Robman. Aired October 15, 2002.

Lorelai's speech at the Stars Hollow High career day takes an unexpected turn. Lane makes a bold play for independence.

Daffy Duck: Animated character in the *Looney Tunes* and *Merrie Melodies* cartoons, created by Tex Avery and Bob Clampett, first appearing in 1937.

Johnny Yune (1936–2020): Korean-American actor, singer, and comedian who hosted *The Johnny Yune Show*, the first Americanized talk show in Korea, from 1989 to 1990.

Lawrence Welk (1903–1992): Bandleader and accordionist who hosted *The Lawrence Welk Show* from 1951 to 1982. He was known for light and bubbly "champagne music."

"Bohemian Rhapsody": A 1975 song by the rock band Queen (see earlier entry).

Pete Best: English musician who was the original drummer for the Beatles before being fired in 1962 in favor of Ringo Starr.

Cornershop: English indie rock band formed in 1991. Rory is listening to their 1997 song "Funky Days Are Back Again."

John Coltrane (1926–1967): Jazz saxophonist and bandleader. Lane is listening to his 1959 song "Naima."

Larry King (1933–2021): Television and radio host who hosted the interview show *Larry King Live* on CNN from 1985 to 2010.

Sultan of Brunei: Head of state and government as prime minister in Brunei in Southeast Asia. Hassanal Bolkiah has served in the role since 1967.

Louis Armstrong (1901–1971): Gravelly voiced jazz vocalist and trumpeter.

"Hello, Dolly": Title track from the 1964 musical of the same name, written by Jerry Herman and first sung by Carol Channing on Broadway.

Pink: Singer-songwriter whose hits include "There You Go" and "Get the Party Started."

Kelly Osbourne: English singer, actress, and daughter of Ozzy Osbourne who came to prominence in the early 2000s when she appeared with her family on MTV's reality show *The Osbournes*.

Gwen Stefani: Singer and TV host who rose to fame in the 1990s as lead singer of the pop band No Doubt before embarking on a successful solo career.

Grunge look: Fashion associated with the grunge era of music in the early to mid-1990s, popularized by bands like Nirvana and including items like flannel shirts and ripped jeans.

Jimmy Buffett, "Margaritaville": Buffett (1946–2023) was a singer-songwriter and popular concert draw whose signature song was 1977's "Margaritaville," with lyrics reflecting a laid-back, tropical lifestyle.

Ace Ventura: Pet Detective: A 1994 comedy film starring Jim Carrey as an eccentric animal detective.

Vin Diesel: Actor known for the *Fast & Furious* film franchise.

Water Salad: Referred to by Lane as Salad Water, this Japanese product is water flavored with green salad.

"Zip-a-Dee-Doo-Dah": Song by Allie Grubel and Ray Gilbert from the 1946 Disney film *Song of the South*.

"If I Only Had a Brain": Song by Harold Arlen and Yip Harburg for the 1939 film *The Wizard of Oz*, performed in the film by actor Ray Bolger as the Scarecrow.

Snoopy: Character in the *Peanuts* comic strip and franchise, the beagle dog owned by protagonist Charlie Brown.

Guy with sunglasses and a dog selling pencils: Trope associated with blind men, particularly in New York City.

Kodak Picture Spot: Locations popular to tourists, especially in Disney theme parks, that were branded with a sign reading Kodak Picture Spot, a recommended place for a photograph. They later became Nikon Photo Spots.

Maxim: Men's magazine founded in 1995.

An Evening at the Improv: Cable TV series that aired from 1982 to 1996, featuring stand-up comedy sets from the Improv comedy club in Los Angeles.

High Noon: A 1952 Western film starring Gary Cooper as a town marshal facing off against a gang of killers.

Sardi's: Famous New York City restaurant founded in 1927, known for its caricatures of celebrities that adorn the walls.

Ward Cleaver, Eddie, Lumpy: Characters from the sitcom *Leave It to Beaver* (see earlier entry). Ward was the family patriarch, and Eddie and Lumpy were friends of his son, Wally.

EPISODE 3.5: EIGHT O'CLOCK AT THE OASIS

Written by Justin Tanner. Directed by Joe Ann Fogle. Aired October 22, 2002. Lorelai pursues a man she meets at Emily's charity auction. The girls are asked to water an eccentric new neighbor's plants.

Norton Critical Edition: Versions of classic literary works published by W. W. Norton & Company that feature annotated texts, context, and criticisms with the manuscript.

Society Matrons League: This reference is a nod to the fictional league for snooty women from an episode of *I Love Lucy* (see earlier entry).

HBO: Home Box Office, a premium cable network launched in 1972. Given its subscription-based accessibility, it has long been able to broadcast more adult content.

Solomon: In the Old Testament, the third monarch of the Kingdom of Israel and Judah, renowned for his wisdom.

Oz: Prison drama series that aired on HBO from 1997 to 2003.

Dead mother sitting in a rocking chair: A reference to the horror film *Psycho* (see earlier entry).

Two wild and crazy guys: A series of sketches from the TV series *Saturday Night Live* that began in 1977, featuring Steve Martin and Dan Aykroyd as two socially inept Czechoslovakian brothers attempting to meet women.

"Escape (The Piña Colada Song)": Lorelai and Rory reference lyrics from this 1979 song by Rupert Holmes.

"Midnight at the Oasis": The song that plays on Dwight's clock (and the episode's title) stem from this 1973 song written by David Nichtern and recorded by Maria Muldaur.

Sign of the Devil: A reference to the Mark of the Beast from the Bible's Book of Revelation.

Andre Cold Duck: Brand of sparkling red wine made in Sacramento, California.

Cardio Salsa: A fitness routine that uses elements of salsa dancing to burn calories.

Augusta National Golf Club: Golf club in Augusta, Georgia, founded in 1932 that operates as a for-profit corporation. For decades it barred membership to African Americans and women before finally admitting members in 1990 and 2012, respectively.

Erin Brockovich: Legal clerk and environmental activist who, despite her lack of law education, successfully built a case against Pacific Gas & Electric Company involving groundwater contamination in a California town in 1993. The lawsuit was the subject of the 2000 film *Erin Brockovich* starring Julia Roberts, who won a Best Actress Oscar for the role.

Trivial Pursuit: Board game in which players compete by answering trivia questions. It was created in 1979.

Blue Crush: A 2002 sports film about three friends in Hawaii who share a passion for surfing.

"Our president said exercise": A reference to then-President George W. Bush's 2002 campaign called the President's Challenge, in which he issued recommendations for people to improve their health and lifestyle.

Marathon Man: A 1976 thriller film based on the William Goldman novel of the same name, starring Dustin Hoffman as a history student and avid runner who becomes embroiled in a plot by a wanted Nazi war criminal, played by Laurence Olivier. The film includes scenes of torture, including using dentistry tools.

"Ground control to Major Tom": The first line of the 1969 song "Space Oddity" by David Bowie about an astronaut accepting the fact that he's stranded in space.

EPISODE 3.6: TAKE THE DEVILED EGGS . . .
Written by Daniel Palladino. Directed by Jamie Babbit. Aired November 5, 2002.
Rory agrees to attend Sherry's baby shower. Jess buys a used car.

US Army: Lorelai quotes a popular recruitment slogan from the US Army, the land service branch of the nation's Armed Services, that said "We do more before 9 a.m. than most people do all day."

Brooke Shields: Actress and model whose credits include *The Blue Lagoon*, *Endless Love*, and *Suddenly Susan*. She has been associated with Mr. Chow, an upscale Chinese restaurant chain.

"Stop the Madness": While a common phrase and not necessarily the source of Rory's quote, "Stop the Madness" was also a Ronald Reagan era anti-drug music video and subsequent public service campaign.

Rosa Parks (1913–2005): Civil Rights–era activist who played a pivotal role in the Montgomery bus boycott when, in 1955, she refused to give up her seat on a Montgomery, Alabama, bus to a white man.

"They're cousins, identical cousins": Lorelai sings a line from the theme song of *The Patty Duke Show*, a sitcom which ran from 1963 to 1966 and starred Duke as a pair of identical cousins.

MotorTrend: A car magazine first published in 1949.

"I'm in good hands": Jess paraphrases the slogan of the insurance company Allstate, whose "You're in good hands" advertising began in the 1950s. The company refers to themselves as the Good Hands People.

SOS: International Morse code signal for distress.

Jan and Dean: Pop-rock duo consisting of William Jan Berry (1941–2004) and Dean Torrence who helped pioneer the "California Sound" music style. Several of their songs were about cars, including "Drag City," "Dead Man's Curve," and "The Little Old Lady (from Pasadena)."

Andrew Jackson (1767–1845): Seventh president of the United States from 1829 to 1837 whose face is on the twenty dollar bill.

Alfred E. Neuman: Fictional mascot of the humor magazine *Mad*, depicted as a red-haired, gap-toothed young man. The image had actually been used much earlier in various advertising campaigns before being adopted by the magazine in the 1950s.

Andy Griffith (1926–2012): Actor and singer best known for *The Andy Griffith Show* and *Matlock*. Jess is referring to the smalltown setting of *The Andy Griffith Show*, the fictional Mayberry.

Lizzie Grubman: Maureen refers to this publicist and socialite who in 2001 backed her Mercedes-Benz into a crowd of people outside an inn in the Hamptons, injuring sixteen people, after a security guard asked her to move it from a fire lane. She served thirty-eight days in jail.

Wang Chung: English New Wave band formed in 1980, whose hits include "Dance Hall Days" and "Everybody Have Fun Tonight."

Billy Joel: Best-selling singer-songwriter and pianist whose hits include "Piano Man" and "We Didn't Start the Fire."

Deenie: A 1973 young adult novel by Judy Blume about a teenage girl with scoliosis.

***For Keeps*, Molly Ringwald, Randall Batinkoff, John Hughes**: *For Keeps* is a 1988 film in which Ringwald and Batinkoff star as two teenagers faced with becoming parents. Ringwald is an actress who had, up until then, been known largely for appearing in teen films directed by Hughes, such as *The Breakfast Club* and *Pretty in Pink*. This was considered among her first mature roles. In 1996, she co-starred with Lauren Graham in the short-lived sitcom *Townies*. Batinkoff's other credits include *School Ties* and *Higher Learning*. Hughes (1950–2009) was a filmmaker whose additional credits include the films *Weird Science*, *Ferris Bueller's Day Off*, *Uncle Buck*, and several others.

Quincy, M.E.: Medical mystery TV series that ran from 1976 to 1983, starring Jack Klugman as a medical examiner who assisted with police investigations.

Aryan breeding: Aryan refers to an obsolete race concept dating back to the late nineteenth century to describe people of Proto-Indo-European heritage as a racial grouping that, by the 1930s, had come to be adopted by Nazis to promote white supremacist ideology portraying Aryans as a "master race."

Uma Thurman: Actress known for *Pulp Fiction* and *Kill Bill*.

Dirk Squarejaw: A reference to the TV series *Mystery Science Theater 3000*, in which characters would provide comedic commentary while watching science-fiction B movies. Dirk Squarejaw was a name prescribed during the commentary to a character in the film *Rocketship X-M*.

"God Bless America": Patriotic song written by Irving Berlin during World War I.

Duane from *Annie Hall*: Duane is a character in the film *Annie Hall* (see earlier entry), portrayed by Christopher Walken, who fantasizes about steering his car into oncoming traffic.

Rand McNally: A company founded in 1868 by William Rand and Andrew McNally that provides mapping for electronic gadgets and produces atlases and road maps.

Haight-Ashbury, *The Electric Kool-Aid Acid Test*: Haight-Ashbury is a San Francisco neighborhood known for being a center of the hippie counterculture of the 1960s. *The Electric Kool-Aid Acid Test* is a 1968 nonfiction book by Tom Wolfe about a group of psychedelic enthusiasts who traveled across the country in a painted school bus.

EPISODE 3.7: THEY SHOOT GILMORES, DON'T THEY?

Written by Amy Sherman-Palladino. Directed by Kenny Ortega. Aired November 12, 2002.
Lorelai is determined to win the annual Stars Hollow dance marathon.

Mad Cow Disease: Common name for Bovine spongiform encephalopathy, an incurable and inevitably fatal neurodegenerative disease of cattle that can also spread to humans.

Tommy Tune: Famous actor, dancer, and choreographer.

Tennessee Williams (1911–1983): Playwright and screenwriter known for *The Glass Menagerie*, *A Streetcar Named Desire*, and *Cat on a Hot Tin Roof*.

Tiny Tim: Character from the 1843 Charles Dickens novella *A Christmas Carol*. He is the son of Scrooge's employee Bob Cratchit and is a sick young boy who needs a crutch to walk.

Señor Wences (1896–1999): Spanish ventriloquist and comedian known for appearing on *The Ed Sullivan Show* and *The Muppet Show*.

Riverdance: Theatrical show consisting primarily of Irish music and dance.

Debbie Reynolds, Eddie Fisher, Fisher Stevens: Lorelai refers to a famous Hollywood love triangle between Elizabeth Taylor (see earlier entry), *Singin' in the Rain* actress Debbie Reynolds (1932–2016), and actor Eddie Fisher (1928–2010). Fisher was married to Reynolds from 1955 until 1959, when it was revealed that he was having an affair with Taylor, who was close friends with Reynolds. Fisher and Taylor were married from 1959 to 1964. The two women eventually rekindled their friendship. Fisher Stevens is an actor and filmmaker known for *Short Circuit* and *Succession*.

Jeff Spicoli: Fictional character from the 1982 coming-of-age high school comedy film *Fast Times at Ridgemont High*—a stoner portrayed by Sean Penn.

Boxing Helena: A 1993 avant-garde thriller film about a woman held captive by a man who amputates her limbs.

"Find a pirate to sit on": A reference to the pirate stereotype of having a parrot sit on their shoulder, stemming from the Long John Silver character in Robert Louis Stevenson's novel *Treasure Island*.

Quadrophenia, **The Who**: *Quadrophenia* is the sixth studio album by English rock band The Who, released in 1973. The band formed in London in 1964. Their classic lineup consisted of lead vocalist Roger Daltrey, guitarist Pete Townshend, bassist John Entwistle, and drummer Keith Moon.

Theme from *Rocky*: The theme song from the film *Rocky* (see earlier entry) is "Gonna Fly Now," composed by Bill Conti with lyrics by Carol Connors and Ayn Robbins, and performed by DeEtta West and Nelson Pigford.

Ted Bundy (1946–1989): Serial killer responsible for kidnapping, raping, and murdering several young women during the 1970s.

Trojan: Brand of condoms introduced in 1916. Its commercials in the 1990s and 2000s featured a song in which the vocalist shouted "Trojan man!"

"Makes me want to ration sugar": A reference to sugar rationing that took place during World War II, in which sugar was rationed to two pounds per person per month.

Howard Roark: Protagonist in the Ayn Rand novel *The Fountainhead* (see earlier entry).

Liam Neeson: Actor known for such films as *Schindler's List*.

The Olympics: International sporting events featuring summer and winter sports in which athletes compete for medals in a variety of competitions.

Martha Graham (1894–1991): Dancer and choreographer who created the Graham Technique style of dancing. The Martha Graham School in New York City is the country's oldest dance school.

Bobby Brady: Fictional youngest son on the TV sitcom *The Brady Bunch* (see earlier entry), portrayed by Mike Lookinland.

Winona Ryder: Actress known for *Beetlejuice*, *Heathers*, *Stranger Things*, and other works. Her personal life has long served as tabloid fodder, including a

2001 arrest for shoplifting designer clothing from Saks, behavior she attributed to clinical depression and painkillers.

Blue Velvet: A 1986 neo-noir mystery thriller directed by David Lynch that blends psychological horror with film noir.

EPISODE 3.8: LET THE GAMES BEGIN

Teleplay by Amy Sherman-Palladino. Story by Amy Sherman-Palladino and Sheila R. Lawrence. Directed by Steven Robman. Aired November 19, 2002.
A visit to Yale with Richard and Emily takes an unexpected turn for Rory.

Donner Party: American pioneers who migrated to California via wagon train in the 1840s but were forced to spend a winter snowbound in the Sierra Nevada mountain range. Members resorted to cannibalism to survive.

Heather Mills: Former model and businesswoman whose leg was amputated below the knee following a motorcycle accident in the early 1990s. She created a trust that sent prosthetic limbs to people who had lost limbs in landmines and also sent discarded prosthetic limbs to people in Croatia.

"Money for Nothing": Lorelai quotes this 1985 song by the British rock band Dire Straits.

Ari Fleischer: Political aid and media consultant who served as press secretary for President George W. Bush from 2000 to 2003.

Frank Lloyd Wright (1867–1959): Famous architect who designed more than one thousand structures. Lorelai relates fairly accurate details of a 1914 incident at a home Wright owned in Wisconsin. Julian Carlton, a servant, set fire to the home and then murdered seven people with an axe as the fire burned. Wright was not present at the time, but among those killed were Mamah Borthwick, a woman for whom he had left his wife.

The Whiffenpoofs: A collegiate a cappella singing group at Yale University formed in 1909.

Perry Como (1912–2001): Famed singer, actor, and TV personality.

"Good to the last drop": Advertising slogan for the Maxwell House brand of coffee, which it began using in 1915.

Søren Kierkegaard (1813–1855): Danish existential philosopher, poet, and religious writer.

Louvre: Famous museum in Paris, France.

Titian (1488–1570): Italian Renaissance painter.

Helena Bonham Carter: English actress known for *A Room With a View* and the *Harry Potter* films. In 1994, while filming Mary Shelley's *Frankenstein*, she began an affair with co-star Kenneth Branagh, who was married to actress Emma Thompson at the time.

George Michael (1963–2016): Pop star who rose to fame as a member of the duo Wham! in the 1980s before embarking on a successful solo career with hits like "Faith" and "Father Figure." In 1998, he was arrested for "engaging in a lewd act" in a public restroom at a Beverly Hills park.

Nantucket: An island off the coast of Massachusetts. Lorelai refers to a famous limerick that begins "There once was a man from Nantucket," of which there are many vulgar versions using certain phrases that rhyme with the word.

Scud missile: Tactical ballistic missile developed by the Soviet Union during the Cold War.

"Lions and tigers and bears": A reference to a famous line in *The Wizard of Oz* (see earlier entry), spoken by characters as they followed the Yellow Brick Road through a darkened forest.

"Slap my face with a glove": The traditional way of challenging someone to a duel.

Oprah's Book Club: A segment originating on *The Oprah Winfrey Show* beginning in 1996, featuring books recommended by the host.

Gloria Estefan: Cuban-American singer who rose to fame as a member of the Miami Sound Machine (see earlier entry) before embarking on a successful solo career.

Mind meld: Vulcan telepathic technique from the *Star Trek* universe (see earlier entry).

Butterfly: Julia Butterfly Hill is an environmental activist who lived in a tent near the top of a 200-foot-tall, 1,000-year-old California redwood tree for 738 days beginning in late 1997 in an effort to stop a lumber company from cutting it down.

EPISODE 3.9: A DEEP-FRIED KOREAN THANKSGIVING

Written by Daniel Palladino. Directed by Kenny Ortega. Aired November 26, 2002.

Lorelai and Rory attempt to juggle invitations to four Thanksgiving dinners.

Grey Gardens: A 1975 documentary film about the everyday lives of an eccentric, reclusive mother and daughter both named Edith Beale (Big Edie and Little Edie), who lived in poverty in a derelict mansion. They were relatives of First Lady Jackie Kennedy (see earlier entry).

***CBS Evening News*, Dan Rather**: Rather is a journalist who anchored the *CBS Evening News* for twenty-four years beginning in 1981. The era referred to the major networks of CBS, NBC, and ABC as the "Big Three."

Ryan Phillippe: Actor known for such films as *I Know What You Did Last Summer* and *Cruel Intentions*.

The Banger Sisters: A 2002 comedy film starring Goldie Hawn and Susan Sarandon as two friends and former groupies.

Manson girl: A reference to the followers of Charles Manson (see earlier entry).

Wes Craven (1939–2015): Filmmaker known for his work in the horror genre, including the *Nightmare on Elm Street* franchise.

Cindy Lou Who: Fictional character from Dr. Seuss's *How the Grinch Stole Christmas*. (See earlier entry for the Grinch.) Cindy Lou Who is a young resident of Whoville whom the Grinch encounters during his exploits. The character has a larger role in the film adaptation of the book.

Michelle Kwan: Retired Olympic figure skater. A fall during the 2002 Olympics netted her a bronze medal instead of the gold she was favored to receive.

Three Stooges: Vaudeville comedy team who starred in short films debuting in the early 1920s, known for slapstick humor. The original trio consisted of Moe Howard, Larry Fine, and Curly Howard.

Frank at the Sands: A reference to Frank Sinatra (see earlier entry), who performed regularly at the Sands Hotel and Casino in Las Vegas.

Quasimodo: Character from *The Hunchback of Notre Dame* (see earlier entry).

Visigoths: An early Germanic people who invaded Italy and sacked Rome. Lorelai refers to a practice from the time of pouring hot oil onto attackers during a siege.

Thunderdome: A reference to the post-apocalyptic, fight-to-the-death arena from the 1985 dystopian film *Mad Max Beyond Thunderdome*.

Smallpox-infested blankets: A reference to the belief that British colonists gave Native Americans blankets infected with smallpox as an act of genocidal biological warfare.

Garrote: A weapon used in capital punishment.

Cold War: The period of political and military tension, albeit absent large-scale fighting, between the United States and the Soviet Union lasting from 1947 until the collapse of the Soviet Union in 1991.

"Free Bird": A 1974 song by the rock band Lynyrd Skynyrd, written by band members Allen Collins and Ronnie Van Zant.

"Lady Marmalade": A 1974 pop song written by Bob Crewe and Kenny Nolan and originally performed by the funk group Labelle. It contains the famous French refrain that Lorelai quotes. In 2001, it was remade by pop singers Christina Aguilera, Mya, Pink, and Lil' Kim.

Five stages of grief: Psychological concept popularized by Swiss psychiatrist Elisabeth Kübler-Ross in her 1969 book *On Death and Dying*. The five stages are denial, anger, bargaining, depression, and acceptance.

The Glad Man: A reference to "The Man from GLAD," the mascot for the trash bag brand Glad. The character was a white-haired man in a white suit used in ads in the 1970s.

Episode 3.10: That'll Do, Pig

Written by Sheila R. Lawrence. Directed by Jamie Babbit. Aired January 14, 2003.
Richard's mother visits with an announcement that stuns Emily.

"Buy ourselves a ranch in Texas": A reference to Prairie Chapel Ranch, located near Waco, Texas, acquired by George W. Bush in 1999 and often referred to during his presidency as "the Western White House" because of the amount of time he spent there.

World War I: Known as the Great War, a global conflict between the Allies and the Central Powers, lasting from 1914 to 1918.

Quaalude: Brand name of methaqualone, a hypnotic sedative discontinued in the 1980s due to concerns relating to recreational use.

Aramis: Luxury men's fragrance introduced in 1964.

Live at the Fillmore Auditorium: A 1967 live album by Chuck Berry (see earlier entry).

Charlemagne (748–814): Former Holy Roman emperor whose titles included king of the Franks from 768, king of the Lombards from 774, and emperor of what is now known as the Carolingian Empire from 800 until his death in 814.

Rain Man: A 1988 comedy-drama film starring Tom Cruise and Dustin Hoffman, about a wheeler-dealer who learns that his estranged father has bequeathed his multimillion dollar estate to his unknown autistic savant brother.

Peloponnesian War: An ancient Greek war fought between Athens and Sparta from 431 to 404 BC.

Minnie Pearl (1912–1996): Country music singer and comedian who appeared at the Grand Ole Opry for more than fifty years and on the TV series *Hee Haw*. She was known for wearing her trademark hat with the price tag still attached.

Korn: Nu metal rock band formed in California in 1993.

Victor Hugo (1802–1885): French writer and politician known for *Les Misérables* and *The Hunchback of Notre Dame*.

New York to London: A reference to the Concorde (see earlier entry), whose flight between New York and London was billed as taking less than three hours.

Wadsworth Mansion: A 16,000-square-foot mansion located in Middletown, Connecticut, built in the early 1900s for businessman Colonel Clarence Wadsworth.

"Be all that you can be": Motto of the US Army.

Betty Boop: Cartoon character created by Max Fleischer featured in theatrical cartoons during the 1930s. She is depicted as a caricature of a Jazz Age flapper.

"What's your damage?": Line from the movie *Heathers* (see earlier entry).

Gidget, Moondoggie: Characters originating in the 1957 Frederick Kohner novel *Gidget, the Little Girl with the Big Ideas*, but best known for a series of successful film and TV adaptations about the titular teenage girl and her surfing friends at a California beach. Gidget becomes infatuated with the surfer Moondoggie when meeting him at the beach.

The Art of War: Ancient Chinese military treatise dating from the fifth century BC, attributed to military strategist Sun Tzu.

Marlo Thomas, Tina Louise: Thomas is an actress and activist known for starring in the 1966–1971 sitcom *That Girl* and for her work with St. Jude Children's Research Hospital, which was founded by her father, actor Danny Thomas. Louise is an actress best known for portraying Ginger on the sitcom *Gilligan's Island*. Rory and Francie refer to one another as the actresses because of their hair color.

Timber!: A call of warning often shouted before a tree falls.

Weezer: Alternative rock band formed in Los Angeles in 1992.

Tattoo: Fictional character from the drama TV series *Fantasy Island*, which aired from 1977 to 1984. It centered around Mr. Roark, a mysterious man who owned an island where people could come and live out their fantasies for a weekend. Tattoo was the diminutive sidekick of Mr. Roark, portrayed by French actor Hervé Villechaize.

Stuart Little: A 1999 live action/computer animated comedy film, loosely based on the 1945 children's novel of the same name by E. B. White, about an anthropomorphic mouse adopted by a couple in New York.

"Standing with an axe next to a cherry tree": A reference to a questionable legend about a young George Washington (see earlier entry), who was supposedly given a hatchet at age six and used it to chop down his father's cherry tree. When confronted, he said he could not tell a lie and confessed to the action.

"That'll do, pig": A line from the movie *Babe* (see earlier entry).

Cheech and Chong: Comedy duo consisting of Cheech Marin and Tommy Chong, known for their stand-up comedy, studio recordings, and feature films often showcasing their love for cannabis.

EPISODE 3.11: I SOLEMNLY SWEAR

Written by John Stephens. Directed by Carla McCloskey. Aired January 21, 2003.
Francie attempts to turn Paris against Rory. A former maid sues Emily.

Jackboot: Military combat boot associated with German forces during World War II.

Munich Beer Hall Rally: The Beer Hall Putsch was a failed coup d'état by Nazi Party leader Adolf Hitler in Munich in 1923. Nearly two thousand Nazis took part in a march that ultimately failed, and Hitler was arrested and charged with treason.

Evel Knievel (1938–2007): Stunt performer and entertainer known for impressive ramp-to-ramp motorcycle jumps.

"It's a bird! It's a plane!": Classic phrase used in various adaptations featuring the comic book superhero Superman, as in "Look up in the sky—it's a bird, it's a plane . . . it's Superman!"

Princess Diana's butler: Paul Burrell is an English former butler of the British Royal Household, as butler to Diana, Princess of Wales (see earlier entry), from 1987 until her death in 1997. He released a memoir in 2003 that Diana's sons called a betrayal of her trust.

Dr. Phil: Phillip McGraw is a TV personality and author best known for hosting the talk show *Dr. Phil*.

Joan Didion (1934–2021): Journalist and author whose works include *The Year of Magical Thinking*.

Eloise: Series of children's books written in the 1950s by Kay Thompson about a young girl who lives in New York City's Plaza Hotel. *Eloise at the Plaza* wasn't technically a name of one of the books, but it was the title of a 2003 made-for-TV film based on the series.

Jerry Garcia (1942–1995): Musician best known for being a member of the band The Grateful Dead.

Ginger Spice: Nickname of singer Geri Halliwell, a member of the pop band the Spice Girls (see earlier entry).

Fletcher Christian (1764–1793): English sailor who led the mutiny on the *Bounty* in 1789, in which he seized command of the merchant ship. He was portrayed by Clark Gable and Marlon Brando in famous film adaptations of the story.

Xanadu: A 1980 musical fantasy film starring Olivia Newton-John as one of the Nine Muses from Greek mythology and Michael Beck as a struggling artist who opens a nightclub called Xanadu. The film was a critical and box office bomb.

John Williams: Composer and conductor known for providing music for many classic films, including *Star Wars*, *Superman*, and many others.

Teutonic: The Teutons were an ancient tribe of people from northern Europe who participated in the Cimbrian War.

David Cassidy (1950–2017): Singer and actor known for the 1970s TV series *The Partridge Family*; half-brother to Shaun Cassidy (see earlier entry).

Cootie Catcher: A folded-paper, fortune-telling children's game.

"I'm crushing your head": A reference to a recurring sketch from the Canadian sketch comedy series *The Kids in the Hall* (1988–1995). Actor Mark McKinney played Headcrusher, a lonely man who would pretend to crush the heads of people he found annoying.

Leavenworth: Refers to the United States Penitentiary in Leavenworth, Kansas.

Shields and Yarnell: Mime team formed in 1972, consisting of married couple Robert Shields and Lorene Yarnell.

***The Great Gatsby*, Daisy**: *The Great Gatsby* is a 1925 novel by F. Scott Fitzgerald about a mysterious millionaire and his desire to reunite with his former lover, Daisy.

"Express Yourself": A 1989 song by Madonna whose video (budgeted at five million dollars) featured the singer commanding muscular men in chains.

People: Weekly magazine specializing in celebrity news and human interest stories.

"Talk to the hand": Slang phrase popularized in the 1990s meaning that the person saying it wasn't interested in hearing what someone else had to say, indicating so by holding up their hand, palm facing the other person.

"Close your eyes and think of England": A phrase meaning to accept one's duty. It is often meant in reference to enduring sex as a marital duty.

Pattycake: A children's nursery rhyme accompanied by a clapping game.

Brutus: Marcus Junius Brutus (ca. 85BC–42BC) was a Roman politician, orator, and participant in the assassination of Julius Caesar. His name has become associated with the betrayal of a friend.

"We'll have it in an Italian restaurant": Reference to a scene in *The Godfather* (see earlier entry).

Creedence Clearwater Revival: CCR is a rock band formed in California who rose to fame in the 1960s with hits like "Bad Moon Rising."

Episode 3.12: Lorelai Out of Water

Written by Janet Leahy. Directed by Jamie Babbit. Aired January 28, 2003. Lorelai prepares for a fishing date with Alex. Lane schemes to go to the prom with Dave.

Ozzfest: A former annual music festival that launched in 1998, featuring hard rock and heavy metal bands. It was founded by Ozzy and Sharon Osbourne.

Joe Namath: Former professional football player who spent most of his career with the New York Jets. He also dabbled in acting and appeared in several commercials, including for Hanes Beautymist pantyhose, which he famously wore in their ads.

Batcave: The secret underground headquarters of the comic book superhero Batman.

Sanford and Son: A TV sitcom that ran from 1972 to 1977, starring Redd Foxx and Demond Wilson as a father and son who ran a junkyard business together.

Hugg-a-Planet: While not referred to by its actual name, this toy is a soft globe that debuted in 1982.

"Good lawyers make for good neighbors": Actually a misquote of the 1914 Robert Frost poem "Mending Wall," which replaces *fences* with *lawyers*.

Pamela Des Barres: Rock and roll groupie, musician, actress, and author best known for her 1987 memoir *I'm With the Band: Confessions of a Groupie*, detailing her time in the California music scene during the 1960s and 1970s.

Tipper Gore: Second lady of the United States from 1993 to 2001 while married to Al Gore, as well as an activist and social issues advocate. In 1985, she launched the Parents Music Resource Center, which advocated for labeling records that contain profanity.

Sundance: Prestigious film festival founded in 1978.

Turncoat: A person who changes their allegiance from one group to another.

Judas: Disciple who, according to the Bible, betrayed Jesus.

Peggy Lee (1920–2002): Singer and actress once known as the "Queen of American pop music."

Encyclopedia of Rock: *The Rolling Stone Encyclopedia of Rock and Roll* is a comprehensive guide to the history of rock and roll music, originally published in 2001.

Smashing Pumpkins: Alternative rock band formed in Chicago in 1988 by frontman and guitarist Billy Corgan.

Jayne Mansfield (1933–1967): Actress, singer, and *Playboy* Playmate who was a popular sex symbol of the 1950s and 1960s.

EPISODE 3.13: DEAR EMILY AND RICHARD
Written by Amy Sherman-Palladino. Directed by Gail Mancuso. Aired February 4, 2003.
As Sherry goes into labor, Lorelai recalls her pregnancy with Rory.

Town & Country: Monthly lifestyle magazine founded in 1846.

"The Rain in Spain": Lorelai quotes this song from the musical *My Fair Lady*.

"Talk into the clown": A reference to the drive-thru clown head that customers placing orders spoke into at Jack in the Box fast-food restaurants from the 1950s to the 1980s.

Kentucky Derby: Annual horse race held at Churchill Downs in Louisville, Kentucky. It is the first leg of the Triple Crown.

Ricard Gere: Actor whose notable works include *Pretty Woman* and *An Officer and a Gentleman*. He is also an advocate for human rights in Tibet.

Glory of Easter: Annual evangelical drama depicting the Passion and Resurrection of Christ, held at California's Crystal Cathedral from 1984 to 2012.

Laura Mercier: A cosmetics and skincare brand founded by its namesake in 1996.

Beanie Babies: A line of stuffed toys created by H. Ty Warner in 1993. The toys became a sought-after collectible fad that dominated the late 1990s.

Adrian Zmed: Actor known for roles in *Grease 2* and *T.J. Hooker*.

Paris and Nicky Hilton: Sisters and celebrity socialites and entertainers who are the granddaughters of Conrad Hilton, the founder of the Hilton Hotel chain.

Myra Waldo (1915–2004): Prolific food and travel writer.

Berlin Wall: Guarded concrete barrier separating West Berlin and East Berlin from 1961 to 1989.

Napoleon III (1808–1873): President of France from 1848 to 1852 and emperor of the French from 1852 until his deposition in 1870.

Marc Chagall (1887–1985): Russian-French modernist artist.

Korean War: Battle fought between North Korea and South Korea from 1950 to 1953.

Barneys: Luxury brand founded in New York in 1923.

Graydon Carter: Journalist who served as editor of *Vanity Fair* from 1992 to 2017.

Don Ho (1930–2007): Hawaiian singer and entertainer known for the song "Tiny Bubbles."

The C&H Pure Cane Sugar Dancers: California & Hawaiian Sugar Company is a brand of processed sugar whose commercials in the 1960s featured Hawaiian children singing and dancing.

Sara Moulton: Cookbook author and TV chef who began her career working with Julia Child.

Sheldon Harnick (1924–2023): Lyricist and songwriter whose notable works include musicals such as *Fiddler on the Roof*.

Howard Stern: Radio and TV host best known for hosting the radio show *The Howard Stern Show*.

Epilady: Brand name of a type of epilator, an electrical device used to remove hair.

Singin' in the Rain: A 1952 musical comedy film starring Gene Kelly, Donald O'Connor, and Debbie Reynolds.

Easter Parade: A 1949 musical film starring Judy Garland and Fred Astaire. Lorelai sings part of the film's theme song later in the episode.

An American in Paris: A 1951 musical comedy film starring Gene Kelly and Leslie Caron.

Saturday Night Fever: A 1977 dance drama film starring John Travolta.

Grease: A 1978 musical film starring John Travolta and Olivia Newton-John as a greaser and the wholesome girl he falls for, respectively.

Episode 3.14: Swan Song

Written by Daniel Palladino. Directed by Chris Long. Aired February 11, 2003. Rory invites Jess to dinner with her grandmother.

"A Fella with an Umbrella": A song by Irving Berlin, performed by Judy Garland in the musical film *Easter Parade*.

The Dean Martin Celebrity Roast: A series of TV specials hosted by actor and singer Martin (1917–1995) that aired from 1974 to 1984 and featured actors and comedians "roasting" a celebrity.

The Talbotts, Deloitte and Touche: The Talbotts is likely a nod to Strobe Talbott, a foreign policy analyst and Yale graduate who served as deputy secretary of state from 1994 to 2001. Deloitte Touche is a professional services network founded in London in 1845.

Lyndon B. Johnson (1908–1973): President of the United States from 1963 to 1969. He was elected to the US Senate in 1948 and is considered a highly effective Senate majority leader.

***The Holy Barbarian*s**: A 1959 nonfiction book by Lawrence Lipton about the Beat Generation subculture.

"Back to the salt mines": An idiom referring to a tedious job.

Andy Warhol (1928–1987): Artist who was a leading figure in the Pop Art movement.

Elaine Stritch (1925–2014): Actress known for her work on Broadway and television. In 2001, she debuted her one-woman show, *Elaine Stritch at Liberty*.

Bette Davis (1908–1989): Actress known for such films as *All About Eve* and *What Ever Happened to Baby Jane?* She is also known for her striking eyes, which became the subject of the 1980s song "Bette Davis Eyes" by Kim Carnes.

Guys and Dolls: A 1950 Broadway musical with music and lyrics by Frank Loesser and book by Jo Swerling and Abe Burrows.

Beantown: Nickname for Boston, Massachusetts.

"One for My Baby (And One More for the Road)": Miss Patty sings this song originally sung by Fred Astaire in the 1943 musical film *The Sky's the Limit* but popularized by Frank Sinatra.

"I toted the barge, lifted the bale": A line from the song "Ol' Man River" from the 1927 musical *Showboat*.

"Baba O'Riley": A 1971 song by the rock band The Who.

Hairspray: Musical with music by Marc Shaiman and lyrics by Shaiman and Scott Wittman, with book by Mark O'Donnell and Thomas Meehan, based on John Waters's 1988 film of the same name.

Encyclopedia Brown: Children's book series by Donald J. Sobol, debuting in 1963, about a boy detective.

Ben and J.Lo.: A reference to Ben Affleck and Jennifer Lopez (see earlier entries), who were in a relationship from 2002 to 2004, then married from 2022 to 2025.

"Toot Sweets": Lorelai makes a pun referencing this song about musical candy from the 1968 family musical film *Chitty Chitty Bang Bang*.

Jonas Salk (1914–1995): Medical researcher who developed a vaccine for polio.

Paulie, The Bada Bing: A character and strip club from the TV series *The Sopranos*.

BunnyRanch: The Moonlite BunnyRanch is a legal brothel in Nevada first opened in 1955.

Norma Desmond: Fictional main character in the film *Sunset Boulevard* (see earlier entry).

Orcs: Fictional humanoid monster characters from *The Lord of the Rings* (see earlier entry).

Bennies and goofballs: Slang terms for the amphetamine Benzedrine and sleeping pills.

Moose Murders: A mystery farce play by Arthur Bicknell that was a notorious flop.

John's of Bleecker Street: Famed pizzeria in New York City, founded in 1929.

"New York Mining Disaster 1921": The 1967 debut single by the pop band the Bee Gees.

Lord Jim: A 1900 novel by Joseph Conrad about a British seaman.

Petey the dog: Dog in the *Our Gang/Little Rascals* short films of the 1920s.

Columbo: Crime drama TV series starring Peter Falk as the titular detective that aired in the 1970s.

Rabbit in *Monty Python*: A reference to the Killer Rabbit of Caerbannog, a character in the film *Monty Python and the Holy Grail* (see earlier entry) that appeared as a cute bunny before revealing itself to be a fierce killer.

Creed: Rock band formed in Florida in 1994 who, despite selling tons of records, have often been labeled among the worst bands of the era.

Amy Grant: Singer-songwriter who got her start in contemporary Christian music before crossing over to pop with hits like "Baby Baby."

Rhett Butler: The love interest of Scarlett O'Hara in the Margaret Mitchell novel and film adaptation *Gone With the Wind*.

Episode 3.15: Face-Off

Written by John Stephens. Directed by Kenny Ortega. Aired February 18, 2003.
Rory discovers that Dean has moved on, while Emily finds her mother-in-law in a surprising situation.

Minutemen: Members of a New England colonial militia during the American Revolutionary War.

Hoosiers: A 1986 sports drama film about a small-town high school basketball team in Indiana that enters the state championship.

Bay of Pigs: A failed 1961 military invasion on the coast of Cuba by Cuban exiles, organized by the United States, aimed at overthrowing Fidel Castro's communist government.

Sadie Hawkins Day dance: A school dance in which girls invite boys, instead of the standard convention of boys inviting girls. It stems from a 1937 *Li'l Abner* comic strip by Al Capp as a day in which women could chase bachelors and marry the one they caught. Hawkins was a character in the strip.

Michael Moore: Filmmaker whose works include *Bowling for Columbine* and *Fahrenheit 9/11*.

"A Mighty Fortress Is Our God": A hymn written by Martin Luther around 1528.

The Big One: Slang term for World War II (see earlier entry).

Full Metal Jacket: A 1987 war film directed by Stanley Kubrick about a US Marine platoon and their abusive drill instructor.

The Wave: An audience participation move done at sporting events where sections of people stand and lift their arms progressively around the arena, creating the look of a "wave."

"Are you ready to rumble?": A phrase used to introduce wrestling and boxing matches, created and trademarked by ring announcer Michael Buffer.

The Beach Boys: Influential pop-rock band formed in California in the 1960s, whose hits include "Surfin' U.S.A." and "I Get Around." The latter is the 1964 song that Lorelai quotes.

Pablo Picasso (1881–1973): Famous Spanish painter and sculptor.

Spanish Civil War: Military conflict fought in Spain from 1936 to 1939.

Love in the Afternoon: A 1957 romantic comedy film about a business magnate and the daughter of a private investigator hired to investigate him.

Israelites: According to the Bible, the Israelites wandered the wilderness for forty years as a punishment from God.

The Distillers: Punk rock band formed in Los Angeles in 1998.

Nike, "Just Do It": Nike is a multinational athletic footwear and apparel company whose slogan, "Just Do It," has been in use since the late 1980s.

Moliere (1622–1673): The stage name of French actor and playwright Jean-Baptiste Poquelin.

EPISODE 3.16: THE BIG ONE

Written by Amy Sherman-Palladino. Directed by Jamie Babbit. Aired February 25, 2003.

Rory awaits her college acceptance letters. Lorelai has an unexpected run-in with Max.

Daniel Day-Lewis: English actor whose works include *My Left Foot* and *There Will Be Blood*. In 1997, he retired from acting for three years and worked as an apprentice shoemaker in Italy.

Al Hirschfeld (1903–2003): Artist known for his black-and-white portraits of celebrities.

Into the Woods: A 1987 musical with music and lyrics by Stephen Sondheim and book by James Lapine whose plot intertwines several Brothers Grimm fairy tales. Paris later sings part of a song from the show.

Mary Martin (1913–1990): Actress known for her stage work, including originating several now-famous roles, including Nellie Forbush in *South Pacific* (1949), the title character in *Peter Pan* (1954), and Maria von Trapp in *The Sound of Music* (1959).

Nathan Lane: Actor known for both stage and screen whose works include *The Producers*, *Angels in America*, and *The Birdcage*.

Les Misérables: Musical adaptation of the Victor Hugo novel of the same name, which premiered in 1980.

Cats: A 1981 musical composed by Andrew Lloyd Webber, based upon the 1939 poetry collection *Old Possum's Book of Practical Cats* by T. S. Eliot.

Chita Rivera (1933–2024): Actress and singer whose work includes *Guys and Dolls* and *West Side Story*.

Jerome Robbins (1918–1998): Dancer and choreographer whose works include *West Side Story* and *Gypsy*.

Ruth Reichl: Chef and food writer who worked as a food critic with the *Los Angeles Times* and the *New York Times*.

"Bolts on the side of your neck": A reference to Frankenstein's monster. (See earlier entry.)

Cowabunga, dude: A phrase associated with California surf culture, as well as characters like *Sesame Street*'s Cookie Monster and the Teenage Mutant Ninja Turtles.

Encyclopedia Britannica: A general knowledge encyclopedia first published in the eighteenth century in Scotland and in the United States since 1901. It went fully online in 2016.

Lock her up in a tower: A reference to *Rapunzel* (see earlier entry).

Mutton chops: A style of sideburns that are bushy and grown down to the chin.

Tears for Fears: English pop-rock band formed in 1981 by Roland Orzabal and Curt Smith, whose hits include "Shout" and "Everybody Wants to Rule the World."

Tasmanian Devil: Character from the *Looney Tunes/Merrie Melodies* cartoons, depicted as short-tempered, ferocious, and generally wild.

Kofi Annan (1938–2018): Ghanaian diplomat who served as secretary-general of the United Nations from 1997 to 2006. He received the Nobel Peace Prize in 2001.

Town crier: A public official who would make pronouncements to the people of a town.

Marxism: Political philosophy and method of socioeconomic analysis originating with nineteenth-century German philosophers Karl Marx and Friedrich Engels that uses historical materialism to understand class relations and social conflict.

Afterschool Special: Television anthology series that aired on ABC from 1972 to 1997, presenting controversial situations targeting teens and children, such as illiteracy and substance abuse.

Lee Iacocca (1924–2019): Automobile executive known for developing the Ford Mustang in the 1960s and for reviving the Chrysler Corporation, of which he served as president from 1978 to 1991.

Malcolm Forbes (1919–1990): Entrepreneur and politician who published *Forbes* magazine.

"Thank you and good night": While not an uncommon phrase, it was also the regular sign-off by TV host David Letterman on *Late Night with David Letterman*.

Billy Carter (1937–1988): Younger brother of President Jimmy Carter known for endorsing brands of beer and liquor.

EPISODE 3.17: A TALE OF POES AND FIRE
Written by Daniel Palladino. Directed by Chris Long. Aired April 15, 2003.
A fire breaks out at the inn during a gathering of the Edgar Allan Poe Society.

Satchmo: Nickname of trumpeter Louis Armstrong (see earlier entry).

Edgar Allan Poe, The Edgar Allan Poe Society: Poe (1809–1849) was a writer and poet whose works are mostly associated with mystery and the macabre. Notable works include "The Raven," "The Tell-Tale Heart," "The Cask of Amontillado," "The System of Doctor Tarr and Professor Fether," and others. These and other Poe works are mentioned in the episode. The

Edgar Allan Poe Society was established in 1923 and consists of volunteers who provide information and resources on the author and his works.

Trekkies: Fans of the *Star Trek* franchise.

I'm an island: Reference to the famous line "No man is an island" from the 1624 prose work *Devotions upon Emergent Occasions* by poet John Donne.

Shari Lewis (1933–1998): Ventriloquist and children's entertainer known as the puppeteer for the sock puppet Lamb Chop, as well as other characters.

Ricardo Montalbán: Mexican-American actor who starred in *Fantasy Island*.

Glinda the Good Witch: Character in the L. Frank Baum novel *The Wonderful Wizard of Oz* and its many adaptations, most notably portrayed by actress Billie Burke in the 1939 film version.

Howard Hughes (1905–1976): Business magnate, pilot, film producer, and philanthropist who exhibited eccentric behavior and adopted a reclusive lifestyle in his later years.

Mira Sorvino: Actress and Harvard graduate whose works include *Mighty Aphrodite* and *Romy and Michele's High School Reunion*.

The Adventures of Gumby and Pokey: Gumby is a cartoon character created in 1953 by Art Clokey, depicted as a blocky green humanoid made of clay, and Pokey is his anthropomorphic orange pony sidekick. They began as clay-animated children's show characters that have evolved into a franchise.

In Search of Lost Time: Novel in seven volumes by Marcel Proust (see earlier entry), published between 1913 and 1927.

Nicholas Nickleby: An 1839 novel by Charles Dickens that is over 340,000 words long.

Hank Williams (1923–1953): Country music singer known for sad songs such as "I'm So Lonesome I Could Cry."

Bedouins: Nomadic Arab tribes.

Ed Wood: A 1994 biographical comedy-drama film starring Johnny Depp as Wood (1924–1978), a filmmaker, actor, and pulp novelist.

Phil Spector (1939–2021): Influential record producer and songwriter who, in 2003, shot and killed actress Lana Clarkson after meeting her in a nightclub. He was sentenced to nineteen years in prison, where he remained until his death.

Family Feud: Game show debuting in 1976 that pits two families against one another, where they guess the most popular answers to survey questions. When a player makes a guess, their family members often clap and shout "good answer!"

Nobel Prize: Named in honor of Alfred Nobel, prestigious awards granted to those who, during the preceding year, have conferred the greatest benefit to humankind in the categories of Physics, Chemistry, Physiology or Medicine, Literature, Peace, and Economics. They were first awarded in 1901.

EPISODE 3.18: HAPPY BIRTHDAY, BABY

Written by Amy Sherman-Palladino. Directed by Gail Mancuso. Aired April 22, 2003.
Lorelai gets a surprise gift from Richard. Luke discovers that Jess is skipping school.

Johnny Marzetti: A casserole-style pasta dish consisting of noodles, cheese, beef or sausage, and tomato sauce.

Renée Estevez: Former actress who appeared in *Heathers* and *The West Wing*.

Dick Van Dyke: Beloved actor known for *The Dick Van Dyke Show*, *Diagnosis: Murder*, and *Mary Poppins* (see earlier entry), the role which Lorelai references in the scene.

Brazil: A 1985 science-fiction dystopian film.

Red Hot Chili Peppers: Rock band formed in Los Angeles in 1992 whose hits include "Give It Away" and "Under the Bridge."

Mrs. Wiggins: Character from a series of sketches in *The Carol Burnett Show*, featuring Burnett as the dim-witted secretary to a frustrated businessman, Mr. Tudball (Tim Conway), who would pronounce her name as "Huh-Wiggins."

Almost Famous: A 2000 comedy-drama film starring Kate Hudson (see earlier entry) about a journalist touring with a fictitious rock band.

Do you Yahoo?: Slogan from a late 1990s-early 2000s advertising campaign for the internet search engine Yahoo.

George Foreman Grill: Brand of tabletop, double-sided grill, introduced in 1994, promoted by Foreman (1949–2025), a heavyweight boxing champion and Olympic gold medalist.

Jimmy Choo: Malaysian fashion designer known for women's shoes.

Roger, Wilco: Procedure phrase in radiotelephone communication meaning "I have heard."

The Eminem Show: A 2002 studio album by rapper Eminem (see earlier entry).

Time-Life Books: Book publisher active from the early 1960s through the early 2000s, among whose offerings were direct-to-consumer titles on such topics as home improvement, nature, geography, and more.

Martha Stewart Living: Women's and lifestyle magazine founded by Stewart (see earlier entry) in 1990. It went fully online in 2022.

Joe Strummer, Pearl Harbour tour: Strummer (1952–2002) was a British musician and founding member of The Clash (see earlier entry). Their first US tour took place in 1979 and was billed as the Pearl Harbour tour.

Hells Angels: An outlaw motorcycle club founded in 1948.

Gangs of New York, **Cameron Diaz, Martin Scorsese**: Diaz is an actress known for such films as *There's Something About Mary*, *Charlie's Angels*, and *Gangs of New York*, a 2002 epic historical drama film set in the 1860s and directed by filmmaker Scorsese, whose additional works include *Raging Bull* and *Goodfellas*. Scorsese first began developing the film in the 1970s after coming across the book *The Gangs of New York: An Informal History of the Underworld* by Herbert Asbury. He originally envisioned Meryl Streep (see earlier entry) in the role that eventually went to Diaz twenty years later.

Polonius: Character in the William Shakespeare play *Hamlet*, who says the famous line "neither a borrower nor a lender be."

EPISODE 3.19: KEG! MAX!
Written by Daniel Palladino. Directed by Chris Long. Aired April 29, 2003.
Lane's band makes their debut at a house party where the rivalry between Dean and Jess comes to a head.

"Shave and a Haircut": A seven-note, call-and-response riff, the response to the first part being "two bits." It dates back to at least 1899.

"1999": A 1982 song by Prince that includes the line "party like it's 1999."

The 700 Club: A newsmagazine television show from the Christian Broadcasting Network in production since 1966.

Dipping girls' hair in inkwells: A form of bullying that schoolboys used to do to girls pre-1950s.

"Forty Miles of Bad Road": A 1959 song by Duane Eddy.

Marriage Encounter: A faith-based marriage-enrichment program designed to help husbands and wives improve their communication.

James Bond: Fictional British secret agent created in 1953 by writer Ian Fleming who used the character in a series of novels. It then expanded into a successful franchise including multiple films.

Cinemax: A pay television cable network launched in 1980, showing feature films, original programming, and beginning in 1984 a late-night block of adult programming known as Cinemax After Dark.

Doug Henning (1947–2000): Canadian magician, illusionist, and escape artist.

Leif Garrett: Singer and actor who was a teen idol during the 1970s.

Milli Vanilli: German pop music duo consisting of Fab Morvan and Rob Pilatus, whose 1988 debut album, featuring songs like "Blame It on the Rain" and "Baby Don't Forget My Number," netted them a Best New Artist Grammy Award. The award was revoked when it was revealed that the pair provided none of the vocals on their album.

Lladró: Spanish company that makes decorative sculptures and porcelain figurines.

Hello, Cleveland!: Phrase shouted by a member of the fictional band Spinal Tap (see earlier entry) in the mockumentary film *This Is Spinal Tap* as the band wanders around a series of tunnels while trying to make their way to the stage for a show.

John Entwistle (1944–2002): English musician who was the bass guitarist for The Who (see earlier entry).

Michelle Branch: Pop singer-songwriter whose hits include "Everywhere" and "All You Wanted."

Matchbox Twenty: Rock band formed in Florida in 1995, whose hits include "Real World," "3AM," and "Push."

Gimli, Legolas: Fictional dwarf and elf characters in *The Lord of the Rings* (see earlier entry).

Neville Chamberlain (1869–1940): Prime Minister of the United Kingdom from 1937 to 1940, who signed the Munich Agreement, ceding a region of Czechoslovakia to Nazi Germany, led by Hitler.

Kenny G: Best-selling jazz saxophonist.

"Trust, but verify": A Russian proverb popularized when then-president Ronald Reagan began using it in the context of nuclear disarmament discussions with the Soviet Union in the 1980s.

Trappists: A Catholic religious order of monks formed in 1664.

EPISODE 3.20: SAY GOODNIGHT, GRACIE

Teleplay by Amy Sherman-Palladino and Janet Leahy. Story by Amy Sherman-Palladino. Directed by Jamie Babbit. Aired May 6, 2003.
Lorelai and Sookie attempt to purchase the Dragonfly Inn. Jess gets a surprise visit from his long-lost father.

"Wind Beneath My Wings": A 1982 song written by Jeff Silbar and Larry Henley that has been recorded by several artists, most notably Bette Midler in 1988, whose version went to number one on the charts.

"Available like an intern": Possibly a joke referencing Monica Lewinsky, who had an affair with then-president Bill Clinton during her days as a White House intern in the mid-1990s.

The Stepford Wives: A 1972 novel by Ira Levin about a town in which the women transform from free-thinking individuals to quiet, compliant wives. It has been adapted into various film versions.

"The Candy Man": Song by Aubrey Woods from the film *Willy Wonka & the Chocolate Factory*, later recorded by Sammy Davis Jr. This is the song Taylor sings when he enters Luke's.

Day of reckoning: The Last Judgment of God in Christian and Islamic belief.

The Day the Music Died: February 3, 1959, the day musicians Buddy Holly, Ritchie Valens, and "The Big Bopper" J. P. Richardson were killed in a plane crash in Iowa.

Sammy Davis Jr.: Davis (1925–1990) was a singer, actor, and dancer whose hits included "The Candy Man."

The Desert Inn: Hotel and casino in Las Vegas, Nevada, that operated from 1950 to 2000 and was a popular performance venue for the likes of Frank Sinatra and others.

Animal House: A 1978 comedy film directed by John Landis about a group of troublemaking fraternity members.

"To be, or not to be": Famous speech from William Shakespeare's *Hamlet*.

The Monkees: Pop-rock band formed in Los Angeles in the 1960s originally created as a fictitious band for the TV sitcom *The Monkees* before eventually becoming successful as a true band.

Doris Day (1922–2019): Actress and singer known for songs like "Sentimental Journey" and films such as *Pillow Talk* and *The Man Who Knew Too Much*.

"Que Será, Será (Whatever Will Be, Will Be)": Song written by Jay Livingston and Ray Evans in 1955, first performed by Doris Day in *The Man Who Knew Too Much*.

Henry VI: Play by William Shakespeare covering the life of King Henry VI of England, which features the words quoted by Mrs. Kim to Dave.

EPISODE 3.21: HERE COMES THE SON
Written by and directed by Amy Sherman Palladino. Aired May 13, 2003.
A recent financial windfall affects Rory's college financial aid. Jess heads to California to find his father.

The Rolling Stones: Influential English rock band formed in London in 1962.

Academy Awards: Also known as the Oscars, annual awards honoring achievement in the film industry, presented by the Academy of Motion Picture Arts and Sciences. Lorelai refers to the 2003 acceptance speech delivered by filmmaker Michael Moore (see earlier entry) after winning Best Documentary Feature for his film *Bowling for Columbine*, in which he openly criticized then-President George W. Bush and the Iraq War, which had just begun a few days earlier.

Peugeot, *Armageddon*: Peugeot is a French automobile brand. *Armageddon* is a 1998 science-fiction disaster film about an asteroid on a collision course with Earth. The actor to whom Lorelai is referring has proven difficult to identify.

Bolshevik Revolution: A series of Russian revolutions beginning in 1917 that established the Soviet Union.

Anne Boleyn (1501 or 1507–1536): Second wife of Henry VIII and Queen of England from 1533 to 1536. She was beheaded for treason.

Kiwanis: An international service club founded in 1915.

Kryptonite: Fictional element appearing primarily in the Superman stories from DC Comics. It is a green, crystalline material that can weaken and kill Superman.

Alfalfa sprouts and a plate of mashed yeast: Dish ordered by Woody Allen's character in the film *Annie Hall* (see earlier entry).

Motown: Record label founded by Berry Gordy Jr. in 1959 that played a vital role in the racial integration of popular music.

Frodo: Protagonist hobbit character in *The Lord of the Rings* (see earlier entry).

Caligula: (12–41) Famous Roman emperor.

General Lee: Robert E. Lee (1807–1870) was a Confederate general during the American Civil War.

Jimmy Jam and Terry Lewis: R&B songwriting and record producing team known for working with Janet Jackson, among other artists.

Marie Claire: French monthly women's magazine.

Vogue: Monthly fashion and lifestyle magazine.

Dante's *Inferno*: The first part of Italian writer Dante Alighieri's fourteenth-century narrative poem *The Divine Comedy*.

Ginger Rogers (1911–1995): Actress and dancer during Hollywood's Golden Age, known for the film *Kitty Foyle* and her performances with Fred Astaire.

Audrey Hepburn (1929–1993): Actress known for *Funny Face*, *Breakfast at Tiffany's*, *My Fair Lady*, and *Sabrina*.

Walter Cronkite: Cronkite (1916–2009) was a broadcast journalist known for anchoring the *CBS Evening News*. His wife was Betsy Maxwell Cronkite.

The Big Bang: A physical theory that describes how the universe expanded from an initial state of high density and temperature.

Tova Borgnine (1941–2022): Founder of Beauty by Tova cosmetics who was married to Ernest Borgnine.

Jimmy Stewart (1908–1998): Beloved actor whose works include *It's a Wonderful Life* and *Mr. Smith Goes to Washington.*

Felicity: Drama series that aired on the WB Network from 1998 to 2002, starring Keri Russell as the titular Felicity, a student navigating college. After the show's first season, Russell—known for her long, curly locks—pranked producers by sending them a photo of herself in a short wig. They liked the idea, and Russell did eventually end up cutting her hair short. The show's ratings soon began to decline, and the media latched onto the haircut as a reason behind the drop.

Natalie Wood (1938–1981): Actress whose credits include *West Side Story* and *Gypsy.*

Olivia de Havilland (1916–2020): Actress whose credits include *Gone With the Wind* and *The Heiress.*

The Lovely Bones: A 2002 novel by Alice Sebold about a teenage girl who was raped and murdered and is watching the life she left behind from heaven. A film adaptation was released in 2009.

Cops: Reality TV documentary program debuting in 1989 chronicling the lives of law enforcement officials.

Ziggy Stardust: Fictional character created by English musician David Bowie, who performed as the character on stage in the early 1970s alongside the release of the album *The Rise and Fall of Ziggy Stardust and the Spiders from Mars.*

Super Bowl: Annual championship game of the National Football League first played in 1967.

Teenage Mutant Ninja Turtles: Franchise created by comic book artists Kevin Eastman and Peter Laird that began as a comic book series in 1984 before branching into a popular cartoon TV series, films, video games, and more. It revolves around four anthropomorphic turtles trained in martial arts.

Aurora Borealis: The play on words refers to the northern lights, the natural light display in Earth's sky visible in northern high-altitude regions.

South Pacific: A 1949 Broadway musical by Richard Rodgers, with lyrics by Oscar Hammerstein II and book by Hammerstein and Joshua Logan, about a nurse stationed on a South Pacific island during World War II who falls in love with a French plantation owner.

Holly Hunter, *Broadcast News*: Hunter is an actress known for such films as *The Piano* and *The Firm*, among many others. *Broadcast News* is the 1987 romantic comedy-drama film in which Hunter plays a determined TV news producer who finds herself in a love triangle with colleagues. She was nominated for a Best Actress Oscar for the role.

EPISODE 3.22: THOSE ARE STRINGS, PINOCCHIO
Written by Daniel Palladino. Directed by Jamie Babbit. Aired May 20, 2003.
Rory graduates from Chilton.

"Peace Train": A 1971 single by Cat Stevens.

The Love Boat, **Captain Stubing, Isaac**: Romantic comedy-drama TV series that aired from 1977 to 1986 about the romantic, dramatic, and humorous adventures of the passengers and crew aboard a cruise ship. Gavin MacLeod portrayed the ship's captain, Captain Stubing, and Ted Lange portrayed Isaac, the ship's bartender.

Ed McMahon (1923–2009): Announcer, game show host, and actor known as Johnny Carson's sidekick on *The Tonight Show Starring Johnny Carson*, as well as for hosting *Star Search* and presenting the American Family Publishers sweepstakes. In 2002, McMahon sued his insurance company for more than $20 million, claiming he was sickened by toxic mold, which he also blamed for the death of his family dog. He was eventually awarded $7.2 million.

Google: Internet search engine founded in 1998. It was around this time that people began using the term "googled" as a verb meaning they searched for something online using the platform.

Deney Terio: Choreographer who hosted the TV series *Dance Fever* from 1979 to 1987.

Armani: Luxury Italian fashion house founded by Giorgio Armani in 1975.

Huey Lewis and the News: Rock band fronted by vocalist Lewis, whose hits include "The Heart of Rock and Roll," "The Power of Love," and others.

Herb Alpert and the Tijuana Brass: Band led by musician Alpert in the 1960s.

Dom Perignon: Brand of vintage champagne introduced in 1921.

Tom Brokaw: Broadcast journalist whose positions have included anchoring the *NBC Nightly News*.

Simone de Beauvoir (1908–1986): French existentialist philosopher and feminist activist.

50 Cent: Rapper, actor, and television producer.

Stephen Sondheim (1930–2021): Composer and lyricist known for his work on Broadway.

"Cherish": A 1966 pop song written by Terry Kirkman and recorded by The Association.

Yoknapatawpha County: Fictional Mississippi county created by author William Faulkner, where he set many of his works.

Pequod: Fictional whaling ship from the Herman Melville novel *Moby-Dick* (see earlier entry).

Huck and Jim: Characters in the Mark Twain novel *The Adventures of Huckleberry Finn* (see earlier entry).

Ignatius J. Reilly: Protagonist of the 1980 novel *A Confederacy of Dunces* by John Kennedy Toole.

Patti Smith: Musician, author, and artist whose most widely known song is "Because the Night." Among her written works is the memoir *Just Kids*.

Robert Frost (1874–1963): Pulitzer Prize–winning poet.

Thomas Edison (1847–1931): Inventor and businessman among whose inventions was a light bulb design that was the first to be long-lasting enough to be practical for widespread use.

Season Four: 2003–2004

Episode 4.1: Ballrooms and Biscotti
Written and directed by Amy Sherman-Palladino. Aired September 23, 2003.
Lorelai and Rory return from their summer backpacking in Europe. Luke shares some surprising news.

"Sk8r Boi": A 2002 pop song by singer Avril Lavigne.

Sandinistas: Socialist political party in Nicaragua founded in the 1960s that ruled the country throughout the 1980s. They came under fire for human rights abuses and were viewed by the US government as a threat to economic interests and national security.

Roman Baths: Preserved public bathing facilities in Bath, Somerset, England, whose construction was completed in 1897. The site includes a Sacred Spring, the Roman Temple, the Roman Bath House, and a museum.

St. Peter's Basilica: Church of the Italian High Renaissance located in Vatican City.

"You were there, and you . . .": A nod to a scene from the 1939 film *The Wizard of Oz* (see earlier entry), in which Dorothy awakens in bed at the end of the film and tells her family and friends about her experience in Oz.

Pietà: Subject in Christian art depicting the Blessed Virgin Mary cradling the body of Jesus Christ after his Descent from the Cross.

The Strand: Bookstore in New York City founded in 1927.

Antoni Gaudí (1852–1926): Famed architect and designer, most of whose works are located in Barcelona.

Anne Frank (1929–1945): German-born Jewish girl who kept a diary while in hiding with her family in an attic amid Nazi persecution during the German occupation of the Netherlands.

Sputnik: The first artificial Earth satellite launched by the Soviet Union in 1957.

Clarence Hotel: Four-star hotel in Dublin, Ireland, opened in 1852. It was purchased by U2 band members Bono and The Edge in 1992. They sold it in 2019.

Esther, Purim: Purim is an annual Jewish holiday that commemorates the saving of the Jewish people from annihilation at the hands of Haman, an official of the Achaemenid Empire, as recounted in the Hebrew Bible's Book of Esther. Haman's plans were foiled by Mordecai of the tribe of Benjamin and cousin, Esther, Queen of Persia.

Barbara Bush, naked party: Barbara Bush is an activist and daughter of former president George W. Bush. In 2002, the Pundits, a secretive Yale University society, alleged that while a student, Bush attended one of what they called "nude parties," presumably nonsexual, exclusive gatherings for select attendees who wear no clothing.

Daria: Animated cynical teenage protagonist of the series *Daria*, which aired on MTV from 1997 to 2002. The character originated on the MTV series *Beavis and Butt-Head*.

Kerry Kennedy: Lorelai references Marilyn Monroe (see earlier entry), who died from a barbiturate overdose and was rumored to have been romantically linked to both President John F. Kennedy (see earlier entry) and his brother, Robert, who served as the US attorney general from 1961 to 1964. (There were also rumors that the Kennedys were involved in her death.) Robert's daughter, Kerry, is a lawyer and human rights activist who married former New York governor Andrew Cuomo in 1990. In 2002, Kennedy demanded a divorce from Cuomo, which became final in 2005. Numerous allegations of sexual misconduct surfaced about Cuomo in 2020, while he was governor, and he resigned in 2021.

Arc de Triomphe: Monument in Paris, France, honoring those who fought in the French Revolutionary and Napoleonic Wars.

Eiffel Tower: Wrought-iron lattice tower in Paris, France, designed by Gustave Eiffel and constructed as the centerpiece of the 1887 World's Fair.

Queen of Hearts: Fictional character and primary antagonist of *Alice in Wonderland* (see earlier entry).

Iran hostage crisis: The comment about Iran and Jimmy Carter (see earlier entry) is a reference to this situation in which a group of Iranian students seized the US Embassy in Tehran on November 4, 1979, and held a group of American diplomats and citizens hostage for 444 days. Carter's handling of the situation was highly criticized, including a failed rescue attempt in 1980. The ordeal left his administration looking weak, and Carter lost his bid for reelection to Ronald Reagan. The hostages were ultimately freed on January 20, 1981, minutes after Reagan was sworn into office.

Corky, Shirley, and Mark Ballas: Corky and Shirley Ballas are professional ballroom dancers who were married from 1985 to 2007. Their son, Mark (not actually named "Corky, Jr."), is also a professional dancer and musician. Both Corky and Mark have appeared on the ABC television series *Dancing With the Stars*.

The Mambo Kings: A 1992 musical drama film based on the 1989 Pulitzer Prize–winning novel *The Mambo Kings Play Songs of Love* by Oscar Hijuelos, about a pair of musician brothers who flee Cuba for New York.

Superman: Caped superhero from DC Comics created by Jerry Siegel and Joe Shuster in 1938 as an alien who crash lands on Earth and, as he grows to adulthood, learns to use his powers—which include flight, x-ray vision, and massive strength—for the good of humanity.

Episode 4.2: The Lorelais' First Day at Yale

Written by Daniel Palladino. Directed by Chris Long. Aired September 30, 2003.
Lorelai helps Rory move into the Yale dorm.

Annie Leibovitz: Photographer best known for innovative celebrity portraits.

Darla: Fictional character and love interest of Alfalfa in the *Our Gang/ Little Rascals* comedy films.

Henry Kissinger (1923–2023): Diplomat and political scientist who served as US secretary of state from 1973 to 1977.

Lady Bird Johnson (1912–2007): First Lady of the United States from 1963 to 1969 as the wife of President Lyndon B. Johnson.

Pat Summerall (1930–2013): Professional football player and sportscaster.

Orson Welles (1915–1985): Director, actor, writer, and producer known for *Citizen Kane*.

Joe Sixpack: Slang term for an average person.

"One": Lorelai quotes a lyric from this 1968 song by Harry Nilsson, also covered by Three Dog Night.

Boston Red Sox: Professional baseball team based in Boston, Massachusetts, founded in 1901.

"Dewey, Cheatem, and Howe": Common gag name used in lawyer jokes as a play on the phrase "Do we cheat them and how?"

9/11: Reference to the September 11, 2001, attacks on the United States in which al-Qaeda terrorists hijacked four commercial airliners, crashing the first two into the Twin Towers of the World Trade Center in New York City and the third into the Pentagon. The fourth plane crashed into a Pennsylvania field during a passenger revolt.

Nancy Sinatra, Frank Sinatra Jr.: The children of singer Frank Sinatra (see earlier entry). Nancy is a singer and actress whose signature song is "These Boots Are Made for Walkin.'" Frank Jr. (1944–2016) was a jazz and big band singer and songwriter.

Henry Box Brown (1815–1897): Virginia slave who escaped to freedom by having himself mailed in a wooden crate to abolitionists in Philadelphia.

"Of all the gin joints . . .": Classic line from the 1942 film *Casablanca*, spoken by Rick Blaine (Humphrey Bogart) when a former lover walks into his bar.

Pupuseria: A restaurant that serves pupusas, stuffed tortillas originating in Central America.

Carmen Electra: Actress, model, and singer whose works include *Baywatch* and *Singled Out*.

Benjamin Franklin (1706–1790): Writer, scientist, inventor, statesman, and one of the Founding Fathers of the United States whose portrait appears on the $100 bill.

Barry White (1944–2003): Singer known for his deep bass voice and romantic image.

Altamont Free Concert: Counterculture rock concert held December 6, 1969, at the Altamont Speedway in Tracy, California, known for using Hells Angels as security. It's also known for significant violence, including the death of a man named Meredith Hunter, who approached the stage during a set by the Rolling Stones, drew a revolver, and was stabbed and beaten to death by a Hells Angels member.

Evanescence: Rock band formed in 1994 whose hits include "Bring Me to Life" and "My Immortal."

"You Can't Hurry Love": A 1966 song by the Supremes.

Episode 4.3: The Hobbit, the Sofa, and Digger Stiles

Written by Amy Sherman-Palladino. Directed by Matthew Diamond. Aired October 7, 2003.

Emily takes it upon herself to redecorate Rory's dorm suite. Richard takes on a business partner.

Pink Floyd, *The Dark Side of the Moon*: Pink Floyd is an English rock band formed in 1965. *The Dark Side of the Moon* is their eighth studio album, released in 1973 and exploring concepts such as greed, time, death, and mental illness.

Uday Hussein (1964–2003): Iraqi politician and eldest son of Saddam Hussein, who, along with his younger brother, died in 2003 in a lengthy and intense gun battle with US troops at his opulent mansion.

Horn of Gondor: An heirloom in *The Lord of the Rings* (see earlier entry) of which it is said that if the horn is blown in need within Gondor, "its voice will not pass unheeded."

Heidi: Children's book by Johanna Spyri published between 1880 and 1881, about a young girl living in the Swiss Alps with her grandfather.

Hydra: While not mentioned by name, Lorelai's line about cutting off a head is a nod to this figure who battled Hercules in Greek mythology. Hydra was a gigantic snake-like creature with multiple heads. Whenever one head was cut off, two emerged in its place.

"My precious!": Line spoken by Gollum, a character in *The Lord of the Rings* (see earlier entry), in reference to the titular ring.

"I'm Julie, your cruise director": A line from the TV series *The Love Boat* (see earlier entry), spoken by the character Julie McCoy (Lauren Tewes).

Mount Doom: Fictional volcano in *The Lord of the Rings* (see earlier entry).

Whoopee cushion: A joke device that is an inflated cushion which emulates fart sounds when sat on.

The Simpsons: Animated sitcom created by Matt Groening that offers a satirical depiction of American life through its titular family. It has aired on Fox since 1989.

Gabor sisters: Trio of Hungarian-American socialite/actress sisters: Magda (1915–1997), Zsa Zsa (see earlier entry), and Eva (1919–1995), who starred on the TV sitcom *Green Acres*.

Osama bin Laden (1957–2011): Militant leader and founder of al-Qaeda who supervised the execution of the 9/11 terrorist attacks (see earlier entry).

Episode 4.4: Chicken or Beef?

Written by Jane Espenson. Directed by Chris Long. Aired October 14, 2003.
Rory is invited to Dean's wedding. Lorelai and Sookie struggle with the necessary construction permits for the Dragonfly.

Yellow Brick Road: Rory's line is a play on this fictional road from the L. Frank Baum novel and its adaptations, *The Wonderful Wizard of Oz*. It is the road that Dorothy and her friends follow to reach the Emerald City.

Persis Khambatta (1948–1998): Indian actress, model, and beauty pageant contestant who was one of the earliest Indian women to compete for Miss Universe. She appeared in *Star Trek: The Motion Picture*.

The Glenn Miller Story: A 1954 biographical film about the life of Miller (1904–1944), a musician and big band conductor whose band was Glenn Miller and his Orchestra. Miller is portrayed by Jimmy Stewart (see earlier entry) in the film.

Dexter Holland: Musician who co-founded the Offspring (see earlier entry).

Greg Ginn, Black Flag: Ginn is the guitarist and primary songwriter of Black Flag, a punk rock band formed in California in 1976.

Bad Religion: Punk rock band formed in Los Angeles in 1980. Rory refers to founding member Greg Graffin. It's a PhD in zoology that he obtained from Cornell.

Calvin Klein: Fashion retail chain founded by its namesake in 1968 and known for advertisements featuring beautiful models and celebrities.

Queer Eye for the Straight Guy: Reality TV show that aired on Bravo from 2003 to 2007 in which a group of gay professionals known as the Fab Five in the fields of fashion, design, food, culture, and grooming, perform a makeover of a straight man. Its title was eventually shortened to *Queer Eye*, and a new version was launched by Netflix in 2018.

Michael, Sonny, Tattaglia, Captain McCluskey: Characters in *The Godfather* (see earlier entry).

Pennysaver: Free community newspaper that features items for sale.

Augustus Gloop: Fictional character in the Roald Dahl novel *Charlie and the Chocolate Factory* and its film adaptation *Willy Wonka & the Chocolate Factory* (see earlier entry). The character is a greedy nine-year-old boy and the first person to find a Golden Ticket.

"Pave paradise and put up a parking lot": A line from the 1970 Joni Mitchell song "Big Yellow Taxi."

"Give the People What They Want": A 1975 song by The O'Jays.

The Manson Family: Cult led by Charles Manson (see earlier entry).

Bud Fox, Gordon Gekko: Characters in the 1987 crime drama film *Wall Street*. Fox is a young stockbroker portrayed by Charlie Sheen who becomes involved with Gekko, a corporate raider portrayed by Michael Douglas.

The Muppets: Cast of comedic puppet characters created by Jim Henson in the 1950s who have starred in a variety of TV shows and films.

Ted Knight (1923–1986): Actor known for *The Mary Tyler Moore Show* and *Too Close for Comfort*.

EPISODE 4.5: THE FUNDAMENTAL THINGS APPLY
Written by John Stephens. Directed by Neema Barnette. Aired October 21, 2003.
Rory goes on her first college date. Lorelai discovers that the decorator she hired for the inn has also worked with her mother.

Charlie, Khe Sanh: Charlie is a nickname for Viet Cong soldiers during the Vietnam War, derived from the radio phonetic alphabet for V and C, Victor and Charlie. Khe Sanh was the site of one of the war's longest and bloodiest battles.

Jake Barnes: Protagonist of the Ernest Hemingway (see earlier entry) novel *The Sun Also Rises*, a man whose war wound has left him unable to have sex.

Woody Guthrie (1912–1967): Singer-songwriter who was among the most notable figures in folk music.

"Workers of the world, unite!": Political slogan and rallying cry from *The Communist Manifesto* by Karl Marx and Friedrich Engels.

National Velvet: A 1944 film, based on the 1935 novel of the same name by Enid Bagnold, starring Elizabeth Taylor as a horse-crazy young girl.

Mel Sharples: The grouchy owner of Mel's Diner, the workplace setting of the TV sitcom *Alice*, which ran from 1976 to 1985. The character was portrayed by Vic Tayback.

John McCain (1936–2018): Statesman and naval officer who represented Arizona in Congress for over thirty-five years. In the late 1960s and early 1970s, he was held as a prisoner of war in North Vietnam for five and a half years.

"The Snows of Kilimanjaro": A 1936 short story by Ernest Hemingway.

F. Scott Fitzgerald, *Tender Is the Night*: Fitzgerald (1896–1940) was an author whose notable works include *The Great Gatsby* and *Tender Is the Night*. The latter is his final novel, published in 1934.

Gunsmoke: Radio and television western drama series that began in 1952.

Jason Voorhees, Freddy Krueger: Fictional horror film characters, Jason from the *Friday the 13th* franchise and Freddy from the *A Nightmare on Elm Street* franchise.

Benji: Fictional canine character created by Joe Camp first appearing in the 1974 film *Benji*.

Lassie: Fictional collie dog from the Lassie franchise that began as a 1938 short story before expanding into film and television adaptations.

Casablanca: A 1942 romance film set during World War II about an American expatriate and his former lover.

Bonnie and Clyde: A 1967 biographical neo-noir film about the titular outlaw couple.

It Happened One Night: A 1934 Frank Capra film about a pampered socialite who falls for a roguish reporter.

His Girl Friday: A 1940 film about a newspaper reporter and his ex-wife who get embroiled in a murder case.

The Treasure of the Sierra Madre: A 1948 neo-western film based on the B. Traven novel of the same name about a trio's search for gold in Mexico.

Diner: A 1982 film about a group of friends who reunite at a Baltimore diner as one of the group prepares to get married.

Mr. & Mrs. Bridge: A 1990 drama film based on a pair of Evan S. Connell novels starring real-life couple Paul Newman and Joanne Woodward.

Shelley Winters (1920–2006): Actress whose works include *The Diary of Anne Frank*, *A Place in the Sun*, and *The Poseidon Adventure*, the latter of which is about a luxury liner that capsizes in a tsunami.

"Shadow Dancing": A 1978 song by Andy Gibb.

Tiffany & Co.: Luxury jewelry and specialty design house founded in 1837.

Little House on the Prairie: Western historical drama TV series that ran from 1974 to 1983.

Hardbodies: A 1984 film about a group of middle-aged men who hire a young man to help them pick up women at the beach.

Arrival of a Train at La Ciotat: This is the film Lorelai references, an 1896 French short silent film. A well-known rumor surrounds the first screening of the film, alleging that the audience was so frightened at the moving image of a life-sized train coming toward the screen that they screamed and fled to the back of the room.

Humphrey Bogart, Ingrid Bergman: Bogart (1899–1957) is an actor whose works include *The Maltese Falcon*, *The Big Sleep*, and *Casablanca*, in which he co-starred with Bergman (1915–1982), an actress whose additional credits include *For Whom the Bell Tolls* and *Gaslight*.

Tony Roma's: Casual dining chain restaurant founded by its namesake in 1952.

The Smiths, *Meat Is Murder*: The Smiths were an English rock band active during the 1980s. *Meat Is Murder* is their second album.

EPISODE 4.6: AN AFFAIR TO REMEMBER

Written by Amy Sherman-Palladino. Directed by Matthew Diamond. Aired October 28, 2003.

Emily hires Lorelai and Sookie to cater her dinner party. Rory searches for a quiet place to study. Kirk goes on a date with Lulu.

Bobbsey Twins: Fictional characters in a series of children's novels by the publisher Stratemeyer Syndicate, written under the pseudonym Laura Lee Hope, the first of which was published in 1904. The books focus on the Bobbsey family, which consists of two sets of fraternal twins.

Trigger (1934–1965): Palomino horse appearing in Western films with its owner, Roy Rogers.

Condoleezza Rice: Diplomat and political scientist who served as US secretary of state from 2005 to 2009 and US national security advisor from 2001 to 2005.

Hans Christian Andersen (1805–1875): Author known for fairy tales such as "The Little Mermaid," "The Ugly Duckling," "Thumbelina," and others.

Liv Tyler, Todd Rundgren: Tyler is an actress whose works include *Empire Records* and *The Lord of the Rings* films. Rundgren is a rock musician who was romantically involved with Tyler's mother in the 1970s, during the time of Tyler's conception and birth, but her father is actually Steven Tyler of Aerosmith.

Tom Cruise: Actor whose films include *Top Gun*, *Rain Man*, *Jerry Maguire*, and many others.

Juicy Couture: Clothing brand founded in 1997.

Jon Cryer, *Pretty in Pink*: Cryer is an actor whose credits include the TV series *Two and a Half Men* and the 1986 John Hughes teen comedy film *Pretty in Pink*, in which Cryer plays Duckie, the outsider best friend of the protagonist Andie, played by Molly Ringwald.

"Try a Little Tenderness": A 1932 song written by Jimmy Campbell, Reg Connelly, and Harry M. Woods. While recorded by several artists, Otis Redding recorded a popular 1966 version.

EPISODE 4.7: THE FESTIVAL OF LIVING ART
Written by Daniel Palladino. Directed by Chris Long. Aired November 4, 2003. As the town prepares to host the Festival of Living Pictures, Sookie and Jackson anxiously await the arrival of the baby.

Scott Joplin (1868–1917): Composer and pianist known as the "King of Ragtime."

Pierre-Auguste Renoir (1841–1919): French Impressionist painter.

Édouard Manet (1832–1883): French modernist painter.

Claude Monet (1840–1926): French painter who founded Impressionism.

John Ashcroft: Lawyer who served as the US attorney general from 2001 to 2005.

The Reaper: A 1937 statue created by Joan Miró.

The Last Supper: Painting by Leonardo da Vinci, dated to the 1490s, depicting the Last Supper of Jesus and the Twelve Apostles, several of whom are mentioned by name in the episode.

Moon landing: A reference to the 1969 *Apollo 11* space mission, the first time humans landed on the Moon.

Angus Young: Co-founder and lead guitarist of the rock band AC/DC.

FICA: Federal Insurance Contribution Act, a US federal payroll tax.

"Rings on my fingers and bells on my toes": A common line dating back to a 1784 nursery rhyme called "Ride a cock horse to Banbury Cross," further popularized in a 1909 song titled "I've Got Rings on My Fingers."

Loaves and fishes: Reference to a story in the Bible, in which, through Jesus Christ's blessing, his disciples were able to feed a crowd of thousands with what was only five loaves of bread and two fish.

Monty Python's The Meaning of Life: A 1983 musical sketch comedy film from the Monty Python comedy troupe.

Rob Roy: Whiskey cocktail named after the operetta of the same name by composer Reginald De Koven and lyricist Harry B. Smith. The operetta was based on the life of Rob Roy MacGregor, a Scottish outlaw and folk hero.

1984: Dystopian novel by George Orwell, written in 1949.

Walkman: Brand of portable audio cassette player from Sony, first released in 1979.

"99 Luftballons": A 1983 song by the West German band Nena.

R.E.M.: Alternative rock band formed in Athens, Georgia, in 1980.

Thompson Twins: British pop band formed in 1977.

Andrew McCarthy: Actor whose works include *St. Elmo's Fire*, *Pretty in Pink*, and *Weekend at Bernie's*.

Emilio Estevez: Actor whose works include *The Outsiders*, *The Breakfast Club*, and *Young Guns*.

Caiaphas (14 BC–46 AD): High Priest of Israel during the first century and an organizer of the plot to kill Jesus.

Antea, **Parmigianino**: Parmigianino (1503–1540) was an Italian Mannerist painter and printmaker whose works include *Antea*, aka *Portrait of a Young Woman*.

Raphael (1483–1520): Italian painter and architect of the High Renaissance.

Leonardo da Vinci (1452–1519): Italian painter and architect of the High Renaissance whose works include *Mona Lisa* and *The Last Supper*.

The House of Blues: Chain of live music halls and restaurants founded in 1992.

The Whiskey a Go Go: Historic night club in Hollywood, California, opened in 1964.

Quiet Riot: Heavy metal band founded in Los Angeles in 1973.

Guernica: A famous 1937 anti-war oil painting by Pablo Picasso (see earlier entry) that portrays the suffering wrought by violence and chaos.

Norma Desmond: Fictional former silent film star in the 1950 film *Sunset Boulevard*, portrayed by Gloria Swanson. Rory paraphrases a famous line from the end of the film, in which a deranged Desmond says, "Alright Mr. DeMille, I'm ready for my closeup," and approaches the camera. Cecil B. DeMille (1881–1959) was a famous filmmaker.

Stevie Wonder: Pioneering blind singer-songwriter and musician.

Weeble: Children's roly-poly toy introduced in 1971, whose advertising jingle was "Weebles wobble, but they don't fall down."

Dance at Bougival: An 1883 painting by Renoir.

EPISODE 4.8: DIE, JERK

Written by Daniel Palladino. Directed by Tom Moore. Aired November 11, 2003. Rory's honest review for the school newspaper creates an enemy.

Siskel and Ebert: Gene Siskel (1946–1999) and Roger Ebert (1942–2013) were a pair of film critics known for their partnership that began in 1979 and lasted until Siskel's death.

Bob Woodward: Investigative reporter and author known for his tenure with the *Washington Post*.

The New Zoo Revue: Children's television show that ran from 1972 to 1977 featuring the puppet characters mentioned in the episode.

Vincent Gallo, *The Brown Bunny*: Gallo is an actor, filmmaker, and musician who starred in, wrote, directed, produced, photographed, and edited the 2003 independent erotic film *The Brown Bunny*. The film features an explicit scene in which a character portrayed by actress Chloë Sevigny performs unsimulated fellatio on Gallo. Critic Roger Ebert proclaimed the film the worst in the history of the Cannes Film Festival.

Stations of the Cross: Series of images depicting Jesus Christ on the day of his crucifixion and accompanying prayers.

Ariel Sharon (1928–2014): Israeli general and politician who served as prime minister of Israel from 2001 to 2006.

Dorothy, Tin Man: Characters in *The Wizard of Oz* (see earlier entry).

East Side 860: A reference to New York gang activity.

Al Capone (1899–1947): Gangster and businessman nicknamed "Scarface" who was charged with income tax evasion in 1931. He was convicted and served around seven and a half years.

Avril Lavigne: Pop-punk singer whose hits include "Complicated" and "Sk8er Boi."

Jason Priestley: Actor best known for his role in the TV series *Beverly Hills, 90210*.

P. Diddy: The "P. Digger" line is a nod to P. Diddy, which was one of many names used by rapper and record producer Sean Combs.

Salvador Dali (1904–1989): Spanish surrealist artist.

8 Mile: A 2002 semi-autobiographical drama film starring rapper Eminem about a rapper attempting to launch a career in hip-hop.

Episode 4.9: Ted Koppel's Big Night Out

Written by Amy Sherman-Palladino. Directed by Jamie Babbit. Aired November 18, 2003.

Lorelai and Rory accompany Richard and Emily to a tailgate party at Yale.

Jessica Simpson: Singer and actress who emerged in the late 1990s. In 2002, she married singer Nick Lachey of the boy band 98 Degrees and the two starred in an MTV reality series from 2003 to 2005 titled *Newlyweds: Nick and Jessica* before divorcing in 2006. In an episode of the show, she is shown saying, "Twenty-three is old. It's almost twenty-five, which is almost mid-twenties."

Survival of the fittest: A phrase originating in Darwinian evolutionary theory to describe natural selection.

Rudolph the Red-Nosed Reindeer: Fictional reindeer created by Robert L. May in a 1939 booklet published by Montgomery Ward department store before going on to be the subject of a beloved holiday song and TV special, as well as other adaptations. Rudolph is the ninth reindeer who uses his red nose to guide Santa Claus's sleigh.

***South Park,* Cartman**: *South Park* is an animated sitcom created by Trey Parker and Matt Stone that debuted on Comedy Central in 1997. It revolves around the exploits of four young boys in a Colorado town. Cartman is one of the show's main characters.

Foreigner: Band formed in New York City in 1976 whose hits include "I Want to Know What Love Is."

Kill Bill: Action film franchise that began with 2003's *Kill Bill: Volume 1*.

Sharon Osbourne: English TV personality and music manager married to heavy metal singer Ozzy Osbourne until his death in 2025. Her hosting credits include *America's Got Talent* and *The Talk*.

Handsome Dan: Bulldog that serves as the mascot of Yale's athletic teams. The original dog dates back to 1889.

Cole Porter (1891–1964): Composer and songwriter responsible for many Broadway standards. While a student at Yale, he was a member of the Whiffenpoofs singing group and wrote several songs, including the Yale Fight Song, "Bulldog."

"Rome wasn't built in a day": An adage with its roots in a medieval French phrase meaning that it takes time to create great things.

Obi-Wan Kenobi: Fictional character in the *Star Wars* franchise, a Jedi Master who trains Luke Skywalker in the ways of the Force. The role was originated by Alec Guinness in the original films.

Paul Wolfowitz: Political scientist and diplomat who served as US Deputy Secretary of Defense from 2001 to 2005 and was considered an architect of the Iraq War.

Ted Koppel: Broadcast journalist known for anchoring *Nightline* from 1980 until 2005.

EPISODE 4.10: THE NANNY AND THE PROFESSOR
Written by Scott Kaufer. Directed by Peter Lauer. Aired January 20, 2004.

Paris's relationship with her professor progresses. Lorelai learns that Jason took another date to a function.

The Sound of Music: A 1965 musical film adaptation of the 1959 musical of the same name, itself based on the 1949 memoir *The Story of the Trapp Family Singers* by Maria von Trapp. It is the retelling of her experiences as governess to seven children. At the beginning of the story, Maria is studying to become a nun.

Harrison Ford, Calista Flockhart: Ford is an actor known for the *Star Wars* and *Indiana Jones* franchises. Flockhart is an actress known for the TV series *Ally McBeal*. The pair met in 2002 and were married in 2010.

Easter Bunny: Folkloric figure and symbol of Easter who brings dyed eggs and other gifts to children. It dates back to a German tradition from the 1800s.

"We'll always have Paris": The episode features a spin on this famous line from the film *Casablanca* (see earlier entry).

Time: News magazine first published in 1923.

Schleprock: Fictional character from the animated series *The Pebbles and Bamm-Bamm Show*, a spinoff of *The Flintstones*, which aired from 1971 to 1972. The character is a depressed teenager with exceptionally bad luck.

Wuthering Heights: Novel by Emily Brontë published in 1847.

The Daily Show: Late-night satirical news and talk show debuting on Comedy Central in 1996.

Fast Times at Ridgemont High: A 1982 coming-of-age comedy film chronicling the lives of students at the school.

Stanford White (1853–1906): Famed architect whose work embodied the "American Renaissance."

Weird-looking Hilton sister: Presumably a reference to Nicky Hilton (see earlier entry).

Fonzie: Fictional character portrayed by Henry Winkler on the TV sitcom *Happy Days*. Epitomizing cool, Fonzie went from being a side character to a breakout lead character with merchandise and an animated spinoff series.

Hugh Hefner (1926–2017): Founder and editor-in-chief of *Playboy* magazine, known for living in luxury mansions surrounded by *Playboy* Playmates.

Eartha Kitt (1927–2008): Singer and actress known for her sex-symbol image and distinctive singing style with songs like "C'est si bon" and "Santa Baby."

EPISODE 4.11: IN THE CLAMOR AND THE CLANGOR

Written by Sheila R. Lawrence and Janet Leahy. Directed by Michael Grossman. Aired January 27, 2004.

Rory learns that she is the subject of gossip on campus. Lane's double life is discovered.

The Witches of Eastwick: A 1984 novel by John Updike about a trio of witches in 1970s Rhode Island. It was adapted into a successful 1987 film.

Prog rock: Progressive rock, a broad genre of rock and roll that emerged in the United Kingdom in the 1960s.

Simon & Garfunkel: Folk-rock duo consisting of Paul Simon and Art Garfunkel, whose hits include "Mrs. Robinson" and "Bridge Over Troubled Water."

Fleetwood Mac: Rock band formed in London in 1967, whose 1977 record *Rumours* has been considered among the best albums of all time.

Sarah McLachlan: Singer-songwriter known for the best-selling record *Surfacing* and for founding the Lilith Fair tour.

Kraftwerk: German electronic band formed in 1970.

CBGB: Music club in New York City that operated from 1973 to 2006. The letters of its name stood for Country, Bluegrass, and Blues—the owner's original vision for the space. It emerged, however, as an iconic venue for punk rock and new wave bands.

Sonic Youth: Rock band active from 1981 to 2011.

Television: Rock band formed in New York City in 1973.

Talking Heads: Rock band formed in New York City in 1975, whose hits include "This Must Be the Place (Naive Melody)" and "Burning Down the House."

Bill Clinton: President of the United States from 1993 to 2001.

The New Pornographers: Canadian indie rock band formed in 1997.

Sparks: Pop-rock duo consisting of brothers Ron and Russell Mael.

Israeli-Palestinian Conflict: Ongoing and complicated military conflict about land and self-determination dating back to the late nineteenth century.

Abraham, Sarah, Hagar: In the Bible, Abraham and Sarah were husband and wife, and Hagar an Egyptian slave and handmaiden to Sarah whom Sarah gave to Abraham as a wife to bear him a child, who was Ishmael, progenitor of the Arab people.

"Cheech growing Thai stick": Thai stick is a type of cannabis cigar, and Cheech is a reference to the marijuana-loving comedian Cheech Marin (see Cheech and Chong).

The Strokes: Indie rock band formed in New York City in 1998.

Hart to Hart: Mystery TV series that aired on ABC from 1979 to 1984, followed by a string of made-for-TV movies in the 1990s. Robert Wagner and Stefanie Powers starred as Jonathan and Jennifer Hart, a wealthy married couple who often found themselves involved in and solving murder cases.

Madeleine Albright (1937–2022): The first woman to hold the position of US secretary of state, serving under Bill Clinton from 1997 to 2001.

Cookie Monster: Cookie-loving blue character from the children's TV series *Sesame Street*.

Seven deadly sins: Group of major vices in the teachings of Christianity, which are pride, greed, wrath, envy, lust, gluttony, and sloth.

Episode 4.12: A Family Matter

Written by Daniel Palladino. Directed by Kenny Ortega. Aired February 3, 2004. Luke's sister visits Stars Hollow. Lorelai attempts to tell her parents about her relationship with Jason.

Arnold Palmer (1929–2016): Popular and charismatic professional golfer and businessman, as well as a fan of the beverage that bears his name, which combines iced tea and lemonade.

Good Morning, Vietnam: A 1987 war comedy starring Robin Wiliams as an Armed Forces Radio Service DJ.

Easy Rider: A 1969 road drama film starring Peter Fonda and Dennis Hopper as two bikers traveling the American Southwest. Jack Nicholson (see earlier entry) stars as a "square" lawyer who befriends the riders and reluctantly tries marijuana at their invitation.

The Doobie Brothers: Rock band formed in California in 1970, whose hits include "Listen to the Music" and "What a Fool Believes."

Nolan Ryan: Former professional baseball player who played for the New York Mets, the Houston Astros, and other teams.

Nancy Spungen (1959–1978): Figure in the 1970s punk rock scene and girlfriend of rock star Sid Vicious. (See *Sid and Nancy*.)

"Vessel with the pestle holds the brew that is true": A nod to a bit in the 1955 musical comedy film *The Court Jester* starring Danny Kaye.

Mrs. Robinson: Character in the 1967 film *The Graduate* (see earlier entry), an older, married woman who seduces the younger protagonist.

"Ask me again, I'll tell you the same": Line from the children's chant and 1963 Alley Cats song "Puddin' n' Tain."

Ted Kennedy (1932–2009): Lawyer and member of the prominent Kennedy family who served as US Senator from Massachusetts from 1962 to 2009.

May–December romance: Phrase used to describe an age disparity in a relationship.

Ming dynasty: Imperial dynasty of China from 1368 to 1644.

"Counting my chickens": Part of the phrase "don't count your chickens before they hatch," meaning to not depend on something that hasn't yet happened.

Neil Kinnock: Welsh politician who was Leader of the Opposition and Leader of the Labour Party from 1983 to 1992 and vice president of the European Commission from 1999 to 2004.

Roger Moore (1927–2017): English actor who played James Bond in seven feature films.

TiVo: Brand of digital video recorder introduced in 1999.

Frontline: Investigative documentary TV program debuting on PBS in 1983.

Donner Pass: Mountain pass in the northern Sierra Nevada range in California, which gets its name from the Donner Party (see earlier entry).

Idi Amin (1928–2003): President of Uganda from 1971 to 1979.

Mr. Goodwrench: Spokes character for the GM Goodwrench auto repair service of General Motors, portrayed by actor Barry Coe in TV commercials in the 1970s and 1980s.

David Blaine: Popular mentalist, magician, and endurance performer.

Bobby McFerrin: Singer-songwriter known for "Don't Worry, Be Happy."

Fortune 500: Annual list of America's largest corporations based on revenue.

EPISODE 4.13: NAG HAMMADI IS WHERE THEY FOUND THE GNOSTIC GOSPEL
Written by Amy Sherman-Palladino. Directed by Chris Long. Aired February 10, 2004.
Car trouble strands Jess in Stars Hollow.

Robert Downey Jr.: Actor known for portraying Iron Man in the Marvel Cinematic Universe and many other roles. His career has seen many addiction-related setbacks. In 1996, while under the influence of a controlled substance, he wandered into a neighbor's home and fell asleep in their bed.

Alive: A 1993 survival drama film about a Uruguayan rugby team's 1972 plane crash in the Andes mountains. Eventually the starving survivors decide to eat the flesh of the deceased in order to stay alive.

Adrian: Fictional love interest in the *Rocky* film franchise, portrayed by Talia Shire.

Budweiser Clydesdales: Group of horses used in promotions for the Budweiser brand of beer. The horses were first introduced in the 1930s.

Ann Jillian: Actress and singer known for the TV series *It's a Living*.

Carnivàle: TV series that aired on HBO from 2003 to 2005 about a Depression-era traveling carnival.

Big Mouth Billy Bass: Animatronic mounted fish prop introduced in 1999 that would wiggle its tail and sing songs like "Don't Worry, Be Happy."

Etch A Sketch: Mechanical drawing toy introduced in 1960.

Demi Moore, Ashton Kutcher: Moore is an actress known for *St. Elmo's Fire*, *Ghost*, and *Indecent Proposal*. Kutcher is an actor known for *That '70s Show* and *Dude, Where's My Car?* The pair were married from 2005 to 2013.

Frances Farmer (1913–1970): Actress whose career was often overshadowed by her mental health struggles and involuntary commitment to psychiatric hospitals.

Nag Hammadi: A city in upper Egypt.

Aquaman: DC Comics undersea superhero first appearing in 1941.

"Mona Lisa": A 2004 song by Grant Lee Phillips. Its name is derived from a well-known painting by Leonardo di Vinci.

Styx: Rock band formed in Chicago in 1972 whose hits include "Come Sail Away."

REO Speedwagon: Rock band formed in Illinois in 1967 whose hits include "Keep on Loving You."

EPISODE 4.14: THE INCREDIBLE SHRINKING LORELAIS
Written by Amy Sherman-Palladino and Daniel Palladino. Directed by Stephen Clancy. Aired February 17, 2004.
Rory deals with self-doubt when a professor suggests she drop a class. The stress of opening the inn affects Lorelai.

Lou Ferrigno: Actor and retired bodybuilder known for playing the title role in the TV series *The Incredible Hulk* from 1978 to 1982.

Taxi Driver: A 1976 Martin Scorsese drama film that follows the deteriorating mental health of a Vietnam veteran taxi driver in New York City.

Basso profondo: Lowest bass type voice.

William Saffire: Journalist, political columnist, and presidential speechwriter for Richard Nixon.

Nattering nabobs of negativism: Phrase used by Vice President Spiro Agnew in the early 1970s to mock journalists, with whom he was angry for their coverage of President Nixon.

Spiro Agnew (1918–1996): Vice president of the United States from 1969 to 1973 under Richard Nixon.

The bird lady from *Mary Poppins*: Fictional character from *Mary Poppins* (see earlier entry), an elderly lady who feeds breadcrumbs to hungry pigeons. She was portrayed by Jane Darwell.

Radioactive spider: A reference to the origin story of the Marvel Comics character Spider-Man. Peter Parker became Spider-Man after being bitten by a radioactive spider.

Bethany Hamilton: The reference to a one-armed surfer girl is a nod to this professional surfer who lost her arm during a shark attack in 2003. She returned to surfing and wrote her memoir in 2004.

André the Giant (1946–1993): Professional wrestler and actor known for his great size. His acting credits include *The Princess Bride*.

Gandalf the Grey: Fictional wizard in *The Lord of the Rings* (see earlier entry).

Potsie: Fictional character from the TV sitcom *Happy Days*, portrayed by Anson Williams.

Jolly Green Giant: Fictional giant mascot of the Green Giant brand of frozen and canned vegetables.

The Carpenters: Singing duo consisting of siblings Karen and Richard Carpenter, active from 1965 to 1983.

The Kids in the Hall: Canadian sketch comedy troupe consisting of comedians Dave Foley, Bruce McCulloch, Kevin McDonald, Mark McKinney, and Scott Thompson. Their eponymous TV series ran from 1989 to 1995 with a revival season airing in 2022.

Charlize Theron: Actress whose works include the 2003 film *Monster*, a biographical crime drama in which she portrayed serial killer Aileen Wuornos.

Sweathogs: Group of fictional students in the TV sitcom *Welcome Back, Kotter*.

Adolphe Menjou (1890–1963): Actor whose career spanned silent films and "talkies."

Nick Nolte: Actor known for *The Prince of Tides*, *48 Hrs.*, and *Down and Out in Beverly Hills*. He is also known for a series of legal troubles and substance abuse. He was arrested on suspicion of drunk driving in 2002, leading to an infamous mugshot in which he appeared bleary-eyed and disheveled.

Episode 4.15: Scene in a Mall

Written by Daniel Palladino. Directed by Chris Long. Aired February 24, 2004. Rory gets a glimpse of Dean's new life. Lorelai and Rory get swept up in Emily's shopping spree at the mall.

Alec Baldwin: Actor whose credits include *Beetlejuice*, *Working Girl*, and *30 Rock*.

Guinness World Records: Reference book listing world records in human achievements and extremes of the natural world.

Big Ben: Famed clock tower in London, England, completed in 1859.

The L Word: TV drama series that aired on Showtime from 2004 to 2009, following the lives of a group of lesbian and bisexual women.

Johnny Carson (1925–2005): Comedian known for hosting *The Tonight Show Starring Johnny Carson* from 1962 to 1992.

Methuselah: Longest-lived figure mentioned in the Bible, dying at 969 years of age.

Moby: Musician known for "South Side," "Porcelain," and other songs.

Love Is . . .: Single-frame comic strip by Kim Casali in 1970, in which the title appears in the upper corner and the thought completed at the bottom, along with an illustration typically depicting a man and woman.

Rosalind Russell (1907–1976): Actress known for *His Girl Friday*, *Auntie Mame*, and *Gypsy*.

Ava Gardner (1922–1990): Actress known for *Mogambo* and *The Night of the Iguana*.

Village People: Costumed disco singing group whose members dress like a construction worker, a policeman, a cowboy, and other figures. Hits include "Macho Man" and "Y.M.C.A."

Hogan's Heroes: TV sitcom set in a World War II Nazi Germany prisoner-of-war camp, airing from 1965 to 1971.

The Libertines: English rock band formed in 1997.

The White Stripes: Rock duo formed in 1997 consisting of Jack and Meg White.

Led Zeppelin, "Stairway to Heaven": Led Zeppelin is an English rock band formed in London in 1968, whose hits include 1971's "Stairway to

Heaven," which has been regarded as among the greatest rock and roll songs of all time.

Teletubbies: British children's TV series focusing on four differently colored characters. The original series debuted in 1997.

Yoda: Fictional character in the *Star Wars* universe, depicted as a small, powerful green humanoid.

Mummenschanz: Swiss theater troupe formed in 1972 who perform in a mask- and prop-oriented style.

Futurama: Animated science-fiction sitcom airing on Fox from 1999 to 2003, followed by revivals in later years.

Sex Pistols, Johnny Rotten: The Sex Pistols are an English punk rock band formed in London in 1975. Rotten was the band's lead vocalist.

Bender, Leela, Nibbler: Fictional animated characters from *Futurama* (see earlier entry).

Giorgio Baldi: Chef and owner of Il Ristorante di Giorgio Baldi in Santa Monica, California. Baldi died in 2011.

Eight maids a-milking: A line from the Christmas carol "The Twelve Days of Christmas."

Vera Wang: Fashion designer who initially gained attention for her wedding gown designs before expanding into a variety of clothing, accessories, and other items.

Manolo Blahnik: Spanish fashion designer and founder of the high-end shoe brand bearing his name.

Valhalla: Majestic hall in Norse mythology presided over by the god Odin.

Orange Julius: Chain of fruit beverage stores founded in 1926, known for its namesake drink, a frothy mixture of ice, orange juice, sweetener, milk, powdered egg whites, and vanilla.

Episode 4.16: The Reigning Lorelai

Written by Jane Espenson. Directed by Marita Grabiak. Aired March 2, 2004.
The family is shocked by the sudden death of Richard's mother.

Stephen Glass: Former journalist for *The New Republic* from 1995 to 1998 until it was revealed that many of his writings were fabricated.

Tobey Maguire: Actor whose works include the *Spider-Man* film trilogy from the early 2000s.

Jayson Blair: Former journalist who worked for the *New York Times* until resigning after revelations of fabrication and plagiarism in his writings.

Welcome to the Dollhouse: A 1995 coming-of-age independent film about an unpopular middle-school girl trying to earn the respect of her peers and family.

Charlie's Angels: Full Throttle: A 2003 action-comedy film starring Cameron Diaz, Drew Barrymore, and Lucy Liu.

Kay Kyser (1905–1985): Band leader and radio personality of the 1930s and 1940s.

Nigella Lawson: English food writer and TV cook.

Brothers Grimm: Duo of German academics, Jacob and Wilhelm, known as storytellers of folklore and for popularizing such tales as "Cinderella," "Hansel and Gretel," and many others.

The Crimson Petal and the White: A 2002 novel by Michel Faber set in Victorian England.

The White Rabbit: Fictional anthropomorphic rabbit in *Alice in Wonderland* (see earlier entry), appearing at the beginning of the story as running late for an appointment. He is followed by Alice down a rabbit hole.

Queen Elizabeth II (1926–2022): Queen of England from 1952 until her death.

EPISODE 4.17: GIRLS IN BIKINIS, BOYS DOIN' THE TWIST
Written by Amy Sherman-Palladino. Directed by Jamie Babbit. Aired April 13, 2004.
Rory and Paris head to Florida for spring break and run into some old friends.

Freshman 15: A term for the weight gain that many college freshmen experience during their first year.

Burmese political prisoners: Activists and anyone outspoken against military rule in this southeast Asian country, now called Myanmar, had long been routinely locked up in prisons for years.

Armin Meiwes: While not mentioned by name, Paris references this German former computer repair technician who received international attention when he murdered and ate a voluntary victim in 2001. Initially arrested and sentenced to eight and a half years in prison, he was later resentenced to life imprisonment.

Gary Gilmore (1940–1977): Convicted murderer who gained attention when he demanded the implementation of his death sentence. He was executed by firing squad.

Al Gore: Vice president of the United States from 1993 to 2001 under the administration of Bill Clinton. Gore unsuccessfully ran for president in 2000, losing to George W. Bush. The "don't endorse me" line refers to the 2004 presidential election, in which Gore made what some called an early move to endorse Vermont governor Howard Dean for the Democratic candidacy. Dean lost out to John Kerry and later cited Gore's endorsement as the beginning of his campaign's decline.

Fagin: Fictional antagonist in the Charles Dickens novel *Oliver Twist*, who leads a group of child pickpockets in exchange for shelter.

Girls Gone Wild: Adult entertainment franchise launched in 1997 that typically featured camera crews documenting supposed wild acts of behavior from college-aged women at spring break parties and similar locations.

"The Twist": A 1958 pop song and accompanying dance craze that was originally released by Hank Ballard and the Midnighters but is best remembered from the 1960 Chubby Checker cover version.

MapQuest: Online web mapping service launched in 1996.

David Caruso: Actor known for *NYPD Blue* and *CSI: Miami*.

Green Party: Political party based on such principles as environmentalism and social justice.

Top Gun: A 1986 action drama film starring Tom Cruise as a young naval aviator.

Casper: Fictional animated friendly ghost debuting in 1945 and appearing in a variety of cartoons, comics, and films.

***The Power of Myth*, Joseph Campbell, Bill Moyers**: Campbell (1904–1987) was a writer who worked in mythology and comparative religion. Moyers is a journalist and political commentator who served as White House Chief of Staff and Press Secretary under President Lyndon B. Johnson in the 1960s. *Joseph Campbell and the Power of Myth* is a six-part documentary broadcast on PBS in 1988, featuring conversations between Campbell and Moyers, focusing on Campbell's views on comparative mythology and the role of myth in human society. A companion book, *The Power of Myth*, was released alongside the documentary series.

Sir Thomas More (1478–1535): Noted Renaissance humanist who served Henry VIII as Lord High Chancellor of England from 1529 to 1532. He authored *Utopia*, in which he described the political system of an imaginary state. After refusing to take the Oath of Supremacy, he was convicted of treason and executed. At his execution, he was reported to have said, "I die the King's good servant, and God's first." He is referenced in the song being performed in the episode by the indie rock band The Shins called "So Says I."

Michael Caine: Noted actor whose long list of credits includes *Hannah and Her Sisters*, *The Cider House Rules*, and *The Muppet Christmas Carol*.

Cialis, Levitra: Medications used to treat erectile dysfunction. An ad for Cialis ran during the Super Bowl in 2003, and an ad for Levitra ran during the game in 2004.

EPISODE 4.18: TICK, TICK, TICK, BOOM!
Written by and directed by Daniel Palladino. Aired April 20, 2004.
Dinner with Jason's parents has disastrous consequences for the Gilmores.

Bilbo Baggins, the Shire: Bilbo Baggins is a fictional hobbit character from J. R. R. Tolkien's *The Hobbit* and *The Lord of the Rings* (see earlier entry). The Shire is the hobbits' homeland in the books.

Amistad: A nineteenth-century two-masted schooner known for a slave revolt in 1839.

Dennis Kucinich: Politician who served as US Representative from Ohio from 1997 to 2013 who unsuccessfully campaigned to be the Democratic nominee for president in the 2004 election. During the campaign, he was criticized for his changing stance on abortion.

Annette Funicello, Frankie Avalon: Funicello (1942–2013) was an actress and singer known for the *Mickey Mouse Club* and for co-starring alongside fellow singer/actor Avalon in a series of beach-themed movies in the 1960s.

Metrosexual: A term that surfaced in the 1990s, and gained popularity in the early 2000s, describing a heterosexual man with meticulous grooming and styling habits.

Wile E. Coyote, the Road Runner: Animated characters in the *Looney Tunes/Merrie Melodies* cartoons, first appearing in 1949. Wile E. Coyote launches elaborate schemes, often involving devices ordered from the Acme Corporation, to try and catch and eat the ever-elusive Road Runner.

Dorf: Fictional character created and performed by actor/comedian Tim Conway, who appeared in a series of direct-to-video films during the 1980s and 1990s, including *Dorf on Golf* and *Dorf Goes Fishing*.

Howard Dean: While not referenced by name, Kirk's impassioned speech at the town square is a nod to this politician who served as governor of Vermont from 1991 to 2003 and chair of the Democratic National Convention from 2005 to 2009. He unsuccessfully campaigned for the Democratic nomination for president in the 2004 election. At the Iowa Democratic caucuses, he gave an impassioned speech and inserted a short, loud "Yeah!" at the end. It was highly criticized as odd and unpresidential and became fodder for comedians and media sound bites, where it was labeled the "Dean Scream" and the "I Have a Scream" speech. Many called it the moment that ended his bid for the nomination.

Harry Chapin (1942–1981): Singer-songwriter known for such songs as "Cat's in the Cradle," about the strained relationship between a father and son.

Oedipus complex: Psychoanalytic theory regarding a son's sexual attitudes toward his mother and hostility toward his father.

Tony Robbins: Self-help author and inspirational speaker.

Disco: A subculture and dance music movement that emerged in the late 1960s and gained momentum during the 1970s. Its popularity rapidly declined in the late 1970s, including an infamous Disco Demolition Night in 1979. It began as a Major League Baseball promotional event in which a crate of disco records was blown up at a game between the Chicago White Sox and the Detroit Tigers. Fans rushed the field after the detonation, resulting in a riot.

Donna Summer (1948–2012): Singer who rose to fame during the disco era of the 1970s with hits like "Last Dance," "Hot Stuff," and "MacArthur Park."

Ruben Studdard, Clay Aiken, Kelly Clarkson: Singers who rose to fame as contestants on the reality singing competition program *American Idol*. Clarkson was the winner of the show's inaugural season in 2002 and has enjoyed a successful career with multiple hit records, Grammy awards, and a daytime talk show. Studdard won the show's second season, and Aiken was that season's runner-up. Both have continued to perform.

Petticoat Junction: Sitcom that aired on CBS from 1963 to 1970 focusing on the goings-on at the fictional rural Shady Rest Hotel.

"Summer Nights": Lorelai misspeaks the title of this song from the musical *Grease* (see earlier entry), written by Jim Jacobs and Warren Casey and most notably performed in the film adaptation by Olivia Newton-John, John Travolta, and the cast.

Groucho, Chico, Harpo, Zeppo: The Marx Brothers (see earlier entry).

Bulldogs: Athletic teams that represent Yale University.

Churchill cigars: Type of cigar named in honor of Winston Churchill (see earlier entry), who was rarely seen without a cigar. It is said that he smoked between eight and ten per day.

Cash on the barrel: An expression meaning money is paid immediately at time of transaction.

EPISODE 4.19: AFTERBOOM
Written by Sheila R. Lawrence. Directed by Michael Zinberg. Aired April 27, 2004.
Lorelai confronts her father regarding his treatment of Jason.

Lucille Ball (1911–1989): Famed actress and comedian known for *I Love Lucy* and other sitcoms.

Bewitched: Fantasy TV sitcom that aired on ABC from 1964 to 1972 about a witch who marries a mortal man and attempts to live the life of a suburban housewife. Lorelai and Kirk discuss several characters from the series.

The Carringtons: Fictional core family on the prime-time TV soap opera *Dynasty*, which aired on ABC from 1981 to 1989.

Zorro: Fictional character portrayed as a dashing masked vigilante in an all-black costume. Zorro was created by writer Johnston McCulley in 1919 and has appeared in multiple stories, films, TV series, and other formats ever since.

Union, Confederate soldiers: Soldiers who fought for the north and south, respectively, during the Civil War (see earlier entry).

Billy Crystal, Oscars: Crystal is a comedian and actor known for *Soap*, *When Harry Met Sally*, and *City Slickers*. He has hosted the Oscars (see Academy Awards) nine times.

Enron: Houston-based energy, commodities, and services company founded in 1985 that gained notoriety in 2001 when it was revealed that their reported financial condition was the result of widespread internal accounting fraud. The scandal led to the company being synonymous with fraud and corruption.

The Trial: Novel by Franz Kafka (see earlier entry) about a man prosecuted by an inaccessible authority. It was published in 1925.

Marsilius of Padua (1270–1342): Italian scholar and political figure who wrote *The Defender of Peace*.

Niccolò Machiavelli (1469–1527): Author, philosopher, and historian during the Italian Renaissance who wrote *The Prince*.

Tante Flickman: The term "tante" refers to an aunt or general elderly woman known to a family. Tante Flickman appears to be one of Lorelai's made-up references.

Timothy Leary (1920–1996): Psychologist and author known for advocating the use of psychedelic drugs.

EPISODE 4.20: LUKE CAN SEE HER FACE
Written by Amy Sherman-Palladino and Daniel Palladino. Directed by Matthew Diamond. Aired May 4, 2004.
Liz announces she's getting married to T.J. Luke tries self-help tapes.

Circle the wagons: An idiom meaning to join forces for protection.

Toby Radloff, *American Splendor*: *American Splendor* is a 2003 biographical film starring Paul Giamatti as comic book writer Harvey Pekar, based on Pekar's comic book series of the same name. Radloff was a colleague of Pekar's—a self-proclaimed "Genuine Nerd" with a love for the film *Revenge of the Nerds*. That love was documented both in the comic book series and the film.

Vanessa Redgrave, *Camelot*: Redgrave is an esteemed English actress whose works include *Julia*, *Howard's End*, and *Camelot*, a 1967 musical fantasy film based on the legend of King Arthur and adapted from the 1960 stage version. Redgrave stars as Guenevere alongside Richard Harris as King Arthur.

***Fatso*, Anne Bancroft**: *Fatso* is a 1980 comedy-drama film examining such issues as obesity, addiction, and self-acceptance. It stars Dom DeLuise and was written and directed by Bancroft (1931–2005). Bancroft was a respected actress whose works include *The Graduate*, *Turning Point*, and *The Miracle Worker* (see earlier entry), in which she played Annie Sullivan (see earlier entry).

Le Cirque: French restaurant in New York City that operated from 1974 to 2018.

Socrates (470–399 BC): Greek philosopher credited as the founder of Western philosophy.

The Lords of Flatbush: A 1974 comedy film starring Sylvester Stallone, Perry King, and Henry Winkler, focusing on a group of lower middle-class Brooklyn street teens in the late 1950s.

"A gay old time": Phrase meaning to have an enjoyable experience, popularized as a line in the theme song to the TV series *The Flintstones*.

The guys with the butterfly nets: A TV and cartoon trope referring to sanitorium workers restraining mental health patients.

EPISODE 4.21: LAST WEEK FIGHTS, THIS WEEK TIGHTS
Written by Daniel Palladino. Directed by Chris Long. Aired May 11, 2004.
Stars Hollow prepares for Liz and T.J.'s wedding in the town square.

"The Safety Dance": A 1982 pop song by Canadian new wave band Men Without Hats. The song's music video features British folk revival imagery and depicts lead singer Ivan Doroschuk, accompanied by a little person and a blonde woman, happening upon a village and dancing alongside Morris dancers, Mummers, a puppet show, and maypole.

Jack LaLanne (1914–2011): Fitness and nutrition guru and motivational speaker who hosted *The Jack LaLanne Show*, a fitness TV series, from 1951 to 1985.

"Clicking their heels": A reference to Dorothy's method for returning home in *The Wizard of Oz* (see earlier entry). While wearing the magical ruby slippers, she was transported back to Kansas by clicking her heels together and saying, "There's no place like home."

Mel Gibson, Jesus: Gibson is an actor and filmmaker whose works include *Mad Max*, *Lethal Weapon*, and *Braveheart*. In 2004, he co-wrote, produced, and directed *The Passion of the Christ*, an epic biblical film violently and graphically depicting the crucifixion and death of Jesus Christ, the central figure of Christianity.

Elihu Yale (1649–1721): Colonial administrator and primary benefactor of Yale University.

"The Lumberjack Song": A 1975 single by the comedy troupe Monty Python.

James Madison (1751–1836): American Founding Father who served as fourth president of the United States from 1809 to 1817.

Blossom Dearie (1924–2009): Notable jazz singer and pianist.

Sun Tzu (544–496 BC): Chinese general and military strategist who wrote *The Art of War*.

Pontius Pilate: Governor of the Roman province of Judaea, known for presiding over the trial of Jesus Christ and ordering his crucifixion.

Julius Caesar, Cleopatra: Caesar (100–44 BC) was a Roman general and dictator. Cleopatra (69–30 BC) was queen of the Ptolemaic Kingdom of Egypt from 51 to 30 BC. The two had an affair which produced a son, Caesarion.

Leslie Van Houton: Convicted murderer and member of the Manson Family cult.

Barrel of Monkeys, Battleship, Whee-lo, Clue, Mouse Trap, Bash!, Spirograph, Kaleidoscope, Yahtzee: These are all children's board games and toys.

Kajagoogoo: English pop band formed in 1978, best known for the 1983 single "Too Shy."

Oingo Boingo: New wave band formed in 1979, best known for the 1985 single "Weird Science."

Geoffrey Chaucer (1343–1400): English poet and writer best known for *The Canterbury Tales*.

Euclid: Ancient Greek mathematician considered the father of geometry.

"Why did Uma wear that dress?": A reference to a bizarre Christian Lacroix gown worn by Uma Thurman (see earlier entry) to the 2004

Oscars. It was later reported that Thurman wore the dress in order to incite criticism.

EPISODE 4.22: RAINCOATS AND RECIPES

Written and directed by Amy Sherman-Palladino. Aired May 18, 2004.
Lorelai recruits friends and family for a test-run night at the Dragonfly Inn.

Brawny paper towel guy: Brawny is a brand of paper towels who in the 1970s began using as its mascot a mustachioed, flannel-shirted lumberjack.

James Spader: Actor whose works include *Sex, Lies, and Videotape*, *Avengers: Age of Ultron*, *Boston Legal*, and *Pretty in Pink* (see earlier entry), in which he played an unlikable, arrogant rich kid.

"Lilly-a-Passion": A 2004 song by Grant Lee Phillips.

Late Show with David Letterman: Late-night TV talk show hosted by David Letterman, which aired on CBS from 1993 to 2015. Lorelai refers to an appearance on the show by actress Farrah Fawcett (see earlier entry) in 1997, in which she appeared distracted and rambled, leading to media speculation.

Aragorn: Fictional character in J. R. R. Tolkien's *The Lord of the Rings* (see earlier entry).

Hayley Mills: Actress known for her dual role portraying separated twin sisters Susan and Sharon in the 1961 film *The Parent Trap*. In the film, the girls scheme to reunite their divorced parents.

Roslyn Kind: Actress, singer, and half-sister of Barbra Streisand (see earlier entry).

The Bad Seed: A 1956 psychological thriller film about a woman who discovers her seemingly sweet daughter is a psychotic killer. Lorelai paraphrases a line from the film.

Blake Edwards (1922–2010): Producer, actor, and director often associated with slapstick and comedy films. His works include *Breakfast at Tiffany's*, *The Party*, and *The Pink Panther* film series.

Season Five: 2004–2005

EPISODE 5.1: SAY GOODBYE TO DAISY MILLER
Written and directed by Amy Sherman-Palladino. Aired September 21, 2004.
Rory deals with the consequences of her actions.

Charlie Chaplin (1889–1977): Actor who rose to fame during the silent film era, well known for his screen persona The Tramp.

Squiggy: Character from the TV sitcom *Laverne & Shirley*, portrayed by David L. Ladner. Squiggy and his roommate, Lenny, were neighbors to the title characters.

"Our Lips Are Sealed": A 1981 song by pop band the Go-Go's, whose lead singer is Belinda Carlisle (see earlier entry).

The Polyphonic Spree: Choral rock band formed in Texas in 2000 by singer-songwriter Tim DeLaughter whose songs are augmented by a large choir.

Al Gilbert: Entertainer known as the Pied Piper of Dance who founded Stepping Tones Records in 1952 and created Training Aid choreographed dance routines in 1971.

Count Dracula: The archetypal vampire and title character in the 1897 gothic horror novel *Dracula* by Bram Stoker.

Page Six: Iconic gossip column from the *New York Post*.

Gigi: A 1958 musical film based on the 1944 Colette novella of the same name about a young woman in Paris groomed as a courtesan by her grandmother.

Daisy Miller: Title character from an 1879 Henry James novella about the courtship of Daisy by a sophisticated compatriot. It was adapted into a 1978 film starring Cybill Shepherd in the title role.

Dean Moriarty: Fictional character in the Jack Kerouac novel *On the Road*, portrayed as enthusiastic and always up for a trip.

Lancelot: Character from Arthurian legend, depicted as a close companion of King Arthur, a Knight of the Round Table, and the secret lover of Guinevere.

Episode 5.2: A Messenger, Nothing More

Written and directed by Daniel Palladino. Aired September 28, 2004.
Rory reconciles with her mother and sends a letter from Europe to Dean.

Rupert Murdoch: Billionaire media magnate who owns a variety of outlets, including Fox Corporation.

The Da Vinci Code: A 2003 mystery-thriller novel by Dan Brown that became a worldwide blockbuster and was adapted into a film starring Tom Hanks. While not mentioned by name, this is the book Zack and Brian are discussing in the diner.

Vietnam War: Armed conflict in Vietnam that lasted from 1955 to 1975.

Mike Mussina, Kevin Brown: Former professional baseball players, both of whom played for various teams, including the New York Yankees.

Deepak Chopra: Author, new-age guru, and popular alternative medicine advocate.

Villa Medici: Historic sixteenth-century villa in Rome, Italy.

Uffizi: Prominent art museum in Florence, Italy.

Piazza Navona: Public square in Rome, Italy.

"We'll leave the light on for you": Slogan from the Motel 6 chain of hotels.

"Fell in Love with a Girl": A 2001 song by the White Stripes (see earlier entry).

"Lithium": A 1992 song by Nirvana (see earlier entry).

Radiohead: English rock band formed in 1985.

The Dandy Warhols: Alternative rock band formed in Oregon in 1994. Their name is a play on the name of artist Andy Warhol.

Men at Work: Australian pop band known for "Down Under" and "Who Can It Be Now?"

Chicago: Rock band formed in 1967 whose hits include "If You Leave Me Now" and "You're the Inspiration." They're known for titling their albums based on its numerical order in their discography.

Wings: Rock band formed in London in 1971 and led by Paul McCartney.

Culture Club: English pop band formed in 1981, led by Boy George, whose hits include "Karma Chameleon" and "Do You Really Want to Hurt Me?"

Quarterflash: Rock group formed in Oregon in 1980, known for "Harden My Heart."

Apocalypse Now: A 1979 war film by Francis Ford Coppola set during the Vietnam War.

"A football for me to kick": Reference to an enduring bit from the *Peanuts* comic strip, in which Lucy (see earlier entry) urges Charlie Brown to run toward her as she holds out a football for him to kick. He protests that she'll pull the ball away as he nears. She promises she won't but ultimately does every time.

E! True Hollywood Story: Documentary TV series airing on the E! network from 1996 to 2021, with topics focusing on various Hollywood subjects, from movies and music to actors to well-known scandals.

Moses: Biblical prophet who led the Israelites out of slavery in the Exodus.

Raging Bull: A 1980 biographical sports film directed by Martin Scorsese, starring Robert De Niro as middleweight boxing champion Jake LaMotta. The film is based on LaMotta's memoir.

Ginchy: Slang term meaning "cool," popularized by the character Kookie, portrayed by Edd Byrnes, on the 1950s–1960s TV series *77 Sunset Strip*.

A Room with a View: Rory and Lorelai watch a clip of this 1985 British film about the budding romance between a young woman and a free-spirited young man. Helena Bonham Carter, Maggie Smith, and Judi Dench star.

Episode 5.3: Written in the Stars

Written by Amy Sherman-Palladino. Directed by Kenneth Ortega. Aired October 5, 2004.

News of Luke and Lorelai's relationship hits the town. Paris hosts a wake for Asher Fleming.

Heather Has Two Mommies: A 1989 children's book by Lesléa Newman.

Arthur Schopenhauer (1788–1860): German philosopher known for his pessimism, atheism, and metaphysical ideas.

Patsy Cline (1932–1963): Influential country music singer whose hits include "Crazy" and "Walkin' After Midnight."

Chicken Dance: An oom-pah song and fad dance popularized in the 1950s.

Carson Kressley: TV personality and designer known for hosting *Queer Eye for the Straight Guy* (see earlier entry).

Some Kind of Wonderful: When discussing their date, Lorelai describes to Luke the plot of this 1987 teen romantic comedy starring Eric Stoltz, Mary Stuart Masterson, and Lea Thompson.

Cecil Beaton and the Duke of Windsor: Beaton (1904–1980) was a famed British photographer, costume designer, and set designer. The Duke of Windsor was Edward VIII (1894–1972), king of the United Kingdom from 1936 until his abdication the same year to marry Wallis Simpson. Beaton photographed the couple.

Nicole Richie: Media personality, actress, and daughter of Lionel Richie. She rose to fame in the early 2000s when starring in the reality TV series *The Simple Life* with Paris Hilton.

***A Midsummer Night's Dream*, Puck**: *A Midsummer Night's Dream* is a comedy by William Shakespeare revolving around the marriage of Theseus and Hippolyta in Greek mythology. Puck, a character in the play, is a mischievous sprite.

Dick Shawn (1923–1987): Character actor who suffered a heart attack and collapsed on stage during a performance at the University of California, San Diego, in 1987. The audience initially thought it was part of the act.

Chippendale: Type of high-end furniture similar to that of English designer Thomas Chippendale.

Maytag Repairman: Known as Ol' Lonely, the Maytag Repairman is a character in advertisements for the Maytag brand of home appliances beginning in the 1960s. The gimmick of the character is that he is lonely and bored because Maytag appliances never need to be repaired.

Mountain Girl trial: Mountain Girl is the nickname given to Carolyn Garcia, former wife of Jerry Garcia, lead singer of the Grateful Dead. She was given the nickname in the 1960s due to her "wild ways." She was married to Garcia from 1981 to 1994. Following Garcia's death in 1995, she entered into litigation with his estate and then-wife Deborah Koons to obtain payments as per their divorce agreement, ultimately settling for $1.2 million.

The Prancing Pony: Fictional pub and inn in *The Lord of the Rings* (see earlier entry).

Paul Thomas Anderson: Filmmaker whose works include *Boogie Nights*, *Magnolia*, and *Punch-Drunk Love*. His works often involve intricate plots with multiple storylines.

Orlando Bloom: Actor known for *The Lord of the Rings* film series.

Judi Dench: Esteemed British actress whose works include *As Time Goes By*, *Shakespeare in Love*, *Chocolat*, and *Iris*.

Master and Commander: The Far Side of the World: A 2003 epic period war film starring Russell Crowe and Paul Bettany set during the Napoleonic Wars.

Samson and Delilah: While not the specific reference in the episode, Samson and Delilah are Biblical figures, Samson being granted immense strength that would be nullified if his long hair were cut. Delilah was the lover who betrayed him by having his hair cut.

"The Times They Are a-Changin'": Song and title of the third album by folk singer Bob Dylan.

Hello!: Magazine specializing in celebrity news and human-interest stories.

"Delta Dawn": A 1971 song written by Larry Collins and Alex Harvey. It has been recorded by several artists, including Bette Midler and Helen Reddy, but is best known as a 1972 hit by country singer Tanya Tucker, who was thirteen at the time of its release.

Episode 5.4: Tippecanoe and Taylor, Too

Written by Bill Prady. Directed by Lee Shallat Chemel. Aired October 12, 2004. Jackson runs against Taylor for town selectman. Rory and Dean struggle to find some privacy. Lane makes a confession to Zack.

MTV Cribs: Documentary TV series that originally aired on MTV from 2000 to 2010 before being revived in 2021. It features tours of the private homes of celebrities.

"In Your Eyes": A 1986 pop song by Peter Gabriel. Lorelai references a famous scene from the 1989 film *Say Anything . . .*, in which a character stands outside the bedroom window of another character, holding up a boombox that plays the song.

Justin and Cameron: Reference to Justin Timberlake and Cameron Diaz (see earlier entries), who were involved in a romantic relationship from 2003 to 2007.

Hoss: Fictional character on the TV Western series *Bonanza*, which ran on NBC from 1959 to 1973. Eric "Hoss" Cartwright, who could be described as a "gentle giant," was portrayed by actor Dan Blocker.

John Nash (1928–2015): Nobel Prize–winning mathematician.

James Caan (1940–2022): Actor whose works included *The Godfather* and *Brian's Song*. For a brief period of time in the 1970s, as he was struggling after a divorce, he lived at the Playboy mansion, hence Lane's reference to Hugh Hefner (see earlier entry).

The Cramps: Rock band formed in 1976, featuring husband-and-wife duo Lux Interior and Poison Ivy.

Yo La Tengo: Indie rock band formed in 1984 by Ira Kaplan and Georgia Hubley.

Kim Gordon and Thurston Moore: Founding members of the rock band Sonic Youth, who were married from 1984 to 2013.

Sonny & Cher: Pop duo consisting of Sonny Bono (1935–1998) and Cher (see earlier entry), whose hits include "I Got You Babe."

X: Punk rock band formed in Los Angeles in the 1970s, whose members include one-time couple Exene Cervenka and John Doe.

Supertramp: British rock band formed in London in 1970 whose hits include "Give a Little Bit."

Jefferson Airplane: Rock band formed in San Francisco in 1965 whose hits include "Somebody to Love" and "White Rabbit."

Heart: Rock band formed in Seattle in 1973 whose roster includes sisters Ann and Nancy Wilson.

Rilo Kiley: Indie rock band formed in Los Angeles in 1998 whose roster includes actors/singers Jenny Lewis and Blake Sennett.

The Tin Man: Lorelai references this character from *The Wizard of Oz* (see earlier entry), who went to the Wizard to get a heart.

Papa Doc: Nickname of dictator and voodooist François Duvalier (1907–1971) who served as president of Haiti from 1957 until his death. He was ruthless about his desire to remain "President for Life."

The Manchurian Candidate: A 1959 Richard Condon thriller novel about the son of a prominent political family brainwashed into being an unwitting assassin. It was adapted into films in 1962 and 2004.

Swift Boat Veterans for Truth: Political group of United States Swift boat veterans formed during the 2004 presidential election campaign to oppose John Kerry's candidacy. The group launched a widely publicized, and eventually discredited, smear campaign against Kerry. Since then, the term "swiftboating" has been used to describe dishonest political attacks.

James Joyce (1882–1941): Irish novelist and poet whose works include *Ulysses* and *A Portrait of the Artist as a Young Man*.

Florida voter harassment: During the 2000 presidential election, allegations arose in Florida that thousands of Black voters were disenfranchised, harassed, and intimidated from voting. Such allegations continued with the 2004 election.

Seals and Crofts: Soft-rock duo consisting of James Eugene Seals and Darrell George "Dash" Crofts, whose hits include "Summer Breeze" and "Diamond Girl."

Prohibition Sally: While the term was used to generally describe female bootleggers during the Prohibition era, it likely stems from Sally Miller Smith, a woman who defied Prohibition in the Adirondacks by providing alcohol to people. Prohibition Sally was also the name of a soda pop–drinking caged bear that was used as a tourist attraction at Point Lookout in Ridgecrest, North Carolina, during the 1920s and 1930s.

Jimi Hendrix, "The Star-Spangled Banner": Hendrix (1942–1970) was an influential guitarist, singer, and songwriter who has been described as "the greatest instrumentalist in the history of rock music" by the Rock and Roll Hall of Fame. In 1969, he headlined Woodstock (see earlier entry), where he performed a famous rendition of "The Star-Spangled Banner," the national anthem of the United States.

"Theme from *The Greatest American Hero* (Believe It or Not)": Hep Alien performs this song written by Mike Post and Stephen Geyer, originally sung by Joey Scarbury, which served as the theme song to the 1980s TV series *The Greatest American Hero*.

Swept Away: A 2002 romantic comedy starring Madonna and Adriano Giannini. It was a box-office bomb and universally panned by critics.

Ken Burns, *Jazz*: Burns is a documentary filmmaker known for works that chronicle American history and culture. *Jazz* is a 2001 documentary series by Burns that aired on PBS and chronicled the history of the music genre.

EPISODE 5.5: WE GOT US A PIPPI VIRGIN

Written by Daniel Palladino. Directed by Stephen Clancy. Aired October 19, 2004. Lorelai and Luke double date with Rory and Dean.

Bill Maher: TV host, comedian, and political commentator whose shows have included *Politically Incorrect* and *Real Time with Bill Maher*, and who has been rumored to have solicited sex workers.

Shell Answer Man: Series of TV commercials from the Shell oil and gas company, running from the 1960s through the 1990s, featuring advice on topics relating to driving, vehicle maintenance, and home heating oil. Various actors played the role of the Answer Man through the decades.

John Hancock (1737–1793): Founding Father and prominent Patriot of the American Revolution best remembered for his large signature on the US Declaration of Independence—so much so that his name has become an enduring colloquialism for a person's signature.

"Et tu, former friend?": Reference to the phrase "et tu, Brute?" from William Shakespeare's play *Julius Caesar*. Meaning "you too, Brutus?," the phrase is spoken by Caesar when he realizes that his friend is among his assassins. The phrase has become common to suggest betrayal by a friend.

Rikers Island: Prison island in the Bronx in New York City.

P. G. Wodehouse (1881–1975): Writer and humorist whose creations include the English gentleman Bertie Wooster and his valet Jeeves.

The History of the Decline and Fall of the Roman Empire: Six-volume work by English historian and writer Edward Gibbon.

Panic Room: A 2002 thriller film starring Jodie Foster (see earlier entry) and Kristen Stewart as a mother and daughter whose home is invaded by burglars.

Suge Knight: Record executive who co-founded Death Row Records, was a central figure in the 1990s success of gangsta rap, and was involved in theories surrounding the deaths of rappers Tupac Shakur and Biggie Smalls. He is currently serving a twenty-eight-year sentence following a 2015 hit-and-run incident.

Barbi Twins: Shane and Sia Barbi are identical twins who rose to fame in the 1990s as a result of their cover modeling career.

Petunia Pig: Animated character in the *Looney Tunes/Merrie Melodies* cartoon series who is the significant other of Porky Pig.

Canvas bag with a big dollar sign: Movie and TV trope, especially in cartoons, in which bank robbers would escape with such bags filled with cash and coins.

Gay fellow whose tiger tried to eat him: See Siegfried & Roy.

"Gas, grass, or ass—no one rides for free": Common phrase that many consider to be the rules of hitchhiking.

"How long is my nose?": See Pinocchio.

Kid Flash: Fictional character from DC Comics, depicted as a junior counterpart to the Flash.

Les Paul (1915–2009): Guitarist, songwriter, inventor, and pioneer of the solid-body electric guitar.

***Brian's Song*, Billy Dee Williams**: *Brian's Song* is a 1971 made-for-TV movie starring James Caan as Chicago Bears football player Brian Piccolo. The film depicts his battle with terminal cancer and friendship with teammate Gale Sayers, portrayed by Williams. Williams is also known for *Batman*, *Nighthawk*, and his role as Lando Calrissian in the *Star Wars* franchise.

"Comme ci, comme ça": French phrase meaning neither good nor bad.

Taj Mahal: Famed Indian marble mausoleum.

Captain Hook: Fictional villain in J. M. Barrie's *Peter Pan*, depicted as a pirate captain with an iron hook replacing a severed hand.

Bionic Man: General reference to a cyborg—part man, part machine. The term is also associated with the 1970s science-fiction TV series *The Six Million Dollar Man*, which starred Lee Majors as a former astronaut who was rebuilt with bionic parts following an injury.

"Super Freak": A 1981 song by Rick James, referring to a sexually adventurous person.

Tex Watson: Convicted murderer and member of the Manson Family cult.

Lurch, *The Addams Family*: Lurch is the fictional tall, gloomy butler in *The Addams Family* franchise, which began in the 1930s as a comic strip created by Charles Addams and has since expanded into various TV, film, and other adaptations. It depicts a wealthy family who delight in the macabre and grotesque.

Penguin: If not the bird, Lorelai is likely referencing this fictional adversary of Batman in DC Comics, who is often depicted wearing a top hat, monocle, and morning suit, and carrying an umbrella.

Cool Hand Luke: A 1967 drama film starring Paul Newman as a prisoner who refuses to submit to the system and George Kennedy as his prison rival.

The Katzenjammer Kids: Comic strip created by Rudolph Dirks in 1897, featuring the misadventures of brothers who rebel against authority.

Richard Pryor (1940–2005): Stand-up comedian and actor known for such films as *Stir Crazy* and *The Wiz*. He also dealt with substance abuse issues and, in a 1980 incident, poured rum all over himself and lit himself on fire.

George Kennedy (1925–2016): Actor whose works include *Cool Hand Luke* and the *Airport* and *Naked Gun* film series.

Last Tango in Paris: A 1972 erotic drama film starring Marlon Brando as a widower who begins an anonymous sexual relationship with a Parisian woman.

Pippi Longstocking: A 1969 film based on the Astrid Lindgren children's book series about a mysterious young girl who moves into an abandoned villa.

An Officer and a Gentleman: A 1982 drama film starring Richard Gere, Debra Winger, and Louis Gossett Jr., about a Navy aviation officer, his girlfriend, and his hard-driving Marine Corps gunnery sergeant.

Bop It: Hand-held audio game launched in 1996 in which players respond to a series of commands to either twist, pull, or bop various parts of the device.

EPISODE 5.6: NORMAN MAILER, I'M PREGNANT!

Written by James Berg and Stan Zimmerman. Directed by Matthew Diamond. Aired October 26, 2004.

The ongoing presence of Norman Mailer at the inn frustrates Sookie. Rory searches for an inspiring story for the newspaper.

The Mothman Prophecies: A 2002 supernatural mystery film, based on the 1975 John Keel book of the same name, starring Richard Gere as a reporter researching the legend of the mysterious Mothman, an unusual creature claimed to have been seen—and responsible for a series of strange phenomena—in a West Virginia town.

"If you build it, they will come": Famous line from the 1989 sports fantasy film *Field of Dreams* starring Kevin Costner as a farmer who builds a baseball field in his cornfield that attracts the ghosts of famous players.

Martin and Hannah Van Buren, Abigail Van Buren, Ann Landers: Martin Van Buren (1782–1862) was the eighth president of the United States, serving from 1837 to 1841. He was married to Hannah (1783–1819), who died from tuberculosis before he became president. Abigail Van Buren is the pen name of advice columnist Pauline Phillips (1918–2013), better known as Dear Abby. Pauline's sister, Eppie Lederer (1918–2002), authored a similar advice column under the pen name Ann Landers. The competing columns led to an estrangement between the sisters.

Boba Fett: Fictional character in the *Star Wars* franchise, depicted as an armored bounty hunter.

R. W. Apple Jr. (1934–2006): Correspondent and editor at the *New York Times*.

***Being There*, Chauncey Gardner**: *Being There* is a 1979 satirical comedy film, based on the 1970 Jerzy Kosinski novel of the same name, starring Peter Sellers as a simple-minded gardener who, through a series of misunderstandings where he is mistaken for a wealthy businessman, rises to national prominence in Washington society.

Norman Mailer, *The Naked and the Dead*: Mailer (1923–2007) was a writer, journalist, and filmmaker whose 1948 debut novel, *The Naked and the Dead*, brought him acclaim. Drawing on his own experiences as a cook during the era, it depicts the experiences of a platoon during World War II.

Gabriel García Márquez (1927–2014): Writer and Nobel laureate whose works include *One Hundred Years of Solitude* and *Love in the Time of Cholera*.

Maureen Dowd: Author and columnist for the *New York Times*.

American letters: Reference to the collective works of the written word in American culture.

Lars Ulrich: Drummer and founding member of the heavy metal band Metallica (see earlier entry).

Talmud: Central text of Rabbinic Judaism and primary source of Jewish religious law and theology.

"Stand By Your Man": A 1968 song by country music singer Tammy Wynette.

Edward James Olmos: Actor known for *Miami Vice*, *Blade Runner*, and *Stand and Deliver*.

Interpol: Rock band formed in Manhattan in 1997.

Paul Weller: English singer-songwriter who was a member of the Jam and Style Council before embarking on a solo career.

Seventeen Seconds: Second studio album by The Cure (see earlier entry), released in 1980.

ABBA: Swedish pop group formed in 1972 whose hits include "Waterloo" and "Dancing Queen." Their music was adapted into the musical *Mamma Mia!*

Frank Zappa (1940–1993): Musician and bandleader whose songs include "Uncle Remus" and "Bobby Brown Goes Down."

Axl Rose: Lead singer of the rock band Guns N' Roses (see earlier entry).

"Manic Monday": A 1986 single by the Bangles (see earlier entry), written by Prince using the pen name Christopher.

Jesse Jackson: Civil rights activist, Baptist minister, and politician.

Skull and Bones: Secret student society at Yale University that has become a cultural institution with powerful alumni and associated conspiracy theories. Among the rumors associated with the group is that of initiates being placed in coffins and forced to masturbate while sharing their sexual histories with other members.

Halston (1932–1990): Fashion designer who rose to fame in the 1970s. He was a fixture at the Studio 54 nightclub and was close friends with Liza Minelli (see earlier entry).

Hoi polloi: Expression borrowed from Ancient Greek meaning "the many" or "the people."

EPISODE 5.7: YOU JUMP, I JUMP, JACK

Written by Daniel Palladino. Directed by Kenneth Ortega. Aired November 2, 2004.

Rory participates in a bizarre event with Logan's secret clique.

Fear Factor: Lorelai's line about making people eat bugs is a nod to this reality TV series that originally ran on NBC from 2001 to 2006, with a couple of revival attempts following in later years. Contestants would compete in a series of extreme stunts, many of which involved eating animal parts or live insects.

O. Henry (1862–1910): Author best known for his short stories, many of which had surprise endings.

Charles Kuralt (1934–1997): Journalist known for his years with CBS News.

All the President's Men: A 1974 nonfiction book by Bob Woodward and Carl Bernstein (see earlier entry) detailing their investigative reporting into the Watergate scandal. It was adapted into a 1976 film starring Robert Redford and Dustin Hoffman. It is the film that Doyle references.

Crash Test Dummy: Anthropomorphic test devices made to simulate humans that are used in automobile crash simulations. While not necessarily the source of Lorelai's reference, in the 1980s the National Highway Traffic Safety Administration created a series of comedic public service announcements encouraging seat belt safety practices using two talking crash test dummy characters—Vince and Larry—and the slogan "You could learn a lot from a dummy." The ads were so popular they spawned a franchise that included action figures, comic books, and video games.

"I see dead people": Famous line from the film *The Sixth Sense* (see earlier entry).

Kalashnikov: A type of assault rifle.

Luciano Pavarotti (1935–2007): Italian operatic singer and member of the Three Tenors.

Stop Making Sense: A 1984 concert film featuring Talking Heads (see earlier entry).

Max Ernst (1891–1976): German painter, sculptor, and poet.

David Byrne: Musician, writer, and lead singer of Talking Heads (see earlier entry).

Motörhead: English rock band formed in London in 1975.

Philip K. Dick (1928–1982): Science-fiction author whose works include *Do Androids Dream of Electric Sheep?* and *The Man in the High Castle*.

George Plimpton, Sugar Ray Robinson, Detroit Lions, Boston Bruins: Plimpton (1927–2003) was a writer known for sports writing and for "participatory journalism" in which he participated in the events he was writing about. He sparred with Robinson (1921–1989), a professional boxer regarded by many as the greatest of all time; served as a backup quarterback with the Detroit Lions, a professional football team founded in 1930; and served as goalie with the Boston Bruins, a professional ice hockey team founded in 1924.

Bill Buford, *Among the Thugs*: Buford is an author whose works include the 1990 nonfiction book *Among the Thugs: The Experience, and the Seduction, of Crowd Violence*, which documented football hooliganism in the United Kingdom. He spent eight years attending matches and witnessing riots to document his findings for the book.

Ernie Pyle (1900–1945): Journalist and war correspondent known for writing about ordinary American soldiers during World War II (see earlier entry).

Richard C. Hottelet, United Press: Hottelet (1917–2014) was a broadcast journalist and war correspondent who worked for the United Press, an international news agency founded in 1907, and was held in a Nazi (see earlier entry) prison for four months in 1941.

"You jump, I jump, Jack": Quote from the 1997 blockbuster film *Titanic*, spoken between the film's lead characters Jack, played by Leonardo DiCaprio, and Rose, played by Kate Winslet.

Richard Diebenkorn (1922–1993): Painter and printmaker.

The Odyssey: Ancient Greek epic poem attributed to Homer.

Happy Gilmore: A 1996 sports comedy film starring Adam Sandler in the title role as a failed ice hockey player who discovers a talent for golf.

EPISODE 5.8: THE PARTY'S OVER

Written by Amy Sherman-Palladino. Directed by Eric Laneuville. Aired November 9, 2004.

Emily and Richard throw a party to introduce Rory to their Yale alumni friends.

"Melrose" Larry Green: Frequent guest on *The Howard Stern Show* who got his nickname from promoting Stern's show on Melrose Avenue in Los Angeles, California, while wearing a sandwich board.

Kelsey Grammer: Actor best known for portraying Dr. Frasier Crane on the TV sitcoms *Cheers* and its spinoff *Frasier*.

Rosemary Clooney (1928–2002): Singer and actress whose songs include "Come On-a My House" and "Mambo Italiano" and whose films include *White Christmas*.

The Little Rascals: Also called *Our Gang*, *The Little Rascals* is a series of short comedy films produced from 1922 to 1944, depicting the adventures of a group of poor neighborhood children. The artichoke quote comes from an episode of the show in which one of the characters, Stymie, attempts to eat an artichoke and proclaims, "It might choke Artie, but it ain't gonna choke Stymie."

Jake Lamotta, Vikki LaMotta: Jake (1922–2017) was a professional boxer whose autobiography was adapted into the film *Raging Bull* (see earlier entry). His personal life includes having been married seven times and being physically abusive. He was married to Vikki (1930–2005) during his peak years of success. They married when she was sixteen and divorced eleven years later. She wrote an autobiography in the 1990s but requested it not be released until after her death because of the information it contained. It was finally released in 2006.

Discovery Channel: Cable television channel launched in 1985.

Barefoot Contessa: Cooking show that aired on the Food Network from 2002 to 2021, hosted by celebrity chef Ina Garten. The name is derived from Garten's specialty foods store, which was already named when she bought it in 1978. The store got its name from a 1954 film starring Humphrey Bogart and Ava Gardner.

Aristotle Onassis (1906–1975): Business magnate who amassed the world's largest shipping fleet.

Prince William, Prince Harry: The children of King Charles III and Diana, Princess of Wales. William is the heir apparent to the British throne. Harry is fifth in line of succession.

Joseph Mitchell (1908–1996): Writer known for creative works of nonfiction published in *The New Yorker*.

The Passion of the Christ: A 2004 graphically violent biblical film co-written, co-produced, and directed by Mel Gibson that depicted the final period before the death of Jesus Christ.

EPISODE 5.9: EMILY SAYS HELLO

Written by Rebecca Rand Kirshner. Directed by Kenneth Ortega. Aired November 16, 2004.
Lorelai and Rory attempt to broker a reconciliation between Richard and Emily.

"Ditch that Audi in Marseilles": A nod to *The Bourne Identity*, a 2002 action-thriller film starring Matt Damon, based on the 1980 Robert Ludlum novel.

Divine Brown, Elizabeth Hurley: Brown is a former sex worker who gained media attention in 1995 when she was caught performing oral sex on actor Hugh Grant (see earlier entry) in his car. Hurley is a model and actress who dated Grant throughout the 1990s. She has appeared in *Austin Powers: International Man of Mystery* and *Bedazzled*.

Associated Press: Also known as A.P., the Associated Press is a not-for-profit news agency founded in 1846.

Bazooka: Brand of chewing gum introduced in 1947 featuring comic strips starring the character Bazooka Joe.

Rumspringa: Amish rite of passage in which teenagers experience life outside their community and either choose to be baptized in the Amish church or leave the community.

Salt mine: An idiom meant to describe one's workplace, especially a dull and tedious one, dating back to the 1800s when Russians would send prisoners into Siberian salt mines for forced labor.

Orpheum Circuit: Former chain of vaudeville and movie theaters founded in 1886.

Abe Vigoda (1921–2016): Actor known for the TV sitcom *Barney Miller* and its spinoff series *Fish*.

Hubbell, Katie, the blacklist: Hubbell and Katie are the lead characters in *The Way We Were* (see earlier entry). The blacklist was the mid-twentieth-century banning of suspected Communists from working in the entertainment industry.

Butterick: Company founded in the 1800s that made sewing patterns.

"Fish on the doorstep," "Horsehead in bed," "Either your signature or your brains": References from *The Godfather* (see earlier entry).

Pauly Shore: Comedian and actor known for *Encino Man* and *Son in Law*.

BUtterfield 8: A 1960 drama film based on the 1935 John O'Hara novel of the same name starring Elizabeth Taylor as a high-class prostitute intent on changing her ways.

Tarantella in A-flat major: Short piano piece by Frédéric Chopin, written in 1841.

Gustav Mahler, Symphony No. 7: Mahler (1860–1911) was a renowned romantic composer among whose works was Symphony No. 7, also called Song of the Night, written in the early 1900s.

The Ed Sullivan Show: Variety show that ran on CBS from 1948 to 1971, hosted by entertainment columnist Sullivan (1901–1974). The series was often a launchpad for acts. The Beatles made their first appearance on American television on the show in 1964—an episode that was watched by seventy-three million viewers and is credited with launching American Beatlemania.

Cleveland Orchestra: Ohio-based orchestra founded in 1918 and considered one of the "Big Five" orchestras.

St. Elmo's Fire: A 1985 coming-of-age film about a group of recent Georgetown University graduates and their adjustment to post-college life. Emilio Estevez, Rob Lowe, Andrew McCarthy, and Demi Moore star.

Rob Lowe: Actor whose works include *The Outsiders*, *St. Elmo's Fire*, *The West Wing*, and *Parks and Recreation*.

Less than Zero: A 1987 drama film starring Andrew McCarthy (see earlier entry) as a college freshman who returns home to spend time with his friend and ex-girlfriend.

Roman Holiday: A 1953 romantic comedy starring Audrey Hepburn (see earlier entry) as a princess who sets out to see Rome on her own and Gregory Peck as the reporter who pursues her.

"Roam": A 1989 single by The B-52's (see earlier entry).

EPISODE 5.10: BUT NOT AS CUTE AS PUSHKIN

Written by Amy Sherman-Palladino. Directed by Michael Zinberg. Aired November 30, 2004.

Rory mentors a Chilton student who is considering attending Yale.

Carrie Bradshaw: Fictional columnist and fashionista on the HBO TV series *Sex and the City* (see earlier entry), portrayed by Sarah Jessica Parker.

"A little song, a little dance, a little seltzer down your pants": Line from a famous 1975 episode of *The Mary Tyler Moore Show* titled "Chuckles Bites the Dust," involving the death and funeral of a children's TV show clown.

Sabrina Fairchild: Protagonist of the 1954 film *Sabrina* (see earlier entry).

Steve Guttenberg: Actor known for the *Police Academy* franchise and *Three Men and a Baby*.

Gutenberg Bible: Earliest major book printed in Europe using mass-produced metal movable type.

"Give me a location": Reference to a common question that performers ask their audience at improvisational acting shows.

Theodore Dwight Woolsey (1801–1889): Author and president of Yale University from 1846 to 1871. The tradition of touching the toe of Yale's Woolsey statue for good luck is true.

Milton Berle (1908–2002): Beloved actor and comedian considered the first major television star, known affectionately as "Mr. Television" and "Uncle Miltie."

Willy Loman: Fictional protagonist of the Arthur Miller play *Death of a Salesman*. He is a salesman whose career is on the decline.

Locust Plague of 1874: Paris references this plague in which hordes of Rocky Mountain locusts invaded the Great Plains in the United States and Canada.

King George I (1660–1727): King of Great Britain and Ireland from 1714 until 1727.

Bob Graham (1936–2024): Lawyer and politician who served as governor of Florida from 1979 to 1987 and a US senator from Florida from 1987 to 2005. He was known for keeping meticulous logs of his daily activities in color-coded notebooks, including such simple things as what he ate for lunch that day.

Maya Lin: Renowned architect and designer who attended Yale University. In 1981, while still a student at Yale, she won a national design competition for the Vietnam Veterans Memorial in Washington, DC.

Sterling Memorial Library: Main library building at Yale University opened in 1931 and named in honor of lawyer and Yale graduate John W. Sterling.

Alexander Pushkin (1799–1837): Russian poet, playwright, and novelist whose works include *The Captain's Daughter*.

Flo, "Kiss my grits": Flo is a fictional waitress at Mel's Diner (see Mel Sharples) on the TV series *Alice*, portrayed by Polly Holliday. Her catchphrase, often directed toward Mel, was "kiss my grits!"

Matthew and Mark: Biblical figures to whom the Gospels of Matthew and Mark are attributed.

Spike and Drusilla: Fictional vampire antagonists in the TV shows *Buffy the Vampire Slayer* and *Angel*, portrayed by James Marsters and Juliet Landau.

Carl Jung (1875–1961): Swiss psychiatrist who founded the school of analytical psychology.

ThighMaster, Suzanne Somers: Somers (1946–2023) was an actress and businesswoman best known for the TV series *Three's Company* and *Step by Step*. In the 1990s, she advertised the ThighMaster, an exercise device used for shaping one's thighs.

Richard Widmark (1914–2008): Actor known for *Kiss of Death*. Lorelai refers to Widmark's guest appearance as himself on the sitcom *I Love Lucy* (see earlier entry), in which Lucy trespasses onto Widmark's property to attempt to steal a grapefruit from his backyard.

Christina Aguilera: Pop singer and TV personality known for the songs "Genie in a Bottle" and "What a Girl Wants" and for appearing on *The Voice* from 2011 to 2016.

Latter-day Saints: The Church of Jesus Christ of Latter-day Saints is a Christian denomination founded in 1830 by Joseph Smith.

Skeletons on the island of Flores: A reference to *Homo floresiensis*, an extinct species of small archaic humans that inhabited the island of Flores in Indonesia. The first remains were found in 2003.

Dylan Thomas (1914–1953): Welsh poet and writer known for the line, "Do not go gentle into that good night."

EPISODE 5.11: WOMEN OF QUESTIONABLE MORALS
Written by Daniel Palladino. Directed by Matthew Diamond. Aired January 25, 2005.
Rory gives Christopher the cold shoulder until she learns that his father has died.

Farewell My Concubine: A 1993 epic historical drama based on the Lilian Lee novel of the same name.

Nathaniel Hawthorne (1804–1864): Novelist whose works include *The Scarlet Letter*.

Baretta: Detective TV series that ran on ABC from 1975 to 1978.

Monty Python: British comedy troupe formed in 1969 consisting of Graham Chapman, John Cleese, Terry Gilliam, Eric Idle, Terry Jones, and Michael Palin.

Jack Frost: Personification of cold weather and a variation of Old Man Winter. The line "Jack Frost nipping at your nose" is from the 1945 Christmas carol "The Christmas Song," written by Robert Wells and Mel Tormé.

Total Request Live: TV series that ran weekday afternoons on MTV from 1998 to 2008 (followed by a brief revival in 2017), featuring the top-ten most requested music videos of the day. Carson Daly was the original host.

"Winter Wonderland": Christmas song written in 1934 by Felix Bernard and Richard Bernhard Smith.

Beverly Hills Cop: A 1984 action-comedy film starring Eddie Murphy as a street-smart Detroit cop who travels to Beverly Hills, California, to investigate a crime. It spawned a popular franchise.

Baba Booey: Catchphrase often shouted as a verbal prank during tense moments on live TV.

Oxford Blues: A 1984 sports film starring Rob Lowe as a young man intent on joining the Oxford University rowing team.

Bing Crosby (1903–1977): Iconic singer and actor known for *Going My Way*, *The Bells of St. Mary's*, *White Christmas*, and other works.

Louis Vuitton: French luxury fashion house founded by its namesake in 1854.

Franz Schubert (1797–1828): Famed Austrian composer.

David Hume (1711–1776): Scottish philosopher best known for his system of empiricism, philosophical skepticism, and metaphysical naturalism. His works include *An Enquiry Concerning the Principles of Morals*.

Benny Hill (1924–1992): English comedian and actor who hosted the slapstick sketch comedy series *The Benny Hill Show*.

Tony Kushner: Author and playwright known for the play *Angels in America*.

From Justin to Kelly: A 2003 musical romantic comedy film starring *American Idol*'s first season winner and runner-up Kelly Clarkson and Justin Guarini. Panned by critics, it has gained a reputation as being among the worst films ever made.

Gilbert du Motier, Marquis de Lafayette: Revolutionary War officer who fought for the Continental Army under George Washington.

Randy Gardner, Tai Babilonia: Figure skating pair who won the 1979 World Figure Skating Championship, as well as five US Figure Skating Championships throughout the 1970s.

Episode 5.12: Come Home
Written by Jessica Queller. Directed by Kenny Ortega. Aired February 1, 2005.
Richard becomes jealous when he discovers Emily is dating another man.

Jon Stewart: Comedian, TV host, and political commentator known for hosting *The Daily Show* on Comedy Central from 1999 to 2015. He returned to the show in 2024.

Pink Lady and Jeff: Variety show that aired on NBC for five weeks in 1980. Pink Lady is a Japanese female pop duo featuring Mie and Keiko Masuda. The titular Jeff refers to Jeff Altman, an actor and comedian known for his multiple appearances on David Letterman's late-night talk shows and his roles on *The Dukes of Hazzard* and *Nurses*. The show lasted five episodes and has been ranked among the worst ever.

"Say goodnight, Gracie": A reference to the popular sign-off at the end of *The George Burns and Gracie Allen Show*, a sitcom that ran from 1950 to 1958 and starred married comedy duo Burns and Allen. Burns would end each show by saying, "Say goodnight, Gracie," with Allen responding, "Goodnight."

Seymour Hersh: Pulitzer Prize–winning investigative reporter and political writer.

Abu Ghraib: City in Iraq and site of a prison where members of the US Army and Central Intelligence Agency committed a series of human rights violations and war crimes against detainees during the Iraq War. The abuses came to public attention in the spring of 2004 when CBS News published photos about the situation.

Sam Ash Music: Musical instrument retail chain founded by its namesake in 1924.

Buddy Holly (1936–1959): Influential singer-songwriter known for "That'll Be the Day" and "Peggy Sue," as well as for the horn-rimmed glasses he wore.

Maroon 5: Pop-rock band whose hits include "Harder to Breathe" and "This Love."

The Slickee Boys: Punk rock band founded in 1976.

My Lai 4: A Report on the Massacre and Its Aftermath: A 1970 book by Seymour Hersh (see earlier entry), detailing his extensive recounting of a 1968 US war crime involving the mass murder of unarmed civilians during the Vietnam War.

Patrick Swayze (1952–2009): Actor known for *Dirty Dancing* and *Road House*.

AC/DC: Rock band known for "Highway to Hell" and "Back in Black."

The Office: British mockumentary sitcom starring Ricky Gervais that ran from 2001 to 2003 and detailed the day-to-day goings-on of office employees at a fictional paper company. It spawned several international versions, including a highly successful American version that ran from 2005 to 2013.

***Dark Shadows*, Barnabus Collins, Maggie Evans**: *Dark Shadows* is a gothic soap opera that ran on ABC from 1966 to 1971, focusing on a wealthy family in Maine where supernatural occurrences take place. Barnabus is a primary character originally portrayed by Jonathan Frid as a 175-year-old vampire in search of his lost love. Maggie, portrayed by Katheryn Leigh Scott, is a waitress who resembles Barnabus's lost love.

"In-A-Gadda-Da-Vida": A 1968 song by Iron Butterfly, its title derived from "In the Garden of Eden."

Oscar de la Renta (1932–2014): Renowned Dominican fashion designer.

Susan Hayward (1917–1975): Actress known for *I'll Cry Tomorrow*, *My Foolish Heart*, and *I Want to Live!*

Clark Gable (1901–1960): Actor known for *It Happened One Night*, *Teacher's Pet*, and *Gone With the Wind*.

Anna Magnani (1908–1973): Italian actress known for *The Rose Tattoo*.

Marlene Deitrich (1901–1992): Actress known for such films as *Touch of Evil* and *Judgment at Nuremberg* and for her androgynous roles and public image that defied sexual norms.

Christian Dior: French luxury goods company founded by its namesake in 1946.

Patrick Stewart: English actor known for *Star Trek: The Next Generation* and many other works.

Episode 5.13: Wedding Bell Blues
Written and directed by Amy Sherman-Palladino. Aired February 8, 2005.
Richard and Emily renew their wedding vows.

Morton Salt Girl: Advertising character for Morton Salt, depicted as a young girl walking in the rain with an open umbrella, scattering salt behind her as she goes. The character has been used since 1914.

Cop Rock: A police procedural musical TV series that had a brief run in 1990.

Super Furry Animals: Welsh rock band formed in 1993.

The Gulag: System of forced labor camps in the Soviet Union.

Arcade Fire: Canadian indie rock band formed in 2001.

Brian Eno: English musician and former member of Roxy Music.

Two shakes of a lamb's tail: Idiom meaning that something will happen quickly.

Miss Gotti: A nod to Gambino crime family boss John Gotti.

Third rung of Hell: From Dante's *Inferno* (see earlier entry), the third rung of Hell is Gluttony.

"Affair with a gardener": Reference to the TV series *Desperate Housewives*, which ran on ABC from 2004 to 2012. One of the early storylines involved a character having an affair with her gardener.

Thora Birch: Actress whose works include *Now and Then*, *Hocus Pocus*, and *Ghost World*.

Culture *Queer Eye* Guy: A reference to Jai Rodriguez, the resident "Culture Vulture" on *Queer Eye for the Straight Guy* (see earlier entry).

Pulp Fiction: A 1994 crime film by Quentin Tarantino, starring John Travolta and Uma Thurman.

Tony Bennett (1926–2023): Renowned jazz and pop singer.

"Wedding Bell Blues": Richard and Emily's song is this 1966 tune written and originally recorded by Laura Nyro. It was a hit for The 5th Dimension in 1969.

Bugsy Malone: A 1976 gangster musical comedy film featuring child actors playing adult roles.

"Girls Just Want to Have Fun": A 1983 single by Cyndi Lauper.

"Hell Is for Children": A 1980 song about child abuse by Pat Benatar.

Anglo-Saxons: Germanic tribes that settled in early medieval England.

EPISODE 5.14: SAY SOMETHING
Written and directed by Daniel Palladino. Aired February 15, 2005.

Lorelai's relationship with Luke is in question following the events of her parents' vow renewal ceremony.

Sherlock Holmes: Famous fictional detective created by Sir Arthur Conan Doyle in 1887.

k.d. lang: Canadian pop and country singer whose hits include "Constant Craving."

B-boy, Mos Def: A b-boy is a young man involved in hip hop culture, especially breakdancing. Mos Def was the former professional name of rapper Yasiin Bey.

Yanni: Greek composer, pianist, and music producer.

Bride of Chucky: A 1998 comedy horror film and the fourth installment of the *Child's Play* franchise.

Katie Couric: Journalist who co-hosted *Today* from 1991 to 2006 and anchored the *CBS Evening News* from 2006 to 2011.

Ludwig Wittgenstein (1889–1951): Austrian philosopher who worked in logic.

Loveline: Syndicated radio call-in program offering relationship and medical advice to listeners. It began in 1983 and has existed in various incarnations ever since, including a popular talk show version that aired on MTV from 1996 to 2000.

Brontë sisters: Nineteenth-century literary family including sisters Charlotte, Emily, and Anne.

The Odd Couple: See Oscar and Felix.

Down to the Turks: Phrase used to describe the final betting round in poker.

Annie: A 1977 Broadway musical and 1982 film adaptation, both based on a 1924 comic strip, about a little orphan girl taken in by a billionaire.

Fanny Brice, Nicky Arnstein: Brice (1891–1951) was a comedian, singer, and actress. Arnstein (1879–1965) was a professional gambler and con artist. The two were married from 1918 to 1927. Their stormy relationship was the inspiration for the musical *Funny Girl*.

Episode 5.15: Jews and Chinese Food

Written by Amy Sherman-Palladino. Directed by Matthew Diamond. Aired February 22, 2005.

Rory attempts to mend her friendship with Marty. Luke agrees to assist with a school play in hopes of running into Lorelai.

Gisele Bündgen: Brazilian fashion model.

Eva Braun (1912–1945): Companion and wife of Adolf Hitler (see earlier entry).

Krav Maga: Israeli self-defense system featuring elements of judo, karate, and boxing.

Plastics: Japanese new wave band who rose to fame in the 1970s.

Dopey: Fictional character in *Snow White and the Seven Dwarfs* (see Seven Dwarfs). Lorelai refers to a poisoned apple created by the Queen and used to lure Snow White into a death-like sleep.

Florence Nightingale (1820–1910): English social reformer and the founder of modern nursing.

Duck Soup: A 1933 comedy film starring the Marx Brothers (see earlier entry).

Joe Lieberman (1942–2024): US Senator from Connecticut from 1989 to 2013.

Tevye: Fictional character from *Fiddler on the Roof* (see earlier entry).

He-Man: Fictional hero and protagonist of the *Masters of the Universe* franchise, noted for his superhuman strength.

"To Life": A song from *Fiddler on the Roof* (see earlier entry). L'chaim is a Hebrew phrase that means "to life."

Jesus Christ Superstar: A 1971 rock opera written by Andrew Lloyd Webber and Tim Rice based on the Gospels' accounts of the Passion of Jesus Christ.

Drew Barrymore: Actress whose works include *E.T. the Extra-Terrestrial*, *Scream*, and *Charlie's Angels*. In 2020 she began hosting her own daytime talk show.

Batman: Comic book superhero from DC Comics, depicted as the bat-like alter ego of wealthy philanthropist Bruce Wayne who protects Gotham City from criminal activity. Mimicking the comic book practice of using words like "pow!" and "bam!" to illustrate fights, the 1960s live-action TV adaptation of *Batman* would display such words on screen during altercations, which is likely the source of Sookie's comment.

Moulin Rouge!: A 2001 musical drama film about an English poet who falls for a cabaret actress.

Ewan McGregor: Actor known for *Trainspotting*, the *Star Wars* prequel trilogy, and *Moulin Rouge!*

Ben Bradlee (1921–2014): Journalist known for his work at *The Washington Post*, including the publishing of the Pentagon Papers and coverage of the Watergate scandal.

Tom Sawyer: Fictional protagonist of Mark Twain's *The Adventures of Tom Sawyer*. The mischievous young boy uses reverse psychology on some neighborhood kids in order to coax them into doing his chores.

"What's up, Doc?": Catchphrase used by Bugs Bunny in the *Looney Tunes/ Merrie Melodies* cartoons from Warner Bros.

Harpo Marx on *I Love Lucy*: Marty discusses this 1955 episode of the sitcom (see earlier entry) in which Marx (see earlier entry) and Ball's character, Lucy Ricardo, reenact a famous mirror scene from *Duck Soup*. The two characters stand facing one another, dressed alike, with Lucy making the same movements as Harpo in an attempt to make him think he's looking in a mirror.

Dore Schary (1905–1980): Dramatist and film producer who was set to play himself in a 1955 episode of *I Love Lucy* but canceled at the last minute and was instead portrayed by actor Philip Ober.

Bosom Buddies: Sitcom that aired on ABC from 1980 to 1982, starring Tom Hanks and Peter Scolari as two single men who disguise themselves as women in order to live in a female-only apartment building because it is all they could afford.

Zydeco: Music genre that blends rhythm and blues with Louisiana Creole elements.

"Do You Love Me?": Song from *Fiddler on the Roof* (see earlier entry), performed by Tevye and his wife, Golde.

Episode 5.16: So . . . Good Talk
Written by Lisa Randolph. Directed by Jamie Babbit. Aired March 1, 2005.

Rory expresses her anger with Emily. Lane realizes her mother has gotten into her head. Luke takes out his frustrations on the diner customers.

Greenpeace: Independent global campaigning network formed by a group of Canadian environmental activists in 1971.

"Priceless": The quick telephone exchange between Lorelai and Rory, in which Rory laments the cost of her cell phone bill and Lorelai says a conversation with her is priceless, is a nod to a 1990s advertising campaign for Mastercard. The TV spots would list the costs involved in preparing for an event, such as the price of a new dress and camera for a family photograph, followed by the notion that the memories created by the activity—multiple generations of a family together in one place—were priceless.

Temple of Apollo: Historical landmark in Greece dedicated to the Greek god Apollo.

Seinfeld: Sitcom that aired on NBC from 1989 to 1998 and starred stand-up comedian Jerry Seinfeld playing a fictional version of himself.

Reno 911!: Mockumentary sitcom that originally aired on Comedy Central from 2003 to 2009, followed by a revival from 2020 to 2022. It followed a group of bumbling police officers in Reno as a parody of *Cops*, with a lot of the dialogue being improvised by the actors. Lorelai references the short shorts worn by the character of Lieutenant Jim Dangle, portrayed by Thomas Lennon.

Augusto Pinochet (1915–2006): While not referenced by name, the "Chilean dictator dude" mentioned by Zack is most likely this politician and military officer who was dictator of Chile from 1973 to 1990.

Mordor: Fictional home base of evil lord Sauron in *The Lord of the Rings* (see earlier entry).

Texas Beef Group vs. Winfrey: Oprah getting mad at beef refers to a 1998 court case involving a lawsuit brought by ranchers against Oprah Winfrey (see earlier entry) and a guest on her talk show in 1996. While discussing mad cow disease on *The Oprah Winfrey Show* in 1996, the plaintiffs argued that disparaging comments about beef were made that damaged the beef industry. The group sued citing a Texas food disparagement law. The jury found that the comments made by Winfrey and her guest did not constitute libel against the cattlemen.

Netflix, *A Star Is Born,* **Janet Gaynor**: Netflix is a streaming service launched in 2007, originally as a mail-based DVD rental platform. The original *A Star Is Born* is a 1937 film starring Gaynor (1906–1984) as an aspiring actress and Fredric March as a fading star who helps launch her career. Gaynor's other works include *7th Heaven*, *Sunrise: A Song of Two Humans*, and *Street Angel*. She was the first woman to win an Academy Award for Best Actress. *A Star Is Born* has been remade multiple times: a 1954 version starring Judy Garland (see earlier entry), a 1976 version starring Barbra Streisand (see earlier entry), and a 2018 version starring Lady Gaga.

Property of Alcatraz: Alcatraz was a maximum security federal prison located in San Francisco, California, in operation from 1934 to 1963 and later reopened as a museum and popular tourist attraction. An Alcatraz gift shop sells apparel featuring the phrase "Property of Alcatraz."

Bob Hope (1903–2003): Pioneering actor, comedian, and entertainer known for a series of *Road to . . .* films with Bing Crosby, his work with the USO, and multiple prime-time comedy specials. He hosted the Academy Awards nineteen times, more than any other host.

Mask of Agamemnon: Gold funerary mask discovered at the Bronze Age archeological site of Mycenae in Greece. It has been described by historians as the *Mona Lisa* of ancient Greece.

Leaves of Grass: Expansive poetry collection by Walt Whitman (see earlier entry) published in 1855.

Acropolis: Ancient citadel located above the city of Athens, Greece.

"Brick House": A 1977 song by the Commodores.

Kris Kristofferson (1936–2024): Actor, singer, and songwriter. His credits include "Me and Bobby McGee" and "For the Good Times." As an actor he was known for *A Star Is Born* and *Songwriter*.

Peter Gabriel: English singer-songwriter who rose to fame as the original frontman of the band Genesis before embarking on a successful solo career. His hits include "Sledgehammer," the video for which featured unique stop-motion animation techniques.

Donna Martin, *Beverly Hills, 90210*: *Beverly Hills, 90210* began as a teen drama television series that aired on Fox from 1990 to 2000 and has spawned a franchise featuring various reboots and merchandise. Donna was a character on the original series portrayed by Tori Spelling. The character was raised a strict Catholic and remained a virgin for much of the show's run.

Hadley Richardson (1891–1979): First wife of Ernest Hemingway (see earlier entry). In 1922, while waiting for a train at Gare de Lyon railway station in Paris, France, she misplaced and lost a suitcase containing Hemingway's manuscripts.

A Woman Under the Influence: A 1974 drama film starring Gena Rowland as a housewife whose unusual behavior leads to conflict with her husband, played by Peter Falk.

Soap: Sitcom that ran on ABC from 1977 to 1981 as a nighttime parody of daytime soap operas, told in serial format with elaborate and melodramatic plotlines.

Episode 5.17: Pulp Friction
Written by James Berg and Stan Zimmerman. Directed by Michael Zinberg. Aired March 8, 2005.
Rory accepts a date with one of Logan's friends. Luke and Lorelai reconcile.

"Favor on this, the day of your daughter's wedding": Nod to a famous scene in *The Godfather* (see earlier entry).

Caroline, or Change: Musical by Jeanine Tesori and Tony Kushner set against the Civil Rights movement.

Angels in America: Play by Tony Kushner set against the AIDS crisis in the 1980s.

Jonathan Swift (1667–1745): Writer and satirist whose works include *Gulliver's Travels*.

Clifford the Big Red Dog: Children's book series by Norman Bridwell about a young girl and her enormous red dog.

He's Just Not That Into You: A 2004 self-improvement book by Greg Behrendt and Liz Tuccillo.

Nick Lachey: Singer, actor, and TV personality who rose to fame as a member of the boy band 98 Degrees.

The Price Is Right: TV game show where contestants compete by guessing the prices of merchandise to win cash and prizes. It debuted in 1972.

Harry & David: Premium food and gift retailer originally founded in 1910 as a premium fruit company called Bear Creek Orchards by Samuel Rosenberg. His sons, Harry and David, took over management in 1914, and it was renamed in 1946.

Tiananmen Square protests: Student-led demonstrations that took place on Tiananmen Square in China in 1989 to mark the death of the popular pro-reform Chinese leader Hu Yaobang. The demonstration grew into protests of inflation and corruption, and troops were eventually deployed to occupy the square, leading to a massacre that reportedly killed approximately three hundred people and wounded thousands. At one point, a column of tanks came upon a lone protester standing in the middle of the street blocking their way, leading to a brief standoff that captured media attention, with the protester being labeled Tank Man.

The $25,000 Pyramid: TV game show and part of the *Pyramid* franchise in which two teams—each consisting of a contestant and a celebrity partner—attempt to convey mystery words and phrases in an effort to win cash and prizes. The *$25,000* version ran from 1974 to 1979 with host Bill Cullen and, more notably, from 1982 to 1988 with host Dick Clark.

Social Origins of Dictatorship and Democracy: Lord and Peasant in the Making of the Modern World: A 1966 book by Barrington Moore Jr.

Renée Zellweger: Actress known for *Jerry Maguire*, *Cold Mountain*, and *Bridget Jones's Diary*.

Quentin Tarantino, Gogo Yubari: Tarantino is a filmmaker whose works include *Pulp Fiction, Inglourious Basterds*, and the *Kill Bill* duology. Gogo Yubari is an antagonist in Tarantino's film *Kill Bill: Volume 1*, depicted as a sadistic and violent schoolgirl. The character was portrayed by Chiaki Kuriyama. (At the party, Robert is dressed as a *Kill Bill* extra, and Logan is dressed as Butch Coolidge, a boxer character from *Pulp Fiction* portrayed by Bruce Willis.)

Reggae Fever: While there are several albums that carry the title *Reggae Fever*, the examples Lorelai provides in the scene appear to be fictitious.

Rastafari: Religion developed in Jamaica in the 1930s.

Harvey Weinstein: Film producer and convicted sex offender.

Spencer Tracy (1900–1967): Actor whose works include *Captains Courageous*, *Boys Town*, and *Guess Who's Coming to Dinner*.

Blast the jam: Slang phrase meaning to loudly listen to music.

EPISODE 5.18: TO LIVE AND LET DIORAMA

Written by Daniel Palladino. Directed by Jackson Douglas. Aired April 19, 2005. Luke volunteers to help convert an old house into a museum. The town celebrates Founders Day. Lorelai is too candid during an interview about the inn.

***Summerland*, Lori Loughlin**: *Summerland* is a drama TV series that aired on The WB from 2004 to 2005 and starred Lori Loughlin as a fashion designer raising her niece and nephew in a California town. Loughlin is an actress best known for the TV series *Full House* and for a 2019 college admissions scandal. She and her husband pleaded guilty to conspiracy to commit fraud in their efforts to get their daughters admitted to the University of Southern California. She was sentenced to two months in prison.

Maxwell tape ad: Maxwell is a Japanese company that manufactures consumer electronics. They were well known for manufacturing blank audio cassettes in the 1980s. Their advertising campaign for the product featured the "Blown Away Guy"—a man sitting low in an armchair, facing a large speaker. His hair and necktie, as well as a lampshade and martini glass, are being blown back by the sound coming from the speaker due to the audio accuracy of the Maxwell tape.

Garrison Keillor: Author, humorist, and radio personality best known for creating the public radio show *A Prairie Home Companion*, which he hosted from 1974 to 2016.

Sheriff Taylor, Otis Campbell: Characters from the TV sitcom *The Andy Griffith Show*. Sheriff Taylor was the show's protagonist, portrayed by Andy Griffith (see earlier entry), and Otis was the town drunk portrayed by Hal Smith.

Muzak: Brand of background music played in retail stores and other public places.

Fortress of Solitude: Fictional fortress and place of solace associated with Superman (see earlier entry) in DC Comics.

Jack Benny (1894–1974): Comedian and actor known for *The Jack Benny Show*.

Redd Foxx (1922–1991): Comedian and actor known for *Sanford and Son* and *The Redd Foxx Show*.

Pol Pot (1925–1998): Cambodian dictator who ruled Democratic Kampuchea from 1976 until 1979. He is considered among the most brutal despots in history.

Barbara Boxer: Politician who served as US Senator from California from 1993 to 2017. In 2005, during the confirmation hearings for US secretary of state nominee Condoleezza Rice (see earlier entry), Boxer challenged Rice to admit to mistakes and false statements made by the Bush administration and leading the United States into the Iraq War.

William Howard Taft (1857–1930): Twenty-seventh president of the United States from 1909 to 1913 and chief justice of the United States from 1921 to 1930.

Garret Hobart (1844–1899): Twenty-fourth vice president of the United States from 1897 to 1899 under President William McKinley.

William McKinley (1843–1901): Twenty-fifth president of the United States from 1897 until his assassination by an anarchist in 1901.

Nederlander Organization: One of the largest operators of live theaters and music venues in the United States, including many Broadway theaters. It was founded in 1912 by David T. Nederlander.

Mamma Mia!: While not mentioned by name, this musical is based on the songs of Swedish group ABBA (see earlier entry). It debuted in 1999 and has been adapted into a successful film version.

EPISODE 5.19: BUT I'M A GILMORE!

Written by Amy Sherman-Palladino. Directed by Michael Zinberg. Aired April 26, 2005.
Rory's dinner with Logan's family takes an unexpected turn. Luke covers for Sookie at the inn when she's placed on bed rest.

Abba-Zaba: Brand of taffy candy bar with a peanut butter center.

Hair of the dog: Expression referring to alcohol consumed to cure a hangover.

House of Flying Daggers: A 2004 martial arts film directed by Zhang Yimou.

Mr. Creosote: Fictional character in Monty Python's *The Meaning of Life*, an obese restaurant customer who is served so much food and alcohol that he vomits repeatedly. He was portrayed by Terry Jones.

The Exorcist: A 1973 supernatural horror film about the demonic possession of a young girl. At one point, the possessed young girl vomits into the face of the priest who is trying to save her.

"When You're Hot, You're Hot": A 1971 song by actor and singer Jerry Reed.

"You had me at hello": Popular romantic line from the 1996 film *Jerry Maguire.*

"Ain't No Mountain High Enough": A 1967 single by Marvin Gaye and Tammi Terrell made more famous when released in 1970 by Diana Ross.

Rob Schnieder: Actor known for *Saturday Night Live* and *Deuce Bigalow: Male Gigolo.*

Alyssa Milano: Actress known for *Who's the Boss?* and *Charmed.*

Han Solo, Luke Skywalker, Tauntaun: Characters from the *Star Wars* franchise. Han and Luke are played by Harrison Ford and Mark Hamill, respectively. In a scene in the original series' second film, *The Empire Strikes Back*, Han rescues a near-death Luke during a snowstorm by cutting open the carcass of a tauntaun, a semi-sentient species of large reptomammal, and using it to keep him warm.

"Very Lucy of you": Reference to a 1952 episode of the sitcom *I Love Lucy* in which Lucy gets locked inside a walk-in freezer.

Ellen DeGeneres: Comedian, actress, and TV host who began each episode of her daytime talk show, *The Ellen DeGeneres Show* (2003–2022), by dancing her entrance.

"You landed the whale," Annette Bening: Landing a whale is a phrase derived from *Moby-Dick* (see earlier entry) and refers to reaching a seemingly unattainable goal. It is often used in sales to mean securing a major customer or business deal. Bening is an actress whose works include *The Grifters* and *American Beauty.* In 1992, she married actor Warren Beatty who, prior to the marriage, had a well-known history of multiple romantic relationships with lots of female celebrities.

Diego Velázquez (1599–1660): Spanish painter considered among the greatest in the history of Western art.

Shanghai: To coerce someone, often by kidnapping or manipulation, into doing something they don't want to do. The term arose through the practice of kidnapping people to serve as sailors.

The Amazing Race: Adventure reality TV show franchise that debuted in 2001 in which teams of two race around the world in competition with other teams.

White knight: Mythological figure and literary stock character depicted as a heroic warrior fighting against evil.

Thumper: Fictional rabbit from *Bambi* (see earlier entry).

The Gambinos: Italian-American mafia crime family.

Julia Roberts, Keifer Sutherland: Roberts is an actress known for *Steel Magnolias*, *Pretty Woman*, *Erin Brockovich* and many other films. Sutherland is an actor known for *The Lost Boys*, *Young Guns*, and *24*. The two co-starred in the 1990 film *Flatliners* and became romantically involved. They planned to marry in 1991 but called off their engagement four days before the ceremony.

Jimmy Breslin (1928–2017): Pulitzer Prize–winning columnist, journalist, and author.

Episode 5.20: How Many Kropogs to Cape Cod?

Written by Bill Prady and Rebecca Rand Kirshner. Directed by Jamie Babbit. Aired May 3, 2005.

Rory begins her internship with Mitchum and brings Logan to Friday night dinner.

"Walking on Sunshine": A 1985 single by the pop band Katrina and the Waves.

Hotel Rwanda: A 2004 biographical historical drama film starring Don Cheadle as human rights activist and hotelier Paul Rusesabagina, who provided shelter for refugees during the 1994 Rwandan genocide.

"Has the town banned dancing and singing?": Paris is referring to *Footloose* (see earlier entry).

"It's hammer time": A phrase that originated with the 1990 song "U Can't Touch This" by MC Hammer.

Deadwood: Western TV series that aired on HBO from 2004 to 2006, notable for its violent depiction of 1870s life in Deadwood, South Dakota.

Lois Lane: Fictional character from DC Comics, depicted as an award-winning journalist and eventual love interest of Clark Kent/Superman.

Empiricists vs. Rationalists: Differing philosophical ideas, with empiricism suggesting that knowledge comes from experience, and rationalism suggesting that knowledge is based on reason and logic.

A posteriori truths, a priori truths: A posteriori truths are facts known from experience. A priori truths are facts known without experience but rather by thought.

Ethics, **Baruch Spinoza**: Spinoza (1632–1677) was a philosopher who authored the philosophical treatise *Ethics* between 1661 and 1675.

Paper Moon: A 1973 road comedy film starring real-life father and daughter Ryan O'Neal and Tatum O'Neal as a pair of Depression-era con artists.

Peter Jennings (1938–2005): Journalist who anchored *ABC World News Tonight* from 1983 until his death in 2005.

Zucker brothers: Filmmaking duo consisting of David and Jerry Zucker who, along with Jim Abrahams, created a variety of slapstick comedy films in the 1980s, including *Airplane!* and *The Naked Gun* films.

TUMI: Brand of high-end travel bags.

Dear Abby: Advice column penned by Abigail Van Buren (see earlier entry).

"My Favorite Things": Song from *The Sound of Music* (see earlier entry).

"My daughter, my sister": Reference to a scene in the film *Chinatown* (see earlier entry), in which a woman claims that a character in the film is both her sister and her daughter.

Kennebunkport: Resort town in Maine known for being the summer home of the Bush family.

Ronald Reagan (1911–2004): Politician and actor who served as president of the United States from 1981 to 1989.

Romeo y Julieta cigars: Brand of premium cigars introduced in 1875.

Kropogs: The Kropog story is fictional but based on an actual tradition at MIT, where the unit of measurement is called a "smoot," a humorous length of measurement developed as part of an MIT fraternity pledge in 1958 by Oliver R. Smoot, who laid down repeatedly on the Harvard Bridge so that his fraternity brothers could use his height to measure its length.

Pete Sampras: Former professional tennis player.

Above the fold: Newspaper phrase referring to the upper half of the front page, where the most important story of the day is placed.

Pinko: Pejorative term referring to a person on the left of the political spectrum, with its origins derived from the word pink, which was suggested to be a lighter shade of red, the color associated with communism. The term was widely used during the Cold War to refer to people supporting the Soviet Union and Communist China.

Roy Cohn (1927–1986): Lawyer who served as chief counsel to Joseph McCarthy during McCarthy's investigations of suspected communists in the 1950s.

National Geographic: Monthly magazine founded in 1888 known for its photography, maps, and in-depth reporting.

EPISODE 5.21: BLAME BOOZE AND MELVILLE

Written by Daniel Palladino. Directed by Jamie Babbit. Aired May 10, 2005.
The article about the Dragonfly Inn is released. Sookie goes into labor. Mitchum reviews Rory's work at her internship.

Easter Island: Island in Chile known for its nearly one thousand monumental statues created by the early Rapa Nui people.

Jose Canseco: Former professional baseball player who admitted to using performance-enhancing drugs.

Spamalot: Stage musical written by Eric Idle and John Du Prez based on the 1975 film *Monty Python and the Holy Grail*.

Father Time: Personification of time.

New Year's Baby: Baby New Year is the personification of the start of a new year.

"She'll Be Coming 'Round the Mountain": Children's folk song.

Marmaduke: Comic strip created in 1954 by Brad Anderson about a family and their giant, messy, lovable Great Dane named Marmaduke.

Sally Forth: Comic strip created by Greg Howard in 1982 about the life of a middle-class mother.

Dennis the Menace, Mr. Wilson: Characters in the *Dennis the Menace* franchise, which began as a comic strip by Hank Ketcham in 1951 and has expanded into various series, films, and other media. Dennis is a mischievous young boy, and Mr. Wilson is his cranky next-door neighbor.

Andy Dick: Comedian and actor known for *Newsradio, Less Than Perfect*, and for eccentric behavior, drug addiction, and sexual misconduct allegations.

Wolf Blitzer: Journalist and TV news anchor known for his work with CNN.

Penélope Cruz: Actress known for *Vicky Cristina Barcelona, Vanilla Sky*, and other films.

Ben Stiller: Actor known for *There's Something About Mary, Zoolander*, and several other works.

Sword of Damocles: Symbolic sword from the Greek tale of Damocles, alluding to the imminent and ever-present danger faced by people in positions of power.

Putting pig vessels in people: A reference to the medical practice, which made news at the time of the episode, of using pig heart valves to replace defective aortic valves in human patients.

Magic 8 Ball: Novelty toy invented in 1946. It is a plastic sphere designed to look like an oversized eight ball from the cue sport of pool, used for fortune telling. The user asks a yes-or-no question and turns the ball over to reveal an answer.

"Drop It Like It's Hot": A 2004 song by the rapper Snoop Dog.

Franz Ferdinand: Scottish rock band formed in 2002.

Chris Rock: Comedian and actor known for *Saturday Night Live, The Chris Rock Show*, and several films.

Rosalynn Carter (1927–2023): Wife of Jimmy Carter and first lady of the United States from 1977 to 1981.

EPISODE 5.22: A HOUSE IS NOT A HOME
Written and directed by Amy Sherman-Palladino. Aired May 17, 2005.
A night of reckless behavior with Logan leads Rory to a major decision.

Caged Heat: A 1974 film about women in prison.

Switchblade Sisters: A 1975 exploitation action film about female gang members.

Andy Sipowitz: Lorelai refers to the TV police procedural series *NYPD Blue*, which ran on ABC from 1993 to 2005 and starred Dennis Franz as Detective Andy Sipowicz. In a first-season episode, Sipowicz's son is mistakenly arrested for drug dealing.

Maxwell Smart, Agent 99: Characters from the comedy TV series *Get Smart*, which ran from 1965 to 1970 and parodied the secret agent genre. Don Adams starred as Agent Maxwell Smart and Barbara Feldon as Agent 99.

Sheryl Crow: Singer-songwriter whose hits include "All I Wanna Do" and "If It Makes You Happy." Lorelai's reference to her in relation to a bike race is because, from 2003 to 2006, she was romantically linked to cyclist Lance Armstrong.

Marc Jacobs: Head fashion designer for the label that bears his name.

Louis B. Mayer (1884–1957): Film producer and co-founder of the Metro-Goldwyn-Mayer studio.

"Mama Tried": A 1968 single by Merle Haggard.

Tom Sizemore, Whizzinator: Sizemore is an actor whose works include *Natural Born Killers* and *Saving Private Ryan*. He has battled drug addiction and, in 2005, he was caught attempting to fake a urine test using a Whizzinator, a device advertised as a sex simulator but often purchased to fraudulently defeat drug tests.

Robert Blake (1933–2023): Actor known for *In Cold Blood* and *Baretta*. In 2002, he was arrested for the murder of his second wife, Bonny Lee Bakley, but was acquitted in criminal court in 2005.

3 Doors Down: Rock band formed in 1996 whose hits include "Kryptonite" and "When I'm Gone."

The Robot: Dance involving stilted movements meant to mimic those of a robot.

Dakota Fanning: Actress whose works include *I Am Sam* and *Uptown Girls*.

Eternal Sunshine of the Spotless Mind: A 2004 film starring Jim Carrey and Kate Winslet as a couple who undergo a memory erasure experiment in order to forget one another.

Match.com: An online dating service launched in 1995.

Peter Pan: Fictional character created in the early 1900s by J. M. Barrie, depicted as a mischievous young boy who never grows up. The iconic character has appeared in a variety of literary, stage, and screen adaptations. A Peter Pan collared shirt is a collar design that is flat in design with rounded collars. It is named after the costume worn by actress Maude Adams in a 1905 stage production of *Peter Pan*.

Festival Express: A 1970 train tour across Canada during which a variety of popular music artists and bands—including Janis Joplin, the Grateful Dead, and The Band, among others—traveled to venues by train.

Cowardly Lion: Character in *The Wizard of Oz* (see earlier entry), a lion who accompanies Dorothy through Oz to the Emerald City so he can ask the wizard for courage.

Season Six: 2005–2006

EPISODE 6.1: NEW AND IMPROVED LORELAI
Written and directed by Amy Sherman-Palladino. Aired September 13, 2005.
Rory learns the consequences of her night out with Logan.

"Funkytown": A 1980 song by the disco-funk group Lipps Inc.

Wonder of wonders, miracle of miracles: Line from the song "Miracle of Miracles" from *Fiddler on the Roof* (see earlier entry).

Zima: Carbonated alcoholic beverage introduced in 1993.

"Pre-Owned Heart": A song by Grant Lee Phillips.

Lollipop Guild: A group of fictional munchkins in *The Wizard of Oz* (see earlier entry) who welcome Dorothy to Oz and present her with a giant lollipop.

Chocolate Factory: See *Willie Wonka & the Chocolate Factory*.

Bob & Carol & Ted & Alice: A 1969 comedy-drama film starring Natalie Wood, Robert Culp, Elliott Gould, and Dyan Cannon.

Frida Kahlo (1907–1954): Mexican painter known for portraits.

Christopher Atkins, *The Blue Lagoon*: Atkins is an actor known for *Dallas*, *The Pirate Movie*, and *The Blue Lagoon*, a 1980 coming-of-age survival film in which he co-starred with Brooke Shields.

Pace car: In motorsports, the pace car is the car that limits the speed of competing cars on a racetrack.

Björn Borg: Swedish former tennis player who was ranked as the world No. 1 in men's singles for one hundred and nine weeks.

"French Foreign Legion": A 1958 song by Frank Sinatra (see earlier entry).

Tim Burton: Notable filmmaker known for gothic horror and dark fantasy films. His works include *Beetlejuice*, *Edward Scissorhands*, *Batman*, and *The Nightmare Before Christmas*.

Breaking Away: A 1979 coming-of-age film about a group of recent high school graduates, one of whom is obsessed with competitive bicycle racing.

Benson: A TV sitcom that aired on ABC from 1979 to 1986. A spinoff of *Soap* (see earlier entry), Robert Guillaume starred as Benson DuBois, who went from being butler to the wealthy Tate family on *Soap* to being head of household for a governor on the spinoff.

The Scorpion and the Frog: Fable dating back to the 1980s about a scorpion who hitches a ride across a river on the back of a hesitant frog who worries that the scorpion might sting him. The scorpion promises not to for, if he did so, they would both sink into the water. Halfway across the river, the scorpion stings the frog, dooming them both, while apologetically saying he couldn't help himself because it is in his nature.

"I smell toast": A common myth in which people say smelling burnt toast is a sign of a serious medical condition such as a stroke or heart attack.

EPISODE 6.2: FIGHT FACE
Written and directed by Daniel Palladino. Aired September 20, 2005.
Rory begins her community service work.

Palace of Versailles: Former royal residence commissioned by King Louis XIV in France. A pivotal event in the French Revolution took place in 1789 when a group of mostly women, angered by food shortages and high prices, marched to Versailles, forcing the king and his family to return to Paris.

Kenny Chesney: Country singer whose hits include "She's Got It All" and "How Forever Feels."

Runaway bride: Not to be confused with the 1999 film of the same name, Sookie refers to Jennifer Carol Willbanks, a woman who ran away from her Georgia home in 2005 to avoid her wedding. Her disappearance sparked a nationwide media frenzy. She eventually surfaced in New Mexico falsely claiming that she had been kidnapped and sexually assaulted—claims that fell apart under FBI investigation. She was ultimately fined and sentenced to community service and probation. Many remarked on Willbanks's prominent eyes, often labeling them "bug eyes."

Star Wars: Episode III: Revenge of the Sith: This film from the *Star Wars* franchise is what Luke and Lorelai are discussing in the diner. It is a 2005 epic space film and the third in a series of three *Star Wars* prequels. Lorelai's comment about George Lucas (see earlier entry) owning San Francisco is a nod to the fact that the city is home to both Lucas and his Lucasfilm studios.

***Bewitched*, Nicole Kidman, Dr. Bombay, Larry Tate**: *Bewitched* is a 2005 comedy film starring Kidman and Will Ferrell, based on the 1960s TV sitcom (see earlier entry). Dr. Bombay and Larry Tate were characters on the original show. Kidman is an actress whose other works include *The Hours* and *Moulin Rouge!*

"Don't cry for me": While not an uncommon phrase, and one that has been used in various songs including by artists such as Whitney Houston, perhaps the most common association is with the song "Don't Cry for Me Argentina" from the musical *Evita*.

Porky Pig: Animated, stuttering pig from the *Looney Tunes/Merrie Melodies* cartoons.

March of the Penguins: A 2005 nature documentary depicting the yearly journey of emperor penguins in Antarctica.

Ann Coulter: Conservative media pundit and author.

Scooter Libby: Lawyer who served as chief of staff under Vice President Dick Cheney from 2001 to 2005.

Burt Bacharach (1928–2023): Composer, songwriter, and producer regarded as an influential figure in popular music.

Paul Anka: Singer and actor whose hits include "Put Your Head on My Shoulder," "Diana," and "(You're) Having My Baby."

"Whassup?": Slurring of the phrase "what's up," originating in an ad campaign for Budweiser beer in 1999 in which a group of friends comically said it to one another while talking on the phone. It gained momentum and became a pop culture catchphrase used for years.

Lladró: Spanish brand of porcelain figurines.

Alexander Hamilton (1755–1804): Military officer, statesman, and Founding Father who served as the first US secretary of the treasury. He is featured on the ten-dollar bill.

Michael Corleone: Fictional character and protagonist of *The Godfather* (see earlier entry).

"Tote that barge": A line from the song "Ol' Man River" from the musical *Showboat*, which has come to be a metaphor for hard work.

Taskmaster: In a biblical context, this word was used to describe Egyptian officials who imposed heavy labor burdens on the Israelites.

"Glue to a horse": A reference to the historic practice of making glue from horse parts, including collagen from hooves and bones.

Episode 6.3: The UnGraduate

Written by David S. Rosenthal. Directed by Michael Zinberg. Aired September 27, 2005.

Construction gets underway at Lorelai's house. Rory begins working for the DAR. Lane's band returns home from their tour.

Ninety-five Theses: List of grievances against the Catholic Church, also known as the *Disputation on the Power and Efficacy of Indulgences*, written by Martin Luther (see earlier entry) in 1517.

"I shot a man in Reno": Famous lyric from the Johnny Cash song "Folsom Prison Blues," about a man incarcerated at Folsom Prison because he "shot a man in Reno just to watch him die."

Tokyo Rose: Name given by Allied troops during World War II to female radio broadcasters of Japanese propaganda. The name, while not actually a person, came to symbolize Japanese villainy for the United States.

Emmanuel Lewis: Actor best known for the TV sitcom *Webster*, which ran from 1983 to 1989. His unusually small stature—he reached only 4'3" in adulthood—allowed him to play much younger characters. In the 1980s, Lewis began a friendship with musician Michael Jackson that many classified as unusual. At the 1984 American Music Awards, when Jackson won the award for Favorite Soul Male Artist, he came to the stage carrying thirteen-year-old Lewis in his arms like a toddler.

"Good to the last drop": Slogan used in advertisements for Maxwell House coffee.

Valerie Plame: Spy and former Central Intelligence Agency officer whose identity was leaked to and published by the *Washington Post* in 2003.

Blogosphere: Term coined in 1999 implying that all blogs consist online in an interconnected community.

BTK: A reference to serial killer Dennis Rader, who murdered at least ten people in Kansas between 1974 and 1991. He gave himself the initials BTK to mean blind, torture, kill. He often sent taunting letters to the police and media describing his crimes. The letters led to his capture in 2005, and he is serving life in prison.

My Left Foot: Lorelai does an impression of Daniel Day-Lewis's (see earlier entry) performance in *Mohicans* with her "I will find you" line. *My Left Foot* is a 1989 autobiographical comedy film in which Day-Lewis stars as Christy Brown, an Irish writer and painter whose cerebral palsy allowed him to only control his left foot, which he would use to write and type.

United Service Organizations (USO): The USO is a nonprofit-charitable corporation that provides live entertainment to members of the United States Armed Forces and their families.

"Hanging on the Telephone": While several artists have recorded it, this song is best known as a 1978 single by Blondie.

Ecclesiastes: Book from the Old Testament of the Christian Bible and the Ketuvim section of the Hebrew Bible.

Katie Holmes: Actress who rose to fame while starring on the TV series *Dawson's Creek*. In 2005, she began dating Tom Cruise (see earlier entry). In an infamous interview on *The Oprah Winfrey Show*, Cruise was so excited talking about his relationship with Holmes that he jumped up on Oprah's couch in what many considered a bizarre show of enthusiasm. The couple wed in 2006 and divorced in 2012.

Captain Ahab: Fictional protagonist in *Moby-Dick* (see earlier entry), a ship captain on a fanatical mission to get revenge on the whale who bit off his leg. See also "You landed the whale."

Jude Law: English actor whose works include *The Talented Mr. Ripley* and *Cold Mountain*. He began dating actress Sienna Miller in 2003 and, in 2005, issued a public apology to Miller for having an affair with his children's nanny.

"Miss Gulch/Witch's theme": Michel hums this song from *The Wizard Oz* (see earlier entry), which is played in the film whenever the Wicked Witch of the West and her Kansas alter ego Miss Gulch appear on screen.

"The *Eagle* has landed": Famous quote spoken by astronaut Niel Armstrong when the *Apollo 11* crew landed the Apollo Lunar Module *Eagle* on the moon on July 20, 1969, marking the first time humans had landed on the moon.

Suzie Q, Shorty George: Kinds of dance moves.

Arthur Murray (1895–1991): Famous ballroom dancer often associated with the dance studio bearing his name.

Cooper's Hill Cheese-Rolling and Wake: Logan describes this famous annual event held near Gloucester, England, in which participants race down a hill chasing a wheel of Double Gloucester cheese. The first recorded occurrence dates back to 1826.

"Until the cows come home": Phrase meaning that something will take a very long time, derived from cows who are let out to pasture staying gone for a long time. Usage of the phrase dates back to the 1690s.

"Working blue": Phrase that often refers to a performance that pushes the envelope with edgy, controversial material. See also "Blue film."

Meet the Press: Weekly Sunday morning news talk show that has aired on NBC since 1947.

Bleach: Debut album by Nirvana (see earlier entry), released in 1989. Producer Jack Endino billed the band for thirty hours of recording at a cost of $606.17.

Dilithium: Fictional crystal in the *Star Trek* universe used in warp drives.

EPISODE 6.4: ALWAYS A GODMOTHER, NEVER A GOD
Written by Rebecca Rand Kirshner. Directed by Robert Berlinger. Aired October 4, 2005.
Sookie asks Lorelai and Rory to be godmothers to her kids.

Deuce Bigalow: Male Gigolo: A 1999 comedy film starring Rob Schneider as the titular male prostitute. A sequel, *Deuce Bigalow: European Gigolo*, was released in 2005.

"Every journey begins with a single step": Common Chinese proverb.

Magnum P.I.: Crime drama TV series that aired on CBS from 1980 to 1988 starring Tom Selleck as private investigator Thomas Magnum.

Knots Landing: Prime-time TV soap opera that aired on CBS as a spinoff of *Dallas* from 1979 to 1993, initially centering on the lives of four married couples. Ginger was part of one of the couples, a kindergarten teacher portrayed by Kim Lankford. Lorelai references "Moments of Truth," an episode from the show's second season in which robbers hold the attendees hostage at Ginger's baby shower.

21 Jump Street: Police procedural TV series starring Johnny Depp that aired on Fox from 1987 to 1991. Michael DeLuise (T.J.) starred on the show during its final season.

Spuds MacKenzie: Fictional bull terrier dog character used during an advertising campaign to promote Bud Lite beer in the 1980s.

Clara Peller (1902–1987): Manicurist and TV personality who rose to fame in her eighties when starring in the "Where's the beef?" advertising campaign for Wendy's fast food restaurants.

"Nothing comes between me and my Calvins": Line from a famous ad campaign for Calvin Klein jeans. The spot sparked controversy because the model in the ad was a fourteen-year-old Brooke Shields.

***Riding the Bus with My Sister*, Andie MacDowell, Anjelica Huston**: Lorelai discussed this 2005 made-for-TV movie based on a 2002 memoir of the same name by Rachel Simon. It is directed by Huston and stars Rosie O'Donnell (see earlier entry) and MacDowell. MacDowell is best known for *Sex, Lies, and Videotape* and *Four Weddings and a Funeral*. Huston is an actress known for playing Maerose Prizzi in *Prizzi's Honor*, as well as starring in *The Grifters* and the *Addams Family* films.

America's Castles: Documentary TV series that aired on A&E Network from 1994 to 2005.

Please Don't Eat the Daisies: Sitcom that aired on NBC from 1965 to 1967, based on the 1957 Jean Kerr book and 1960 film of the same name.

Gilbert Stuart (1755–1828): Painter and portraitist best known for the *Athenaeum Portrait*, an unfinished portrait of George Washington.

Entertainment Weekly: Entertainment magazine that launched in 1990. It became a digital publication in 2022.

Flatt and Scruggs: Bluegrass duo consisting of Lester Flatt and Earl Scruggs, active from 1948 to 1969.

Mount Vernon: Former Virginia residence and plantation estate of George Washington.

Clara Barton (1821–1912): Civil War nurse who founded the American Red Cross.

Carrot Top: Red-haired actor and stand-up comedian known for prop comedy.

Jefferson Davis (1808–1889): Politician who served as president of the Confederate States from 1861 to 1865.

Susan Powter: Motivational speaker, nutritionist, and trainer who rose to fame in the 1990s with a weight-loss infomercial and the catchphrase "Stop the Insanity!" She was known for wearing a bleached blonde, buzzed hairdo.

Stradivarius: High-quality string instruments crafted by the Stradivari family in Italy during the seventeenth and eighteenth centuries.

Mad Hot Ballroom: A 2005 documentary film about a group of kids in a New York City ballroom dance program.

R2-D2: Fictional robot character from the *Star Wars* franchise.

"Make her an offer she couldn't refuse": Brian paraphrases a famous line from *The Godfather* (see earlier entry).

Greta Garbo (1905–1990): Actress during Hollywood's silent and early golden eras, known for *Romance*, *Anna Christie*, and *Grand Hotel*.

The Lion, the Witch, and the Wardrobe: A 1950 children's novel by C. S. Lewis, the first in *The Chronicles of Narnia* series.

Mary Is My Homegirl: Slogan that appeared on merchandise in the 2000s, alongside "Jesus Is My Homeboy" items.

The Brian Jonestown Massacre: Rock band formed in San Francisco in 1990.

Nicodemus: Figure in the New Testament of the Bible who is drawn to the teachings of Jesus.

The Pierre: Luxury hotel in Manhattan.

EPISODE 6.5: WE'VE GOT MAGIC TO DO
Written by Daniel Palladino. Directed by Michael Zinberg. Aired October 11, 2005.
Rory organizes an event for the DAR.

"Gunga Din": An 1890 poem by Rudyard Kipling about an Indian water-carrier and the British soldier whose life he saves.

Scarlett O'Hara: Fictional protagonist in Margaret Mitchell's *Gone With the Wind*.

Mutt and Jeff: Newspaper comic strip by Bud Fisher about two mismatched characters. Regarded as the first daily comic strip, it ran from 1907 to 1983.

Grover Norquist: Political activist and anti-tax advocate who founded Americans for Tax Reform.

Babe Ruth (1895–1948): Professional baseball player regarded as one of the greatest of all time.

Samuel Beckett (1906–1989): Nobel Prize–winning writer whose works include *Waiting for Godot* (see earlier entry).

Hollywood Canteen: A club that operated from 1942 to 1945 in Los Angeles, California, offering food, dancing, and entertainment to enlisted men and women typically on their way overseas to fight in World War II. It was created when a group of entertainers joined forces to organize it, among them Bette Davis (see earlier entry). Rory later passes by a large photo of Davis ("Bette's life was tough enough.")

J. Paul Getty Museum: Art museum in Los Angeles, California, established in 1974.

"Attica! Attica!": Famous line from the 1975 biographical drama film *Dog Day Afternoon* starring Al Pacino, chronicling a 1972 bank robbery and hostage situation. The line is yelled by Pacino's character to invoke the real-life 1971 Attica prison riot, during which inmates took control of the prison to protest inhumane conditions.

John "Grizzly" Adams (1812–1860): Famous California mountain man and grizzly bear trainer whose life has been portrayed in various literary and screen adaptations.

Mortimer J. Adler (1902–2001): Philosopher, encyclopedist, and author who founded the Institute for Philosophical Research.

***Just Shoot Me*, Wendie Malick**: *Just Shoot Me* is a workplace sitcom that ran on NBC from 1997 to 2003, set in the offices of a fictional, *Vogue*-like fashion magazine. Malick portrayed former model Nina Van Horn, the magazine's fashion editor. Her other works include *Dream On*, *Hot in Cleveland*, and *Night Court*.

Swan Lake: Famous 1877 ballet by Pyotr Ilyich Tchaikovsky.

Krumping: Type of street dance popularized in the early 2000s.

"Magic to Do": Opening song from the musical *Pippin*.

Radar O'Reilly: Fictional character on the TV sitcom *M*A*S*H*, portrayed by Gary Burghoff. The character was known for anticipating the needs of his commanding officer and for his excellent hearing. He was able to hear incoming helicopters before anyone else could.

Dave Navarro: Guitarist best known as a member of the bands Jane's Addiction and Red Hot Chili Peppers. During the time of this episode, he was also a co-host and judge on the reality TV series *Rock Star: INXS*, where contestants competed to become the lead vocalist of the band INXS.

T. S. Eliot (1888–1965): Nobel Prize–winning poet and playwright whose works include "The Love Song of J. Alfred Prufrock" and "The Hollow Men."

The Andrews Sisters: Singing group from the swing and boogie-woogie eras consisting of sisters LaVerne, Maxene, and Patricia Andrews, whose songs included "Boogie Woogie Bugle Boy," "Bei Mir Bist Du Schoen," "Don't Sit Under the Apple Tree (with Anyone Else but Me)," and "I'll Be With You in Apple Blossom Time." Most of these songs are performed by the group in the episode.

Benny Goodman (1909–1986): Bandleader known as the "King of Swing."

Glenn Miller (1904–1944): Famous big band conductor and composer. He and his band entertained troops during World War II, and he eventually joined the US Army Air Forces. He went missing in action in 1944 while flying over the English Channel. He was declared dead a year and a day later (which was standard military procedure).

Karl Marx (1818–1883): German-born philosopher best known for writing the 1848 pamphlet *The Communist Manifesto*.

Desmond Tutu (1931–2021): South African bishop and anti-apartheid activist.

"A Hard Rain's a-Gonna Fall": A 1962 song by Bob Dylan.

Abigail Adams (1744–1818): Wife of President John Adams and First Lady of the United States from 1797 to 1801.

Donald Rumsfeld (1932–2021): Politician who served as US secretary of defense from 1975 to 1977 under President Gerald Ford and again from 2001 to 2006 under President George W. Bush.

The Swing Dolls: The group performing at the benefit are an actual 1940s-style vocal trio who perform in tribute to the Andrews Sisters.

Episode 6.6: Welcome to the Dollhouse

Written by Keith Eisner. Directed by Jackson Douglas. Aired October 18, 2005. When Stars Hollow changes its street names to their original eighteenth-century monikers, Lorelai worries about the fate of the Dragonfly Inn.

Scooby-Doo: Animated talking Great Dane who solves mysteries along with his owner, Shaggy, and friends. The character debuted in the 1969 Hanna-Barbera Saturday morning cartoon series *Scooby-Doo, Where Are You!* and has become an enduringly popular franchise consisting of multiple series, films, and merchandise endeavors.

Arthur Godfrey (1903–1983): Popular radio and TV broadcaster and entertainer.

Charing Cross Road: Street in London renowned for its specialty and secondhand bookshops. It is widely known for the 1970 book *84, Charing Cross Road* by Helene Hanff, which chronicles Hanff's long-standing correspondence with the Charing Cross bookshop Marks & Co.

Abbey Road: Thoroughfare in London best known as the name (and location of the famous cover image) of the Beatles' eleventh studio album, *Abbey Road*.

"Gang up on that light bulb": Reference to the enduring joke that asks how many people of a certain group are needed to screw in a light bulb.

New England Journal of Medicine: Peer-reviewed medical journal founded in 1812.

Bring Me the Head of Alfredo Garcia: A 1974 neo-Western film starring Warren Oates, Isela Vega, and Kris Kristofferson. A commercial and critical failure, it has gained a cult following in the years since its release.

Birkin bag: Prestigious luxury bag introduced in 1984 by French goods maker Hermés. Costs vary widely, ranging from around fifteen thousand to several hundred thousand dollars.

"Crash landed in the Andes": Reference to the film *Alive* (see earlier entry).

Home Shopping Network: Group of cable networks launched in 1982 that sell items such as jewelry, clothing, and shoes.

John le Carré (1931–2020): English author known for writing spy novels.

Norma Rae: A 1979 drama film starring Sally Field as a factory worker who becomes involved in union activities as a result of poor working conditions.

"The South will rise again": Rallying cry popularized after the Civil War suggesting that the Confederacy would be revived. The phrase has been used frequently in literature and song.

Anthony Michael Hall: Actor known for *National Lampoon's Vacation*, *The Breakfast Club*, *Weird Science*, and *Sixteen Candles* (see earlier entry), which is the film Lorelai is referencing.

Sotheby's: International auction house dealing in fine goods.

"Let down your hair": A reference to Rapunzel (see earlier entry).

EPISODE 6.7: TWENTY-ONE IS THE LONELIEST NUMBER
Written by Amy Sherman Palladino. Directed by Robert Berlinger. Aired October 25, 2005.
Emily plans an elaborate twenty-first birthday party for Rory.

The Mad Hatter: Fictional character in *Alice in Wonderland* (see earlier entry), a top hat-clad man whom Alice encounters at a tea party.

Hercules: In classical mythology, a man known for his great strength.

Don King: Boxing promoter known for "The Rumble in the Jungle" and the "Thrilla in Manila" matches, as well as for his outrageous hair that stood straight up.

Pia Zadora: Actress and singer known for "The Clapping Song" and *Butterfly*.

"It's De-Lovely": Lorelai paraphrases this 1936 Cole Porter song, which includes the line "it's de-lightful, it's de-licious, it's de-lovely."

Mutual Admiration Society: While a phrase often used idiomatically to refer to people who express esteem for one another (as in Rory's case), it was originally an actual literary circle of women at Somerville College at the University of Oxford, as well as the title of a song from the 1956 Broadway musical *Happy Hunting*.

The 40-Year-Old Virgin: A 2005 romantic comedy film starring Steve Carell as the titular forty-year-old virgin.

My Little Pony: Toy line of colorful plastic ponies introduced in 1981. It has expanded into a media franchise including TV and film adaptations.

The Rat Pack: Group of entertainers in the 1960s who often appeared together on stage and screen, including Frank Sinatra, Dean Martin, and Sammy Davis Jr.

John O'Hurley: Actor and game show host known for his recurring role on *Seinfeld*, hosting *Family Feud*, and winning the first season of *Dancing with the Stars* in 2005.

EPISODE 6.8: LET ME HEAR YOUR BALALAIKAS RINGING OUT
Written by Daniel Palladino. Directed by Kenneth Ortega. Aired November 8, 2005.
Jess visits with a surprise for Rory. Luke sponsors a youth soccer team.

Cone of Silence: While a phrase used in navigation and radar, it also has pop culture elements, such as a device used for privacy in the 1965 novel *Dune* and a fictional transparent hemisphere lowered over the head of characters on the TV sitcom *Get Smart* to keep conversations private.

"Better dead than red": Cold War anticommunist slogan.

Lullaby League: Fictional troupe of ballerina Munchkins in *The Wizard of Oz* (see earlier entry).

Tom Thumb: Character in English folklore and fairy tales whose small stature (he's the size of his father's thumb) lands him in various jams, such as being baked in a cake and stolen by a crow.

Cylons: Race of sentient robots in the *Battlestar Galactica* science-fiction franchise.

Daddy Warbucks: Fictional billionaire who adopts Annie in the *Little Orphan Annie* franchise.

Viggo Mortensen: Actor whose works include the *Lord of the Rings* film trilogy.

Donald Sutherland (1935–2024): Actor known for *The Dirty Dozen*, *Ordinary People*, and *Six Degrees of Separation*.

"Tom Dooley": Traditional folk song based on the real-life murder of a woman by a man named Tom Dula, whose name was pronounced in local dialect as "Dooley."

Snuff film: Type of film showing scenes of an actual homicide.

INXS: Australian rock band whose hits include "Need You Tonight" and "New Sensation." The lead singer, Michael Hutchence, died in 1997 and, in 2005, remaining members participated in the reality singing competition series *Rock Star: INXS*, in which vocalists competed to become their lead singer. J. D. Fortune won the competition and performed with the band until 2011.

Stingo: Character in the 1982 drama film *Sophie's Choice*, a Brooklyn writer. In slang terms, stingo also refers to a strong ale.

Soccer moms: Lorelai's comment about soccer moms being concerned with issues like national security stems from the term's widespread media usage during the 1996 presidential election, when they were described as key swing voters who would decide the election.

Bend It Like Beckham: A 2002 sports film about a girl who dreams of playing professional soccer. The title references David Beckham (see earlier entry).

Sam Peckinpah (1925–1984): Filmmaker whose works were known for their explicit depiction of violence.

Scarface: A 1983 crime drama film known for its violence.

"Rock Around the Clock": A 1954 song by Bill Haley & His Comets.

John Dos Passos: Novelist best known for his *U.S.A.* trilogy.

Robert Musil (1880–1942): Austrian writer whose unfinished work, *The Man Without Qualities*, is considered important and influential.

EPISODE 6.9: THE PRODIGAL DAUGHTER RETURNS

Written and directed by Amy Sherman-Palladino. Aired November 15, 2005.
Lorelai and Rory begin to reconcile. Luke gets an unexpected visitor.

"Duck, duck, goose": Children's chasing game.

Yao Ming: Basketball executive and former professional player who at one point was the tallest active player in the NBA.

"Saturday Night's Alright for Fighting": A 1973 song by Elton John.

Valerie Cherish, *The Comeback*: Cherish is a fictional sitcom actress portrayed by Lisa Kudrow in the HBO series *The Comeback*, which ran for one season in 2005 and a second season in 2014. A final third season is slated for 2026. Lorelai quotes a popular catchphrase from Cherish's character.

Bernardo: Fictional gang leader in *West Side Story* (see earlier entry).

Wisteria Lane: Fictional suburban setting of the TV series *Desperate Housewives*.

Laa-Laa: Fictional character on the *Teletubbies* children's series (see earlier entry).

Erik Estrada: Actor and police officer known for the TV series *CHiPs*.

Joe Klein, *Primary Colors*: Klein is a political commentator and author known for his column in *Time* magazine and for the 1996 book *Primary Colors*, a novel based on the 1992 presidential campaign of Bill Clinton. Published anonymously, Klein was identified as its author several months after publication.

Episode 6.10: He's Slippin' 'Em Bread . . . Dig?
Written by Daniel Palladino. Directed by Kenneth Ortega. Aired November 22, 2005.
Liz attempts to prepare Thanksgiving dinner.

"The guys get shirts!": Rory discusses an infamous mid-1980s recording of Paul Anka berating his crew and band for what he considered unprofessional behavior. It was recorded secretly and shared with the media. A number of quotes from the tirade became widely used.

Louis Prima (1910–1978): Famous trumpeter and bandleader.

Hokey Pokey: Participation-style dance and song with roots dating back to the 1800s but popularized in the 1940s.

Lenny Kravitz: Singer-songwriter and musician known for "American Woman" and other songs. He briefly dated and was engaged to Nicole Kidman (see earlier entry) in 2003 and 2004.

"Ring of Fire": A 1963 song by Johnny Cash.

Beowulf: Old English epic poem written anonymously and produced sometime between 975 and 1025 AD.

Seamus Heaney (1939–2013): Nobel Prize–winning poet and playwright whose works include *Death of a Naturalist*.

Waiting for Guffman: A 1996 mockumentary comedy film about the production of a stage musical, where the cast and crew await the arrival of a Broadway producer to critique the production.

The Police: English rock band whose hits include "Roxanne" and "Every Breath You Take."

The Knack: Rock band known for the song "My Sharona."

D. A. Pennebaker (1925–2019): Documentary filmmaker known for, among other things, his work with musicians, including Bob Dylan, Little Richard, and David Bowie.

Fountains of Wayne: Rock band known for the song "Stacy's Mom."

The Shins: Indie rock band formed in New Mexico in 1996.

The Zombies: English rock band formed in 1961. Zack references their second studio album, *Odessey and Oracle*, released in 1968.

The Replacements: Rock band formed in Minnesota in 1979.

Kill 'Em All: Debut album by the heavy metal band Metallica, released in 1983.

Yakov Smirnoff: Stand-up comedian and actor who has appeared in *The Money Pit*, *Brewster's Millions*, and *Night Court*.

Wash & Brush Up Co.: Fictional salon and spa from *The Wizard of Oz*, where Dorothy and her friends are sent to freshen up after arriving in the Emerald City.

Bill Gates: Businessman known as co-founder of Microsoft.

Narnia: Fantasy world created by C. S. Lewis as the setting for the children's book series *The Chronicles of Narnia*.

Oscar Mayer: Brand of meat products, such as hot dogs and bologna, created by its namesake in 1883.

Buddy Hackett (1924–2003): Comedian and actor known for *The Music Man* and *It's a Mad, Mad, Mad, Mad World*.

"A priest, a rabbi, and a Mormon missionary": Lorelai refers to a common joke setup involving various combinations of religious figureheads, often depicted as walking into a bar.

Jack White: Musician and record producer who rose to fame as a member of the rock duo The White Stripes.

"Free Bird": A 1974 single by Lynyrd Skynyrd.

Warren Beatty: Actor known for *Bonnie and Clyde* and *Shampoo* and for his notorious reputation as having had relationships with multiple women.

Ryan Seacrest: TV and radio personality known for hosting *American Idol*, *Live with Kelly and Ryan*, and *Wheel of Fortune*.

EPISODE 6.11: THE PERFECT DRESS

Written by Amy Sherman-Palladino. Directed by Jamie Babbit. Aired January 10, 2006.

Lorelai shops for her wedding dress. Luke visits April's mother.

Trump Taj Mahal: Hotel and casino in Atlantic City, New Jersey, inaugurated in 1990 by Donald Trump (see earlier entry). In 2015, it faced a $10 million fine for "willfully violating" anti-money-laundering regulations. It closed in 2016 and was converted into a Hard Rock Hotel & Casino.

Wendy & Lisa: Music duo consisting of Wendy Melvoin and Lisa Coleman who got their start working with Prince in the 1980s.

The Supremes, Diana Ross: The Supremes were an all-female Motown singing group whose hits include "Baby Love," "Stop! In the Name of Love," "You Can't Hurry Love," and many others. Ross is a singer and actress who was the original lead singer of the Supremes until her departure in 1970. She went on to have multiple chart hits ("Ain't No Mountain High Enough") and film credits (*The Wiz*).

James Brown (1933–2006): Singer-songwriter known for funk and soul music, whose hits include "I Got You" and "Papa's Got a Brand New Bag."

Tony Danza: Actor known for *Who's the Boss?* and *Taxi*.

Dolly Parton, "Jolene": Parton is an iconic singer, songwriter, actress, and philanthropist whose hits include "9 to 5," "I Will Always Love You," "Coat of Many Colors," and "Jolene," a 1973 song inspired by a woman who flirted with Parton's husband.

It takes a village: Proverb suggesting that a community of people must come together to interact with and provide for children to ensure they grow up in a safe and healthy environment. The phrase rose to prominence in the 1990s when Hillary Clinton used it as the title of a best-selling book.

Rush Limbaugh (1951–2021): Conservative political commentator and talk radio host.

John Steinbeck (1902–1968): Nobel Prize–winning novelist whose works include *The Grapes of Wrath* and *Of Mice and Men*.

William Saroyan (1908–1981): Pulitzer Prize–winning novelist and playwright known for *The Human Comedy*.

Barbara Mandrell: Country music singer and actress whose hits include "I Was Country When Country Wasn't Cool" and "Sleeping Single in a Double Bed."

"You have the golden ticket": Reference to *Willy Wonka & the Chocolate Factory* (see earlier entry).

Divine (1945–1988): Actor, singer, and drag queen known for appearing in the films of John Waters.

Aleksandr Solzhenitsyn, *One Day in the Life of Ivan Denisovich*: Solzhenitsyn (1918–2008) was a Nobel Prize–winning author and dissident who helped raise awareness about political repression in the Soviet Union with his work *The Gulag Archipelago*. *One Day in the Life of Ivan Denisovich* is his 1962 political novella about a day in the life of a Gulag prisoner.

Doo-wop: Style of rhythm and blues music originating in the 1940s.

Angela's Ashes: A 1999 biographical film based on the 1996 Pulitzer Prize–winning memoir of the same name by Frank McCourt, detailing his childhood in Ireland and struggles with poverty and his father's alcoholism.

"Spur of the Moment": Without mentioning it by name, Lorelai explains the plot of this 1964 episode of *The Twilight Zone* (see earlier entry).

Macauley Culkin: Actor best known for *Home Alone* and *Uncle Buck*.

"Those are some big ears you have there, grandma": Paraphrased line from *Little Red Riding Hood*. (See "Very big eyes for you, Grandma.")

Martin Luther King Jr. (1929–1968): Baptist minister and activist who was a prominent leader in the civil rights movement until his assassination in 1968. He participated in the 1963 March on Washington, where he delivered the famous "I Have a Dream" speech.

Pete Townshend: English musician and co-founder of the Who. In the early 2000s, he was placed on a sex offenders registry for five years following an investigation after he used his credit card to access a website with child sexual abuse imagery. He claimed to have accessed the site while conducting research in a campaign against child sexual abuse. Authorities could not prove that the website he accessed involved children, and no incriminating evidence was found on his computer.

Episode 6.12: Just Like Gwen and Gavin

Written by Daniel Palladino. Directed by Stephen Clancy. Aired January 17, 2006.

April asks to spend a day at the diner. Paris's reign of terror at the newspaper leads to a pending staff coup.

Rubik's Cube: A 3D combination puzzle toy introduced in 1974.

Matt Lauer: TV news personality known for his work with NBC News, including co-hosting *Today* with Katie Couric (see earlier entry) for many years. He was terminated in 2017 when allegations of inappropriate sexual behavior in the workplace surfaced.

Matthew McConaughey: Actor known for *Dazed and Confused*, *Dallas Buyers Club*, and many other roles.

***People*'s Sexiest Man Alive**: Annual designation from *People* magazine (see earlier entry) naming the sexiest male celebrity. Since it began in 1985, recipients have included Richard Gere, Brad Pitt, Matthew McConaughey, and John Krasinski.

Flowers for Algernon: A 1959 short story by Daniel Keyes, which he later expanded into a novel, about a lab mouse who undergoes surgery to increase his intelligence.

Aaron Brown (1948–2024): Journalist recognized for his coverage of the 9/11 terror attacks. He hosted *NewsNight with Aaron Brown* on CNN until it was replaced by *Anderson Cooper 360°* in 2005.

Howell Raines: Journalist who served as executive editor of the *New York Times* from 2001 to 2003, when he was dismissed amid the reporting scandal related to Jayson Blair (see earlier entry). Raines was faulted for continuing to publish Blair's work after being alerted to the issues with his writing.

"The Rain in Spain": A 1956 song from the musical *My Fair Lady*.

"Margaret, I'm home!": Famous recurring line from the sitcom *Father Knows Best*, starring Robert Young and Jany Wyatt, which began on radio in 1949 and ran on television from 1954 to 1960. Young's character, Jim, would say the line to Wyatt's character, his wife Margaret, upon coming home from work.

Gavin Rossdale: British musician and lead singer of the band Bush. From 2002 to 2016, he was married to Gwen Stefani (see earlier entry). In 2004, a paternity test revealed that Rossdale was the father of fashion designer Pearl Lowe's daughter, Daisy, who was born in 1989.

The Smurfs: Comic franchise centering on the adventures of a colony of small, blue humanoid creatures living in mushroom-shaped houses. It began as a Belgian comic series in the 1950s but expanded into multiple comics, toys, films, and cartoon series, rising to particular fame in the 1980s with a Saturday morning cartoon show.

EPISODE 6.13: FRIDAY NIGHT'S ALRIGHT FOR FIGHTING

Written by Amy Sherman Palladino. Directed by Kenneth Ortega. Aired January 31, 2006.

Rory steps into a leadership position when the Yale newspaper faces a tight deadline. Friday night dinners are reinstated.

"Hurt So Good," John Mellencamp: Mellencamp is a singer-songwriter whose hits include "Jack & Diane," "Pink Houses," and "Hurt So Good," a 1982 single that won a Best Male Rock Vocal Performance Grammy.

"Once more with feeling": A common phrase used to suggest repeating an action or statement with additional emotion or enthusiasm. It's often used in show business and is the title of various works of song and screen, including a popular musical episode of the TV series *Buffy the Vampire Slayer*.

Nora Ephron (1941–2012): Filmmaker known for romantic comedies like *When Harry Met Sally . . .* and *Sleepless in Seattle*.

Rita Wilson: Actress, singer, and wife of Tom Hanks, whose works include *Now and Then* and *Sleepless in Seattle*. Logan references a famous scene from *Seattle* in which Wilson's character gives a passionate and emotional explanation of the plot of *An Affair to Remember* (see earlier entry).

Taboo: Stage musical about the London club scene in the 1980s, written by and partially focusing on pop singer Boy George. Rosie O'Donnell financed a Broadway production of the show, which had originally run in London. It opened in 2003 and was a critical and commercial flop, with O'Donnell reportedly losing her entire investment.

"Ice Ice Baby": A 1990 single by rapper Vanilla Ice.

Naomi Campbell: British model, actress, and TV host.

Rowan and Martin: Dan Rowan (1922–1987) and Dick Martin (1922–2008) were comedians and actors who hosted *Rowan & Martin's Laugh-In*, a sketch comedy TV series that ran from 1968 to 1973.

Christopher Isherwood (1904–1986): Novelist and playwright whose works include *Goodbye to Berlin*, a novel that inspired the musical *Cabaret* (see earlier entry).

Mildred Pierce: A 1945 film starring Joan Crawford. Lorelai describes part of the film's plot involving Mildred and her daughter, Veda.

The Bridges of Madison County: A 1995 romantic drama film, based on the 1992 Robert James Waller novel of the same name, starring Clint Eastwood and Meryl Streep (see earlier entry). It flashes between present day and a 1965 love affair between the two lead characters.

Kabbalah bracelets, matzah: This is a reference to Passover, a Jewish holiday celebrating the Exodus of the Israelites from slavery in Egypt. Kabbalah is a type of Jewish mysticism, and Kabbalah bracelets are an ancient practice of warding off bad luck and the "evil eye." Matzah is a form of bread seen as a bread of faith and a reminder of the spiritual state of the Jewish people at the time of the Exodus.

D-Day: A military term meaning the day on which a combat attack will commence. The term is most commonly used to reference June 6, 1944, the day of the Normandy landings during World War II.

Sweeney Todd: The Demon Barber of Fleet Street: Stage musical debuting in 1979 about a serial killer barber whose victims' remains are used in a meat-pie shop.

Punxsutawney Phil: Groundhog who is the central figure in the annual Groundhog Day celebration in Punxsutawney, Pennsylvania.

Alan Greenspan: Economist who served as chairman of the Federal Reserve from 1987 to 2006.

"Rob Peter to pay Paul": Phrase meaning to take from one person to give to another, as in eliminating one debt by incurring another.

For Dummies: Extensive series of reference books on various topics, intended to present information in a non-technical, easy-to-understand format.

"Asteroid toward Earth": While stopping an asteroid from hitting Earth has been the focus of actual research and of Hollywood projects, one famous depiction is the 1998 film *Armageddon*, in which a group of blue-collar drillers are sent into space to destroy an asteroid on a collision course with Earth.

Episode 6.14: You've Been Gilmored

Written by Jordan Nardino. Directed by Stephen Clancy. Aired February 7, 2006. Emily invites Luke to dinner. Paris isn't thrilled when Rory is chosen editor of the paper.

Solaris: A 2002 science-fiction film starring George Clooney (see earlier entry), based on the 1961 Stanisław Lem novel of the same name, set almost entirely on a space station orbiting the fictional planet Solaris. It was a box office failure.

Bullets Over Broadway: A 1994 Woody Allen film about a playwright forced to cast a mobster's girlfriend in his newest play.

Robert's Rules of Order: Manual of parliamentary procedure by US Army officer Henry Martyn Robert (1837–1923).

Judith Miller: Journalist known for writing about Iraq's alleged weapons of mass destruction program.

"Good night and good luck": Famous catchphrase of broadcast journalist and war correspondent Edward R. Murrow, who began ending his reporting segments with the phrase during World War II in 1940. It became the title of a 2005 historical drama film about Murrow's conflict with US Senator Joseph McCarthy in the 1950s.

Hanging chad: Fragment of a punch-card ballot not detached fully, resulting in an incomplete and invalid ballot. They were partly responsible for a high proportion of invalid votes in Florida during the 2000 presidential election.

Erhard Seminars Training: Seminar series operating between 1971 and 1984 that used concepts loosely based on Buddhism for self-improvement. The strict six-day, sixty-hour sessions drew criticism, including allegations of mind control, authoritarianism, and cult behavior.

K Street: Thoroughfare in Washington, DC, known as the center for lobbying.

Peanuts: Comic strip created by Charles M. Schulz in 1950, focusing on a group of children including Charlie Brown and his dog, Snoopy.

Ginsu knives: Brand of direct-marketed knives that were heavily promoted through TV infomercials in the 1970s and 1980s.

Endicott Peabody (1857–1944): Educator and episcopal priest who founded Groton School in 1844.

Walden: An 1854 book by Henry David Thoreau in which he reflects on simple living in natural surroundings.

Grand Ole Opry: Country music live radio broadcast founded in 1925 and originating from Nashville, Tennessee.

W. Somerset Maugham (1874–1965): English writer whose works include *Of Human Bondage*.

Vaudeville: Theatrical genre of variety entertainment dating back to nineteenth-century France.

Trotskyism: Political ideology and branch of Marxism developed by Russian revolutionary Leon Trotsky.

7th Heaven: Family drama TV series that ran on The WB and The CW from 1996 to 2007.

Hester Prynne: Protagonist of the Nathaniel Hawthorne novel *The Scarlet Letter*, portrayed as a woman condemned by her Puritan neighbors for having a child out of wedlock.

Episode 6.15: A Vineyard Valentine
Written and directed by Daniel Palladino. Aired February 14, 2006.
Rory and Logan invite Luke and Lorelai to the Huntzbergers' vacation house for Valentine's Day weekend.

"Nothing new under the sun": Phrase originating in the Bible's Book of Ecclesiastes, meaning that everything has already been done before.

"Zydeco Boogaloo": A 1983 song by zydeco artist Buckwheat Zydeco.

Dixieland: Style of jazz originating in New Orleans at the start of the twentieth century.

Led Zepagain: Hard rock Led Zeppelin tribute band formed in 1991.

"Early in the Mornin'": Jazz and blues standard originally recorded in 1947 by Louis Jordan and covered by many others over the decades.

Pete Doherty: English musician best known as frontman for the Libertines.

Thucydides (460–400 BC): Athenian historian and general who wrote *The History of the Peloponnesian War.*

Partridge in a pear tree: Famous line from the holiday song "The Twelve Days of Christmas."

Betty Friedan (1921–2006): Feminist writer and activist who wrote *The Feminist Mystique.*

"Hot Blooded": Lorelai paraphrases this 1978 song by the band Foreigner, which includes the line "hot blooded, check it and see."

Gospel of John: Book in the New Testament that focuses on the ministry of Jesus.

John Philip Sousa (1854–1932): Composer and conductor known for military marches.

Bergdorf Goodman: Luxury department store based in New York City.

Mario Batali: Chef and former restaurateur who appeared on the Food Network. In 2017, allegations of sexual misconduct surfaced, and Batali sold all his restaurant holdings in the wake.

Ina Garten: Chef known as the *Barefoot Contessa* (see earlier entry).

EPISODE 6.16: BRIDESMAIDS REVISITED
Written by Rebecca Rand Kirshner. Directed by Linda Mendoza. Aired February 28, 2006.
Rory learns some unsettling news about Logan at his sister's wedding.

"White Rabbit": A 1967 single by the rock band Jefferson Airplane.

Ming-Na Wen: Actress known for *The Joy Luck Club* and *ER.*

David Foster Wallace (1962–2008): Author whose works include the very lengthy novel *Infinite Jest.*

Saw II: A 2005 horror film about a group of ex-convicts trapped in a house by a serial killer.

"Riding in My Car": Zack is performing this 1940s children's song written by Woody Guthrie at the music shop.

Faye Dunaway, *Network*: *Network* is a 1976 comedy-drama film about a veteran news anchor who learns he's being put out to pasture. Dunaway stars as the network's ambitious producer. Her other credits include *Bonnie and Clyde*, *The Thomas Crown Affair*, and *Mommie Dearest.*

Brigitte Nielsen: Danish actress and model whose credits include *Red Sonja* and *Rocky IV*. She is six feet tall, providing context to Christopher's remark.

Kareem Abdul-Jabbar: Former professional basketball player who is seven feet and two inches tall.

Richard C. Levin: President of Yale University from 1993 to 2013.

Gatorade: Brand of sports drink introduced in 1965. Lorelai refers to the Gatorade shower, a sports tradition popularized in the 1980s in which players on a winning team sneak up behind their head coach with a cooler full of Gatorade and pour it over their head at the end of a game.

Sienna Miller: Actress known for *The Girl* and *American Sniper*. For a time, she was romantically involved with actor Jude Law (see earlier entry), who cheated on her with his children's nanny.

"Hollaback Girl": A 2005 single by Gwen Stefani.

"My Humps": A 2005 single by the Black Eyed Peas.

Royal Albert Hall: Famous concert hall in London, England.

Soulcalibur III: Video fighting game introduced in 2005.

"If I Could Turn Back Time": A 1989 single by Cher (see earlier entry).

Brokeback Mountain: A 2005 film, based on the 1997 short story of the same name by Annie Proulx, depicting the complex romantic relationship between two cowboys.

"Hava Nagila": Traditional Jewish folk song often sung at weddings and bar and bat mitzvahs.

Carolina Herrera: Venezuelan-American fashion designer.

Bridezillas: While the term bridezilla—a combination of bride and Godzilla used to refer to an unreasonably demanding bride—is used commonly, it was also the name of a reality TV series that aired on the WE network beginning in 2004.

"Dead man walking": A phrase originally used in the prison system to describe a condemned prisoner being led to execution, but expanded to refer to a person in a doomed situation. It has also been the name of various books, films, and songs.

Full House, **Mary-Kate and Ashley Olsen**: *Full House* is a TV sitcom that aired on ABC from 1987 to 1995, about a widowed father raising his three daughters with the help of two friends. Among the cast were the Olsen twins, who together played the role of Michelle. They went on to various films and series, becoming hugely successful, and entered into the fashion industry in adulthood.

Lynda Carter: Actress and singer best known for portraying the title character in the *Wonder Woman* TV series from 1975 to 1979.

Mia Farrow: Actress known for *Peyton Place* and *Rosemary's Baby* and for her long relationship with Woody Allen (see earlier entry). Their relationship ended when Allen's intimate relationship with Farrow's adopted daughter was publicized.

Invasion of the Body Snatchers: A 1978 science-fiction horror film about an alien invasion starring Donald Sutherland (see earlier entry).

Milk carton kids: A reference to the 1980s and 1990s practice of putting photos and details about missing children on the backs of milk cartons.

Noh: A form of Japanese dance-drama dating back to the fourteenth century.

Dr. Benjamin Spock (1903–1998): Famed pediatrician whose 1946 book *Baby and Child Care* became an enduring bestseller.

Abraham Lincoln (1809–1865): Sixteenth president of the United States from 1861 until his assassination in 1865. Lorelai's comment refers to the fact that Lincoln was largely self-educated.

EPISODE 6.17: I'M OK, YOU'RE OK
Written by Keith Eisner. Directed by Lee Shallat Chemel. Aired April 4, 2006.
Luke chaperones a school trip for April. Zack asks Mrs. Kim's permission to marry Lane.

Danny Bonaduce: Actor, radio personality, and wrestler best known for the 1970s sitcom *The Partridge Family*, on which he starred as a child. As an adult, he got into boxing and wrestling and also had a 1991 arrest for beating and robbing a transgender sex worker.

Sheila E.: Singer and instrumentalist known for her percussion work and for the songs "The Glamorous Life" and "A Love Bizarre."

Janet Leigh: Actress best known for *Psycho* (see earlier entry), in which her character was stabbed to death while in the shower during a famous scene.

Little Man Tate: A 1991 drama film about a child prodigy who struggles in social settings.

Charlotte's Web: Lorelai's reference to a talking pig is a nod to this 1952 children's book by E. B. White (and its popular 1973 animated adaptation) about a farm pig named Wilbur and his friendship with Charlotte the spider.

Shriners: Masonic society described as a global fraternity, founded in 1872.

Babyshambles: English rock band formed by Pete Doherty in 2003. During the era of this episode, their shows were often marred by Doherty's dependence on drugs.

Lindsay Lohan: Actress known for *Freaky Friday* and *Mean Girls*.

Curious: Fragrance from pop singer Britney Spears (see earlier entry), developed in collaboration with Elizabeth Arden and released in 2004.

Taken: Science-fiction TV miniseries about alien abduction that aired on the Sci-Fi Channel in 2002.

Publishers Clearing House: Lorelai's line about Ed McMahon (see earlier entry) showing up with a large cardboard check is a reference to his time as spokesperson for the American Family Publishers direct marketing sweepstakes company. In an example of the kind of false memory known as a "Mandela Effect," she is confusing him with a competing sweepstakes company, Publishers Clearing House, whose winners would be notified when members of the "Prize Patrol" would show up at their door with a giant check. In actuality, McMahon and American Family Publishers never did this.

Mata Hari (1876–1917): Dutch exotic dancer convicted of being a spy for Germany during World War I.

Nanny McPhee: A 2005 fantasy film starring Emma Thompson as a magical nanny to a group of unruly children.

Final Destination: Horror movie franchise that consisted of three films at the time of this episode, but has since gone on to include several additional films, as well as novels and comic books.

"Make my bones": Idiom meaning to take action in order to establish respect.

Scott Baio, Florrie Dugger: Baio is an actor known for *Happy Days*, *Joanie Loves Chachi*, and *Charles in Charge*. Dugger is a former actress who appeared in *Bugsy Malone* (see earlier entry), the film referenced in the scene.

Bill Blass (1922–2002): Famed fashion designer.

Nancy Grace: Legal commentator and TV journalist who hosted *Nancy Grace* on HLN from 2005 to 2016.

Ray Davies: English musician known as lead singer of the Kinks (see earlier entry).

The Dave Clark Five: English rock band formed in 1958.

The Jam: English rock band formed in 1972.

The Futureheads: English post-punk band formed in 2000.

Syd Field (1935–2013): Author who wrote several books on screenwriting, including *Screenplay: The Foundations of Screenwriting*.

"Papa's Got a Brand New Bag": A 1965 single by James Brown.

EPISODE 6.18: THE REAL PAUL ANKA
Written and directed by Daniel Palladino. Aired April 11, 2006.
Rory visits Jess in Philadelphia. Lorelai spots her parents house hunting in Stars Hollow.

American Tourister: Lorelai refers to a famous ad campaign for this brand of luggage, whose TV spots in the 1970s featured a gorilla attempting to destroy the bags.

Ulysses S. Grant (1822–1885): General who led the Union Army to victory in the American Civil War then served as the eighteenth president of the United States from 1869 to 1877.

"The Elements": A 1959 song by Tom Lehrer that recites the name of all the chemical elements.

Johnny Damon: Former professional baseball player who played for the Boston Red Sox (see earlier entry) from 2002 to 2005 and the New York Yankees from 2006 to 2009.

George Steinbrenner (1930–2010): Businessman who owned the New York Yankees (see earlier entry) from 1973 until his death in 2010.

Harry Whittington (1927–2023): While not mentioned by name, Whittington was "the old guy" shot by Dick Cheney (see earlier entry). He was a lawyer and political figure who was accidentally shot in the face, neck, and torso while on a hunting trip with Cheney in 2006.

Willem de Kooning (1904–1997): Abstract expressionist artist.

Jackson Pollock (1912–1956): Abstract expressionist artist.

Cedar Bar: A 1986 work by artist Red Grooms depicting members of the New York School as they might have looked during the heyday of American expressionism.

Golda Meir (1898–1978): Prime Minister of Israel from 1969 to 1974.

Episode 6.19: I Get a Sidekick Out of You
Written and directed by Amy Sherman-Palladino. Aired April 18, 2006.
Lane and Zack's wedding day approaches.

Jimmy Kimmel: Late-night talk show host who has hosted *Jimmy Kimmel Live!* since 2003.

Mark Herron (1928–1996): Actor and fourth husband of Judy Garland (see earlier entry).

Deney Terrio: Choreographer who hosted the TV dance show *Dance Fever* from 1979 to 1987.

Consumer Reports: Nonprofit consumer organization dedicated to product testing.

Buddha: Founder of Buddhism.

American Gigolo, **Richard Gere**: *American Gigolo* is a 1980 crime drama film starring Gere as a high-priced escort who becomes involved with a politician's wife. There is a full-frontal nude scene featuring Gere, an actor whose other credits include *Pretty Woman* and *An Officer and a Gentleman*.

Jenna Jameson: TV personality and former adult film star.

Chico and the Man: Sitcom that aired on NBC from 1974 to 1978 about the owner of a run-down garage and the young Mexican-American who comes looking for a job.

Rhoda Morgenstern: Fictional best friend character on *The Mary Tyler Moore Show*, and its spinoff series *Rhoda*, portrayed by Valerie Harper.

"I'm a Believer": A 1966 song by the Monkees, written by Neil Diamond.

Calamity Jane (1852–1903): American frontierswoman, sharpshooter, and storyteller.

EPISODE 6.20: SUPER COOL PARTY PEOPLE
Written by David S. Rosenthal. Directed by Ken Whittingham. Aired April 25, 2006.
Luke throws April a birthday party at the diner. Rory rushes to the hospital to be with an injured Logan.

America's Next Top Model: Reality competition TV series that debuted in 2003, in which contestants compete to launch their career in the modeling industry.

Buttercup: Fictional young woman in the film and novel *The Princess Bride*.

"40 Years": A 1987 song by the rock band House of Freaks.

"Endless Love": A 1981 song by Lionel Richie and Diana Ross.

Colin Farrell: Actor known for *Minority Report* and *The Batman*. He struggled with drug and alcohol addiction, once claiming he had been drunk or high since age fourteen.

Lawrence Summers: Economist who served as US secretary of the treasury from 1999 to 2001 and president of Harvard University from 2001 to 2006.

Hagrid: Fictional character in the *Harry Potter* series (see earlier entry), depicted as a large, burley groundskeeper at Hogwarts.

Mad Libs: Word game invented in 1953, in which a player prompts other players to fill in word blanks in a story before reading it aloud.

RoboCop: A 1987 science-fiction action film about a murdered cop who is revived as a cyborg law enforcer.

Secretariat (1970–1989): Champion thoroughbred racehorse who won the American Triple Crown and holds the fastest time record for the events.

Emack & Bolio's: Ice cream shop chain founded by lawyer Robert Rook in 1975. It is named after two homeless men for whom Rook did pro bono work.

Sophia Loren: Italian actress known for *Two Women* and *Marriage Italian Style*.

Vanessa Minnillo: TV host, model, and actress who hosted MTV's *Total Request Live* from 2003 to 2007.

Harold and the Purple Crayon: A 1955 children's picture book by Crockett Johnson about a young boy on an imaginative adventure.

Us Weekly: Celebrity and entertainment magazine founded in 1977.

The New Way Things Work: A 1998 revision of a 1988 nonfiction book by David Macaulay that discusses in relatable terms how machines work.

Two and a Half Men: TV sitcom that ran on CBS from 2003 to 2015, starring Jon Cryer and Charlie Sheen as brothers and Angus T. Jones as the young son of Cryer's character.

Wet n Wild, Sun-In, Aqua Net: Wet n Wild is a brand of cosmetics, Sun-In is a brand of hair lightener spray, and Aqua Net a brand of hairspray, all of which were popular in the 1980s.

Red Badge of Courage: An 1895 war novel by Stephen Crane set during the American Civil War.

Sister Wendy (1930–2018): British Catholic nun and art historian who rose to fame presenting a series of BBC documentaries on the history of art.

EPISODE 6.21: DRIVING MISS GILMORE

Written by Amy Sherman-Palladino and Daniel Palladino. Directed by Jamie Babbit. Aired May 2, 2006.
Lorelai assists Emily following an eye surgery.

Ashlee Simpson: Lorelai and Rory are presumably discussing this singer and actress at the dinner table in the opening scene. The younger sister of singer Jessica Simpson (see earlier entry), Ashlee famously dyed her blonde hair black in 2004.

Marcus Welby, M.D.: Medical drama TV series that aired on ABC from 1969 to 1976.

Scarlett Johansson: Actress and singer known for *Lost in Translation* and the *Avengers* films.

Beyoncé: Singer and actress whose songs include "Crazy in Love" and "Single Ladies (Put a Ring on It)."

The Allman Brothers Band: Rock band formed in 1969 whose songs include "Midnight Rider" and "Ramblin' Man."

"Me and Julio Down By the Schoolyard": A 1972 single by Paul Simon.

Dr. Moshe Abramowitz: Staff member at an Israeli psychiatric hospital who was charged in 2006 with alleged acts of sadism and brutality conducted against hospital patients. The other name Logan says could be referring to Dana Ben-Meir, a nurse also charged in the case, although it sounds as though he is saying Dina. Dina Abramowitz (1909–2000) was a Jewish librarian and Yiddish language expert; however, the Ben-Meir reference fits the context best.

Mount Rushmore: National memorial in South Dakota centered around a giant sculpture of four former presidents—George Washington, Abraham Lincoln, Theodore Roosevelt, and Thomas Jefferson.

Alberto Gonzales: US Attorney General from 2005 to 2007 whose tenure was marked by controversy surrounding legal authorization of "enhanced interrogation techniques," which was eventually regarded as torture, during the post–9/11 War on Terror.

Helen Keller (1880–1968): Author and activist who was blind and deaf. She worked with her teacher and life-long companion Anne Sullivan (see earlier entry).

Mrs. Onassis: A nod to the fashion style of Jacqueline Kennedy Onassis (see John and Jackie).

Saddam Hussein (1937–2006): Iraqi dictator who served as president of Iraq from 1979 until his overthrow in 2003. That year, a large statue of Hussein located in Baghdad was overturned and destroyed by Iraqi citizens and US Marines—an action that came to symbolize the end of his rule.

60 Minutes: TV news magazine program airing on CBS beginning in 1968.

"Frosty the Snowman": Holiday song written by Walter "Jack" Rollins and Steve Nelson, about a snowman brought to life by wearing a magical silk hat. The hat allows him to have adventures with a group of children until the sun threatens to melt him.

Jay-Z: Rapper, record executive, and husband of Beyoncé.

Broadway Danny Rose: A 1984 film by Woody Allen about a theatrical agent who gets involved in a love triangle involving the mob. The woman in the love triangle is played by Mia Farrow (see earlier entry).

Sarah Bernhardt (1844–1923): French stage actress known as "the queen of the pose and the princess of the gesture."

Give 'Em Hell Harry!: Biographical play and 1975 film by Samuel Gallu, a one-man show about former US President Harry S. Truman.

Dollywood: Theme park in Pigeon Forge, Tennessee, opened by Dolly Parton in 1986.

Episode 6.22: Partings

Written by Amy Sherman-Palladino and Daniel Palladino. Directed by Amy Sherman-Palladino. Aired May 9, 2006.
Stars Hollow is invaded by troubadours. Logan graduates from Yale.

"Amazing Glow": A 2005 song by the Pernice Brothers. Joe Pernice is the troubadour performing the song.

Alfred Stieglitz (1864–1946): Famed photographer and art promoter.

Henri Cartier-Bresson (1908–2004): French artist and humanist photographer.

"Perfume": A 2006 song by Sparks, who perform it as troubadours.

"Last Train to Clarksville": A 1966 single by the Monkees.

Pat Boone: Singer-songwriter whose hits include "Love Letters in the Sand" and "A Wonderful Time Up There."

Iraq War: Rory references this conflict that saw the US National Guard being deployed to Baghdad to aid military efforts.

Mikhail Baryshnikov: Dancer, choreographer, and actor.

The Turning Point: A 1977 film about the world of New York City ballet.

"The Story of Yo La Tengo": A 2006 song by the band Yo La Tengo, who perform it as troubadours.

Insane Clown Posse: Hardcore hip-hop duo formed in Detroit in 1989.

Ice Cream Room: Lorelai references the fact that President George W. Bush had a personal ice cream room in the White House during his presidency.

"What a Waste": A 2006 song by the band Sonic Youth, who perform it as troubadours.

Barney Fife: Fictional deputy on *The Andy Griffith Show*, portrayed by Don Knotts.

"Heart of Gold": A 1972 single by Neil Young (see earlier entry).

***The Sopranos*, Adriana La Cerva**: *The Sopranos* is a crime drama TV series that aired on HBO from 1999 to 2007. Adriana was a character on the show portrayed by Drea de Matteo.

"Chim Chim Cher-ee": A song from the 1964 film *Mary Poppins* (see earlier entry).

Gwenyth Paltrow, *Shakespeare in Love*: Paltrow is an actress known for *The Talented Mr. Ripley* and *Shakespeare in Love*, a 1998 period romantic comedy film for which she won an Academy Award.

Skull Mountain: An enclosed roller coaster at the Six Flags theme park in New Jersey.

"Taking Pictures": A 2001 song by Sam Phillips, who scored the series and performs the song as a troubadour.

Season Seven: 2006–2007

EPISODE 7.1: THE LONG MORROW
Written by David S. Rosenthal. Directed by Lee Shallat Chemel. Aired September 26, 2006.
After her night with Christopher, Lorelai attempts to rid the house of reminders of Luke.

"We Are the Champions": A 1977 single by Queen.

"Time for your closeup, Mr. Demille": See Norma Desmond.

"Rocket Man," "Crocodile Rock," "Bennie and the Jets," "Candle in the Wind," Elton John: These songs are all hits by British singer-songwriter Elton John, one of the best-selling artists of all time.

The final frontier: A phrase used to describe outer space in the opening narration of *Star Trek*.

Winnie-the-Pooh: Fictional anthropomorphic teddy bear created by author A. A. Milne and illustrator E. H. Shephard, first appearing in 1925 and expanding into a multifaceted franchise of books, TV and film adaptations, and merchandise.

Big Brother: Character and symbol from the George Orwell dystopian novel *Nineteen Eighty-Four*. The phrase "Big Brother is watching" has become ubiquitous with the notion of being under constant surveillance.

Fast & Furious: Action media franchise consisting of a series of films about street racing, heists, and spies. The first film was released in 2001. The tenth was released in 2023.

Jarhead: A 2005 biographical war film based on the 2003 memoir of the same name by Anthony Swofford.

Cormac McCarthy (1933–2023): Author known for *Blood Meridian*, *The Road*, and *All the Pretty Horses*.

In Cold Blood: A 1966 nonfiction novel by Truman Capote recounting the 1959 Clutter family murders in Kansas.

"The Long Morrow": A 1964 episode of *The Twilight Zone* (see earlier entry), about an astronaut who falls in love on the eve of a forty-year-long space voyage.

Miss Moneypenny: Fictional character in the James Bond novels and films, depicted as the secretary to Bond's superior officer.

EPISODE 7.2: THAT'S WHAT YOU GET, FOLKS, FOR MAKIN' WHOOPEE

Written by Rebecca Rand Kirshner. Directed by Bethany Rooney. Aired October 3, 2006.

Lorelai attempts to cheer up Rory by recreating Rory's planned trip to Asia. Lane returns from her honeymoon with a surprising discovery.

Terracotta Army: Collection of terracotta soldiers depicting the armies of Chinese emperor Qin Shi Huang.

Tony Roma: Founder of his namesake restaurant chain specializing in baby back ribs, established in 1972.

"Teach a man to fish": Part of the common phrase "give a man a fish, and you feed him for a day; teach a man to fish, and you feed him for a lifetime."

Arigato: "Thank you" in Japanese. Sookie could be referring to the 1983 song "Mr. Roboto" by the band Styx. It features the line "Domo arigato, Mr. Roboto."

Linda Blair: Actress best known for *The Exorcist*.

Hockettes: Synchronized ice skating team.

The Rockettes: Precision dance company founded in 1925 who perform at Radio City Music Hall in New York City.

Laura Bush: First lady of the United States from 2001 to 2009 and wife of President George W. Bush (see earlier entry).

Mao Zedong (1893–1976): Leader of China from 1949 to 1976.

Sandra Oh: Actress known for *Grey's Anatomy* and *Killing Eve*.

The Bridge on the River Kwai: A 1957 war film about prisoners of war who are forced to construct a railway bridge.

The Karate Kid: A 1984 martial arts film about a teenager who learns karate to help protect himself from bullies.

Shanghai Surprise: A 1986 adventure-comedy film starring Sean Penn and Madonna.

Bruce Lee, *Enter the Dragon*: *Enter the Dragon* is a 1973 martial arts film starring Lee (1940–1973), a famous martial artist and actor.

Tom Selleck, *Mr. Baseball*: Selleck is an actor known for *Magnum, P.I.* and *Blue Bloods*. *Mr. Baseball* is a 1992 sports comedy film in which Selleck stars as an American baseball player traded to a Japanese team.

***Breakfast at Tiffany's*, Mickey Rooney, Holly Golightly**: *Breakfast at Tiffany's* is a 1961 romantic comedy film based on the Truman Capote novella of the same name, about a young woman named Holly Golightly. Rooney (1920–2014), a white man, portrays Holly's Japanese landlord. Rooney's other works include *National Velvet* and the *Andy Hardy* film series.

Munchkin cat: Breed of cat characterized by its very short legs.

"Makin' Whoopee": A 1928 song originally popularized by Eddie Cantor and recorded by multiple artists in the years since.

Shallow Hal: A 2001 film by the Farrelly brothers starring Gwenyth Paltrow and Jack Black about a man who falls in love with an obese woman after being hypnotized to only see her inner beauty.

View from the Top: A 2003 romantic comedy film in which Gwyneth Paltrow portrays a flight attendant.

June Cleaver: Fictional matriarch of the Cleaver family in the TV sitcom *Leave It to Beaver*, portrayed by Barbara Billingsly.

"Blanket" Jackson: Nickname of the youngest son of pop star Michael Jackson (see earlier entry), born Prince Michael Jackson II in 2002 and now going by Bigi. His father adopted the nickname Blanket during his infancy. When he was nine months old, his dad held him over a balcony in Berlin with a towel over his face to show off his infant to fans, a move that sparked much controversy.

Pillow: Lane and Rory reference the media speculation that actress Katie Holmes (see earlier entry) was not actually pregnant with the child of her husband Tom Cruise (see earlier entry) but was instead wearing a pillow. Their daughter, Suri, was born in 2006.

Apple Martin: Media personality, actress, and daughter of Gwenyth Paltrow (see earlier entry) and singer Chris Martin.

Rachel Griffiths: Australian actress known for *Six Feet Under, Brothers and Sisters,* and *Hilary and Jackie.* In 2003, she gave birth to a son she named Banjo.

Ronan Farrow: Journalist and son of Mia Farrow and Woody Allen (see earlier entries), whose full name at birth was Satchel Ronan O'Sullivan Farrow.

Pilot Inspektor Lee: Son of actor and skateboarder Jason Lee and actress Beth Riesgraf.

Battlestar Galactica: Science-fiction military TV series that aired from 2004 to 2009.

Keanu Reeves, Sandra Bullock, *Speed*, *The Lake House*: Reeves is an actor known for *The Matrix, Point Break,* and *Bill & Ted's Excellent Adventure.* Bullock is an actress known for *Miss Congeniality, The Blind Side,* and *Hope Floats.* The two co-starred in the 1994 action film *Speed* and the 2006 fantasy romance film *The Lake House.* Liz is referring to the latter in the scene.

EPISODE 7.3: LORELAI'S FIRST COTILLION
Written by Rina Mimoun. Directed by Lee Shallat Chemel. Aired October 10, 2006.
Michel accompanies Lorelai to Emily's cotillion dance.

C. Z. Guest (1920–2003): Actress, fashion designer, and socialite who achieved fame as a fashion icon.

Count Basie (1904–1984): Jazz musician and composer.

Tanglewood: Music venue in Massachusetts.

The Princeton Review: Company founded in 1981 that provides tutoring and test preparation services.

IM'ing: Internet slang for instant messaging.

Edward Hopper, the Met: Hopper (1882–1967) was a realism painter and printmaker whose notable works include *Automat* and *Nighthawks.* The Met is a nickname for the Metropolitan Museum of Art in New York City.

***Rigoletto*, Lincoln Center**: *Rigoletto* is an opera in three acts by Giuseppe Verdi. Lincoln Center is a performing arts venue in New York City.

Giacomo Casanova (1725–1798): Venetian adventurer and writer whose many sexual affairs with women has led to his name being a byword for a male seducer.

Imogene Coca (1908–2001): Comic actress known for *Your Show of Shows* and *National Lampoon's Vacation*.

Madame Alexander Doll Company: Manufacturer of collectible dolls founded in 1923 by Beatrice Alexander.

What to Expect When You're Expecting: Pregnancy guide written by Heidi Murkoff, originally published in 1984.

Henry Miller, *Sexus*: *Sexus* is a 1949 work by the author Miller (1891–1980), part of his *The Rosy Crucifixion* trilogy that presents a fictionalized account of his life in Brooklyn. *Sexus* is the first part, which chronicles the breakup of his first marriage as he meets and falls in love with his second wife.

Noël Coward (1899–1973): English playwright and composer known for his wit and flamboyance.

Slim Keith (1917–1990): Socialite and fashion icon.

Episode 7.4: 'S Wonderful, 'S Marvelous
Written by Gayle Abrams. Directed by Victor Nelli Jr. Aired October 17, 2006.
Lorelai begins dating Christopher. Rory makes some new friends. April pays a visit to Luke.

Snakes on a Plane: A 2006 action thriller film about venomous snakes loose on a passenger plane.

The Nutcracker: An 1892 ballet by Pyotr Ilyich Tchaikovsky.

Anna Pavlova (1881–1931): Famous Russian ballet dancer.

Ephron and Bernstein: Reference to filmmaker Nora Ephron and journalist Carl Bernstein (see earlier entries), who were married from 1976 to 1980.

Bullitt: A 1968 action thriller film starring Steve McQueen as Frank Bullitt, a San Francisco police lieutenant. It is notable for its stunt work and location shooting, including a famous car chase scene.

Funny Face: A 1957 romantic musical comedy film, based on the 1927 stage musical, starring Audrey Hepburn (see earlier entry) and Fred Astaire.

Kwik-E-Mart: Fictional convenience store in *The Simpsons*.

Fred Astaire (1899–1987): Dancer, actor, and singer known for *Holiday Inn*, *Easter Parade*, and *Funny Face*.

"S'wonderful": A 1927 song by George Gershwin from the musical *Funny Face*.

"Jailhouse Rock": A 1957 single by Elvis Presley.

"Folsom Prison Blues": A 1955 single by Johnny Cash.

"Chain Gang": A 1960 single by Sam Cooke.

Peter Brook (1925–2022): English theater and film director.

"Life is too important to be taken seriously": Famous quote by Oscar Wilde (see earlier entry).

California Suite: A 1976 play by Neil Simon set in the Beverly Hills Hotel.

EPISODE 7.5: THE GREAT STINK
Written by Gina Fattore. Directed by Michael Schultz. Aired October 24, 2006. Lorelai brings Christopher to Friday night dinner with her parents.

Salvatore Ferragamo: Italian luxury fashion house founded by its namesake in 1927.

BBC: British Broadcasting Corporation, the British public service broadcaster founded in 1922.

Girlfriends: TV sitcom that aired on UPN and The CW from 2000 to 2008.

Sábado Gigante: Spanish-language TV variety show originating in Chile in 1962 and broadcast in the United States beginning in 1986.

Pedro Almodólvar: Spanish film director, screenwriter, and author.

Dangerous Liaisons: A 1988 romantic drama film starring Glenn Close and Michelle Pfeiffer.

Samuel Johnson (1709–1784): English writer known for *A Dictionary of the English Language*.

James Boswell (1740–1795): Scottish biographer and diarist best known for his biography *The Life of Samuel Johnson*, with whom he had a long and enduring friendship. The book is said to be the greatest biography written in the English language.

Myspace: Social networking website founded in 2003.

Ira Glass: Public radio personality known for hosting *This American Life*.

Danger Mouse: Stage name of musician and record producer Brian Joseph Burton.

William Bligh (1754–1817): Royal Navy officer best known for his role in the mutiny on HMS *Bounty*, when the ship was under his command.

Carnegie Deli: Jewish delicatessen in New York City founded in 1937.

Dr. Brown's Cel-Ray Soda: Celery-flavored soda introduced by the Dr. Brown's brand in 1869.

Stay Puft Marshmallow Man: Fictional character from the *Ghostbusters* franchise.

Fo shizzle: Slang phrase meaning "for sure," popularized by the rapper Snoop Dogg.

Icehotel: Hotel in northern Sweden opened in 1990, rebuilt each year with snow and ice.

Archduke Franz Ferdinand (1863–1914): Archduke of Austria whose assassination was a cause of World War I.

Maria Sharapova: Russian professional tennis player.

Bobby Kennedy (1925–1968): US attorney general from 1961 to 1964 and US senator from 1965 until his assassination in 1968.

Bobby Knight (1940–2023): Men's college basketball coach whose career included coaching for the Indiana Hoosiers and the Texas Tech Red Raiders.

Bobby Brown: Singer, songwriter, and rapper who rose to fame as a member of New Edition before embarking on a successful solo career.

Great Wall of China: Series of fortifications in China dating to the seventh century BC and spanning more than thirteen thousand miles in length.

Egyptian pyramids: Ancient masonry structures in Egypt built between 2600 and 2500 BC.

Twelfth of Never: Popular expression meaning a date that will never come to pass and the title of a 1956 Johnny Mathis song.

Episode 7.6: Go, Bulldogs!

Written by David S. Rosenthal and Rebecca Rand Kirshner. Directed by Wil Shriner. Aired November 7, 2006.

Lorelai and Christopher attend Parents' Weekend at Yale. Luke meets April's swimming instructor.

Antiques Roadshow: TV show in which people bring in their antiques to have them appraised by experts. The American version debuted in 1997 and is based on the original British version, which debuted in 1979.

Pleasantville: A 1998 teen fantasy-comedy film about two siblings who find themselves trapped in a 1950s TV show.

Laverne & Shirley: TV sitcom that ran on ABC from 1976 to 1983 and starred Penny Marshall and Cindy Williams as the titular friends and roommates.

Mark Antony (83 BC–30 BC): Roman politician and general who was married to Cleopatra (see earlier entry) from 32 to 30 BC.

Facebook: Social media platform launched in 2004.

Riddler: Supervillain from DC Comics debuting in 1948. The character is an enduring nemesis of Batman who incorporates riddles, puzzles, and schemes into his crimes in an effort to thwart Batman and the authorities.

Hubble Space Telescope: Space telescope launched into low Earth orbit in 1990, named after astronomer Edwin Hubble.

Nick "Goose" Bradshaw, Pete "Maverick" Mitchell: Fictional friends from the film *Top Gun* (see earlier entry), portrayed by Anthony Edwards and Tom Cruise.

"You've Lost That Lovin' Feelin'": Kirk sings a line from this 1964 song by the Righteous Brothers.

"Zombie Jamboree": A 1962 song by Harry Belafonte.

Project Runway: Reality competition TV series about fashion design in which contestants compete to create the best clothes. It debuted in 2004.

Touch of Evil: A 1958 film noir by Orson Welles, starring Charlton Heston, Janet Leigh, and Marlene Dietrich (see earlier entry).

The Lady Is Willing: A 1942 screwball comedy film starring Marlene Dietrich and Fred MacMurray.

Destry Rides Again: A 1939 Western comedy film starring Marlene Dietrich and James Stewart. Coach Bennett recites one of Dietrich's lines from the film.

Clark Kent: Fictional alter ego of Superman in the DC Comics universe.

"Livin' on a Prayer": A 1986 single by the rock band Bon Jovi.

Episode 7.7: French Twist

Written by David Babcock. Directed by Lee Shallat Chemel. Aired November 14, 2006.

Lorelai and Christopher take Gigi to visit her mother in Paris. Mrs. Kim has big plans for Lane and Zack.

Boho-chic: Fashion style drawing on bohemian and hippie influences popular during the mid-2000s.

"The Charge of the Light Brigade": An 1854 narrative poem by Alfred, Lord Tennyson about the titular military action that took place during the Crimean War.

"Rebel Rebel": A 1974 song by rock star David Bowie.

Nevermind: A 1991 studio album by the rock band Nirvana. The famous album cover depicts a baby boy swimming underwater with a dollar bill on a fishhook just out of his reach.

Madeline: Children's book series (which has since expanded into a multimedia franchise) by Ludwig Bemelmans about a little girl attending boarding school in Paris.

Harry's New York Bar: Famous bar in Paris established in 1911 that has played host to multiple international celebrities and birthed many famous cocktails.

Gauloises: Brand of French cigarettes founded in 1910.

Cubism: An avant-garde art movement that began in Paris in the early twentieth century.

Tour de France: Annual men's multi-stage bicycle race held primarily in France.

Brahms' "Lullaby": Famous piece by composer Johannes Brahms, first published in 1868.

The Real World: Denver: The eighteenth season of the MTV reality TV series that placed seven diverse strangers into a shared house for several months as camera crews followed their activities. Each season took place in a different city beginning with New York City in 1992. The Denver season aired in 2006–2007.

Mr. Snuffleupagus: Puppet character on *Sesame Street*, depicted as a large mammoth-like creature. Snuffy was originally portrayed as Big Bird's imaginary friend.

Gérard Depardieu: Famous French actor.

Everybody Loves Raymond: TV sitcom that aired on CBS from 1996 to 2005, starring stand-up comedian Ray Romano.

"Bigger than a breadbox": Common phrase popularized by comedian Steve Allen on the 1950s TV game show *What's My Line?*

Conan O'Brien: TV host, comedian, and actor known for hosting late-night talk shows such as *Late Night with Conan O'Brien* from 1993 to 2009.

Snap, Crackle, and Pop: Cartoon elf-like mascots of the Rice Krispies brand of breakfast cereal.

Edvard Munch (1863–1944): Norwegian painter known for *The Scream*.

Tony Orlando and Dawn: Pop group consisting of lead singer Orlando backed by the vocal group Dawn. Hits include "Knock Three Times" and "Tie a Yellow Ribbon Round the Ole Oak Tree."

"Professor" Harold Hill: Fictional con man and protagonist of the 1957 stage musical *The Music Man*, depicted as a con man who poses as a boys' band organizer in an attempt to sell musical instruments to naïve townspeople.

4-H: Network of youth organizations dedicated to advancing the field of youth development, administered by the US Department of Agriculture's National Institute of Food and Agriculture. The four H's stand for head, heart, hands, and health.

EPISODE 7.8: INTRODUCING LORELAI PLANETARIUM
Written by Jennie Snyder. Directed by Lee Shallat Chemel. Aired November 21, 2006.
Rory learns surprising news about her parents. A judgmental article written by Rory leads to an argument with Logan.

"Don't Worry, Be Happy": A 1988 single by Bobby McFerrin.

"Take Me to the River": A 1974 song written by Al Green and Mabon "Teenie" Hodges and recorded by several artists since.

"Meet George Jetson, his boy Elroy": Line from the theme song to the animated TV sitcom *The Jetsons*, which originally aired from 1962 to 1963 as a counterpart to *The Flintstones*, focusing on the life of a space-age family in the future.

Water Lilies: A series of oil paintings by French artist Claude Monet (see earlier entry).

Paris Hilton: Media personality and socialite whose works include the reality TV series *The Simple Life*.

John Turturro: Actor and filmmaker whose works include *Do the Right Thing*, *The Big Lebowski*, and *O Brother, Where Art Thou?*

Roland Barthes (1915–1980): French literary theorist and essayist.

Barack Obama: President of the United States from 2009 to 2017 and US senator from Illinois from 2005 to 2008.

Slate: Online magazine covering current events, politics, and culture, launched in 1996.

Marie Antoinnette (1755–1793): Queen of France from 1774 to 1792. The title of Rory's article is a play on the line "Let them eat cake" (see earlier entry).

Ironweed: A 1983 Pulitzer Prize–winning novel by William Kennedy set during the Great Depression.

An Inconvenient Truth: A 2006 documentary film about former vice president Al Gore's campaign to educate people about global warming.

Darfur: Region in Sudan that was the site of a major armed conflict known as the War in Darfur beginning in 2003 and continuing for sixteen years.

Synchronicity: The fifth and final album by the rock band The Police, released in 1983.

Lynn Hirschberg: Journalist who has worked for *Rolling Stone*, *Vanity Fair*, and the *New York Times*.

Fran Liebowitz: Author, essayist, and public speaker known for her social commentary on American life.

Tama Janowitz: Novelist and short story writer known for *Slaves of New York*.

"The pen is mightier than the sword": Common expression dating back to 1839, meaning that the written word is more effective than violence.

EPISODE 7.9: KNIT, PEOPLE, KNIT!
Written by David Grae. Directed by Lee Shallat Chemel. Aired November 28, 2006.
Stars Hollow hosts a knitathon festival. Liz has her baby.

Tip O'Neill (1912–1994): Politician who served as speaker of the US House of Representatives from 1977 to 1987.

Kiki Smith: German-born American artist.

Madame Defarge: Fictional character and primary antagonist in the Charles Dickens novel *A Tale of Two Cities*.

UGG boots: Brand of sheepskin footwear founded in 1978 that rose to pop culture prominence after being featured as one of Oprah's Favorite Things in 2003.

A Brief History of Time: A 1991 biographical documentary film about physicist Stephen Hawking, derived from the title of Hawking's 1988 bestselling book.

Joaquin Phoenix: Actor known for portraying dark and eccentric characters. His works include *Hotel Rwanda*, *Walk the Line*, and *Joker*. For context to Lorelai's comment, he wore a monochromatic black tuxedo at the 2006 Oscars.

Arnold Schwarzenegger: Actor, former politician, and former bodybuilder who served as governor of California from 2003 to 2011. His acting credits include *The Terminator* and *Kindergarten Cop*.

EPISODE 7.10: MERRY FISTICUFFS
Written by David S. Rosenthal. Directed by Jackson Douglas. Aired December 5, 2006.
Luke consults a lawyer about partial custody of April. Christopher and Luke get into a fight.

Benjamin Britten (1913–1976): English composer, conductor, and pianist responsible for a range of operas including, as Emily mentions, an opera adapted from William Shakespeare's *A Midsummer Night's Dream* (see earlier entry).

Renée Fleming: Famed soprano singer and actress.

"Man's inhumanity to man": Phrase originating in the 1784 Robert Burns poem "Man Was Made to Mourn."

Survivor: Reality competition TV series debuting in 2000 in which contestants are placed in an isolated location and must provide food, fire, and shelter for themselves.

La bohème: An 1896 opera by Giacomo Puccini.

Franco Zeffirelli (1923–2019): Italian filmmaker whose works included multiple Shakespearean adaptations.

Rent: American rock musical loosely based on *La bohème* about a group of struggling artists in Manhattan.

Al Gore and the internet: Logan's reference to buying the internet from Al Gore (see earlier entry) stems from Gore's comments in a TV interview that, as a congressman, he was involved in the creation of the internet. The claim became fodder for late-night comedy punchlines.

The Merchant of Venice, **Portia**: *The Merchant of Venice* is a play by William Shakespeare about a merchant who deals with the consequences of defaulting on a large loan. Portia, whom Lucy says she played, is a female protagonist in the play.

John Abizaid: US Army general who served as commander of the US Central Command from 2003 to 2007.

Men Are from Mars, Women Are from Venus: A 1992 book by relationship counselor John Gray that asserts that most relationship problems are the result of fundamental differences between the sexes.

Episode 7.11: Santa's Secret Stuff

Written by Rebecca Rand Kirshner. Directed by Lee Shallat Chemel. Aired January 23, 2007.

Christopher and Lorelai have a belated Christmas celebration with Rory. Luke asks Lorelai for a character reference in his fight for custody of April.

Gallagher (1946–2022): Comedian known for prop-based comedy. His best-known routine involved using a large, mallet-like tool to smash various items, most notably watermelons.

Ebenezer Scrooge: Crotchety protagonist of the Charles Dickens novella *A Christmas Carol*.

"Angels We Have Heard on High": Christopher sings the well-known "Gloria" line from this Christmas song dating back to 1862.

I Have a Dream: Famous 1963 speech by civil rights activist Martin Luther King Jr. (see earlier entry).

Robert J. Van de Graaff (1901–1967): Physicist known for constructing the Van de Graaff generator, an electrostatic generator that creates very high electric potentials.

History Channel: Cable TV network launched in 1995.

The Muse: A 1999 comedy film starring Albert Brooks and Sharon Stone (see earlier entry).

Ashley Judd, Morgan Freeman: Judd and Freeman are actors who appeared together in thriller films like *Kiss the Girls* (1997) and *High Crimes* (2002).

Tom Hanks: Actor, filmmaker, and author whose works include *Forrest Gump*, *Big*, *Philadelphia*, and many others.

Joe Versus the Volcano: A 1990 romantic comedy film starring Tom Hanks and Meg Ryan. While not a huge success upon release, it has since achieved a bit of cult status.

Art Brut, "Formed a Band": Art Brut is an English indie rock band formed in 2003. "Formed a Band" is a song they released in 2004.

"Little Ghost": A 2005 song by the White Stripes (see earlier entry).

The Decemberists: Indie rock band formed in Portland, Oregon, in 2000.

Gulag Orkestar: A 2006 album and song by the rock band Beirut.

"Losing My Religion": A 1991 single by the rock band R.E.M.

Kenneth C. "Jethro" Burns, Steve Goodman: Burns (1920–1989) was a mandolinist and half of the comedy duo Homer and Jethro alongside Henry D. "Home" Haynes. Goodman (1948–1984) was a folk and country singer-songwriter whose songs include "City of New Orleans." Burns and Goodman were longtime collaborators, and Burns played on multiple Goodman albums.

"The Battle of Evermore": A 1971 song by Led Zeppelin.

"Rock-a-bye Baby": Traditional children's nursery rhyme and lullaby dating back to the 1700s.

Pluto: Dwarf planet discovered in 1930 and long considered the ninth planet until its status was questioned when it was discovered to be much smaller than originally thought. In 2006, the International Astronomical Union formally redefined its definition of planet to exclude dwarf planets like Pluto. Many astronomers, however, still consider Pluto a planet.

Pearl Harbor: Harbor in Hawaii that was the site of a surprise attack by the Imperial Japanese Navy in 1941, which marked the United States' entry into World War II.

Christmas in July: A 1940 screwball comedy film about a clerk who mistakenly thinks he has won a large sum of money which he proceeds to spend before receiving.

EPISODE 7.12: TO WHOM IT MAY CONCERN
Written by David Babcock. Directed by Jamie Babbit. Aired January 30, 2007. Luke and Anna attend a custody hearing. Richard has a health scare during a lecture.

Sue Grafton, Kinsey Millhone: Grafton (1940–2017) was a writer known for her "alphabet series" of detective novels featuring fictional sleuth Millhone that began with *"A" Is for Alibi* in 1982. *"R" Is for Ricochet* and *"S" Is for Silence* were part of the series, which saw the publication of *"Y" Is for Yesterday* before Grafton's death in 2017.

Reggie Bush: Former professional football player whose career included playing for the New Orleans Saints and Miami Dolphins.

Bush daughters: A reference to Jenna and Barbara Bush (see earlier entry), the twin daughters of President George W. Bush and his wife, Laura.

Dan Abrams: Media personality, TV host, author, and the Chief Legal Analyst for ABC News, whose career has included hosting *The Abrams Report* on MSNBC from 2001 to 2006.

Scott Peterson: Man who murdered his wife, Laci, in 2002 while she was eight months pregnant with their child. He was eventually found guilty of first-degree murder.

Sanjay Gupta: Neurosurgeon, medical reporter, and writer who serves as the chief medical correspondent for CNN.

John Maynard Keynes (1883–1946): English economist and philosopher for whom the Keynesian economic theories are named.

Episode 7.13: I'd Rather Be in Philadelphia

Written by Rebecca Rand Kirshner. Directed by Lee Shallat Chemel. Aired February 6, 2007.

Luke provides comfort and support during Richard's hospital stay, while Christopher is noticeably absent.

"I'd rather be in Philadelphia," W. C. Fields: Fields (1880–1946) was an actor, comedian, juggler, and writer. The Philadelphia quote is derived from a fictional epitaph he proposed for himself to suggest that he'd rather be living in Philadelphia than in the grave. President Ronald Reagan (see earlier entry) used the phrase in 1981 while hospitalized in Washington following an assassination attempt.

Rubber Man: While not an uncommon phrase to describe a supposed flexible superhero, a notable version is the DC Comics hero actually named Plastic Man, who first appeared in 1941.

Sean Connery (1930–2020): Scottish actor whose credits include being the first to portray James Bond.

Chad Hurley, Steve Chen, YouTube: Hurley and Chen are businessmen who co-founded the video-sharing platform YouTube in 2005. In 2006, they sold it to Google Inc. for $1.65 billion.

Mark Zuckerberg: Businessman who co-founded Facebook.

The Apprentice: Reality TV game show franchise in which contestants compete to become apprentice to a businessperson. It debuted in 2004.

Bobby Short (1924–2005): Singer and pianist who interpreted songs by popular composers.

George Gershwin, "Rhapsody in Blue" (1898–1937): Composer and pianist whose works include the 1924 orchestral composition "Rhapsody in Blue."

Claude Debussy (1862–1918): Influential French Impressionist composer.

Gary Crosby, "When You and I Were Young, Maggie Blues": Crosby (1933–1995) was an actor, singer, and son of Bing Crosby (see earlier entry). The pair had a hit duet in 1951 of "Maggie Blues," a popular folk standard written by George W. Johnson and James Austin Butterfield.

Imelda Marcos: First lady of the Philippines from 1965 to 1986.

***A Monetary History of the United States*, Milton Friedman**: *A Monetary History* is a 1963 book by Friedman (1912–2006), a Nobel Prize–winning economist, and Anna Schwartz.

"Spirit in the Sky," Norman Greenbaum: "Spirit in the Sky" is a 1969 song by singer-songwriter and one-hit wonder Greenbaum.

Arthur Conan Doyle (1859–1930): British writer and physician best known as the creator of Sherlock Holmes.

J. Press: Traditional men's clothier founded on the Yale University campus in 1902.

EPISODE 7.14: FAREWELL, MY PET

Written by Jennie Snyder. Directed by Jamie Babbit. Aired February 13, 2007. Rory develops a crush on a new professor. Lorelai plans a memorial service for Michel's dog.

Ben Bernanke: Economist who served as chairman of the Federal Reserve from 2006 to 2014.

Gloria Steinem: Journalist and activist who emerged in the 1960s and 1970s as a leader of the feminist movement.

Nadine Strossen: Lawyer and former president of the American Civil Liberties Union from 1991 to 2008.

Harlequin: Canadian publisher of romance novels and women's fiction founded in 1949. Their paperback romances are among the most popular in the world.

"Peace out, yo": Idiomatic phrase meaning goodbye.

***Gender Trouble*, Judith Butler**: *Gender Trouble: Feminism and the Subversion of Identity* is a 1990 book by gender theorist and philosopher Butler which argues that gender is performative.

Geoff Tabin: This is presumably the Tabin, a travel author, that Paris refers to.

Shen Congwen (1902–1988): Famed Chinese writer.

Tony Griffiths: History and travel writer.

***Eva Luna*, *The House of the Spirits*, Isabel Allende**: *Eva Luna* is a 1987 novel, and *The House of the Spirits* a 1982 novel, by Chilean writer Allende.

Snoop Dogg: Rapper and actor whose songs include "Gin and Juice" and "What's My Name?"

Herbie Flowers (1938–2024): English musician known for bass guitar, double bass, and tuba.

Aynsley Dunbar: English drummer who has performed with Journey and other artists.

Diamond Dogs: A 1974 studio album by David Bowie (see earlier entry).

Johann Sebastian Bach (1685–1750): German composer and musician.

"My Heart Will Go On": A 1997 single by Celine Dion (see earlier entry) popularized as part of the *Titanic* soundtrack.

"My Heart Belongs to Daddy": A 1938 Cole Porter song.

"My Heart Belongs to You": A 1948 single by Arbee Stidham.

"Tears in Heaven": A 1992 single by Eric Clapton.

"My Heart Stood Still": A 1927 song by Richard Rodgers and Lorenz Hart.

"I Will Always Love You": A 1974 song by Dolly Parton. Whitney Houston recorded a hit version in 1992.

William Payne Whitney (1876–1927): Influential businessman and philanthropist.

EPISODE 7.15: I'M A KAYAK, HEAR ME ROAR
Written by Rebecca Rand Kirshner. Directed by Lee Shallat Chemel. Aired February 20, 2007.
Lorelai avoids telling her mother about her separation from Christopher. Liz and T. J. stay with Luke.

Roy Rogers (1911–1998): Singer, actor, TV host, and rodeo performer nicknamed "King of the Cowboys."

Howdy Doody: Children's TV program featuring circus and Western themes that aired from 1947 to 1960. The titular Howdy Doody was a childlike puppet controlled by host Buffalo Bob Smith.

Captain Kangaroo: Children's TV series that aired from 1955 to 1984. The titular captain was portrayed by Bob Keeshan.

Tony Jacklin: Champion English golfer.

Jack Nicklaus: Champion professional golfer nicknamed the "Golden Bear."

Ryder Cup: Biennial men's golf competition between the European and US teams.

Hamlet: William Shakespeare tragedy written between 1599 and 1601.

Stonehenge: Ancient prehistoric monument in England consisting of an outer ring of vertical standing stones connected by horizontal stones.

Celtics: Professional basketball team based in Boston, Massachusetts.

Bob Tway: Champion professional golfer.

Greg Norman: Champion Australian golfer.

PGA: Professional Golfers Association of America.

Durga: Hindu goddess associated with protection, strength, motherhood, destruction, and wars, depicted with multiple arms.

Pandora's box: Greek mythological artifact that, when opened, released curses upon mankind.

James Reston (1909–1995): Journalist who wrote for the *New York Times*.

Philip Meyer, *The Vanishing Newspaper*: Meyer (1930–2023) was a noted journalist, author, and scholar who wrote *The Vanishing Newspaper: Saving Journalism in the Information Age* in 2004.

Poor little rich boy: Rory uses this spin on the common phrase "poor little rich girl" (see Barbara Hutton).

Teetotalism: The practice of voluntarily sustaining from the consumption of alcohol.

EPISODE 7.16: WILL YOU BE MY LORELAI GILMORE?

Written by Gayle Abrams and Gina Fattore. Directed by David Paymer. Aired February 27, 2007.
Lorelai and Rory host a baby shower for Lane. Logan reveals a failed business venture.

A Beautiful Mind: A 1988 biography and 2001 film adaptation about the life of Nobel Prize–winning economist and mathematician John Nash (see earlier entry).

Top Chef: Reality TV competition that debuted in 2006 in which chefs compete against each other in culinary challenges.

Shiloh Jolie-Pitt: The first biological child of actors Angelina Jolie and Brad Pitt (see earlier entries), the baby that Sookie mentions being born.

Kevin Federline: Sookie refers to this dancer, actor, and DJ who was married to Britney Spears (see earlier entry) from 2004 to 2007 and is the father of her two children. Sookie also refers to a 2006 incident in which Spears was photographed driving with her baby on her lap instead of in his car seat.

In Touch Weekly: Celebrity gossip magazine founded in 2002.

Jane's Addiction: Rock band formed in Los Angeles in 1985.

Exodus, Deuteronomy: Books of the Bible.

Dirty Dancing: A 1987 film starring Patrick Swayze, Jennifer Grey, and Kelly Bishop about a young woman who falls in love with a dance instructor at a vacation resort.

Joseph and the Amazing Technicolor Dreamcoat: A 1972 musical by Andrew Lloyd Webber and Tim Rice, based on Joseph from the Bible's Book of Genesis.

John Lennon (1940–1980): English musician best known as a member of the Beatles. He was married to Yoko Ono (see earlier entry) from 1969 until his death.

George J. Maloof Jr.: Entrepreneur, businessman, and member of the prominent Maloof family who own several business properties.

The River Styx: In Greek mythology, the ferryman Charon transports the souls of the dead across the River Styx in the Underworld.

Anthony Quinn (1915–2001): Actor known for *Viva Zapata!* and *Lust for Life*.

Davy Jones, Peter Tork: Jones (1945–2012) and Tork (1942–2019) were members of the pop band the Monkees (see earlier entry).

Dean Martin (1917–1995): Singer and actor known for *The Dean Martin Celebrity Roast* (see earlier entry).

"Mambo Italiano": A 1954 song by Bob Merrill made famous by Rosemary Clooney.

Rorschach test: Psychological test in which subjects' perceptions of inkblots are recorded and analyzed.

Pretty Girls Make Graves: Post-hardcore band formed in Seattle in 2001.

Ginger Grant, Mary Ann Summers: Fictional castaways on the 1960s TV sitcom *Gilligan's Island*, about a group of castaways shipwrecked on an island after setting sail for what was to be a three-hour tour. Tina Louise portrayed movie star Ginger and Dawn Wells portrayed Mary Ann, a wholesome farm girl.

"Hush, Little Baby": A traditional lullaby whose author and date of origin are unclear.

Episode 7.17: Gilmore Girls Only

Written by David Babcock. Directed by Lee Shallat Chemel. Aired March 6, 2007.
Lorelai, Rory, and Emily take a road trip to attend Mia's wedding. Lane goes into labor.

Brenda Starr, Reporter: Comic strip about an adventurous reporter that ran from 1940 to 2011.

I spy: Children's guessing game where one player chooses an object within sight and the other players have to guess the object based on its first letter.

W. B. Yeats (1865–1939): Irish poet, dramatist, and writer.

Richard the Lionheart: Nickname of Richard I (1157–1199), King of England from 1189 to 1199, because of his reputation as a great military leader.

Hitch: A 2005 romantic comedy film starring Will Smith and Kevin James.

My Morning Jacket: Rock band formed in Louisville, Kentucky, in 1998.

Wolfmother: Australian hard rock band formed in 2004.

A Prairie Home Companion: Radio variety show created and hosted by Garrison Keillor that aired live from 1974 to 2016.

The Pursuit of Happyness: A 2006 biographical drama film starring Will Smith as homeless salesman Chris Gardner.

Will Smith: Actor and rapper whose songs include "Gettin' Jiggy wit It" and whose screen credits include *The Fresh Prince of Bel-Air* and *Men in Black*.

Episode 7.18: Hay Bale Maze

Written by Rebecca Rand Kirshner. Directed by Stephen Clancy. Aired April 17, 2007.
The Spring Fling festival leads to a chance encounter for Luke and Lorelai. Rory shows Logan around Stars Hollow.

Fabien Baron: French art director and magazine editor.

Outtie 5000: Slang phrase popularized in the 1990s film *Reality Bites*, used to announce one's departure, and a play on the car model Audi 5000.

Jake Gyllenhaal: Actor whose works include *Donnie Darko* and *Brokeback Mountain*.

That Girl: TV sitcom that ran on ABC from 1966 to 1971, starring Marlo Thomas as an aspiring actress trying to make it in New York City.

Jay McInerney: Novelist whose works include *Bright Lights, Big City* and *Brightness Falls*.

Louise Erdrich, *Love Medicine*: Erdrich is a Native American author whose works include the 1984 novel *Love Medicine*, which follows the lives of five interconnected Ojibwe families.

Sally Jessy Raphael: Tabloid talk show host who hosted her own show from 1983 to 2002.

Alexander Haig (1924–2010): US Secretary of State under President Ronald Reagan and White House chief of staff under presidents Richard Nixon and Gerald Ford.

René Magritte (1898–1967): Belgian surrealist artist.

Wailing Wall: Also known as the Western Wall, a portion of the retaining wall of the ancient Temple Mount in Jerusalem where Jewish people traditionally go to pray.

Food Network: Cable network launched in 1993, focusing on food-related content.

Bozo: Clown character used for children's TV entertainment, introduced in 1946.

Don Corleone: Reference to the fictional character Vito Corleone, leader or "Don" of the Corleone family in *The Godfather* (see earlier entry).

Roswell incident: Roswell is a city in New Mexico where the discovery of military balloon debris in 1947 became the basis for UFO and alien-related conspiracy theories.

eBay: Online commerce and auction-style site launched in 1995.

Second Life: Multiplayer virtual world launched in 2003.

World of Warcraft: Multiplayer online role-playing video game released in 2004.

EverQuest II: 3D fantasy multiplayer video game released in 2004.

David Hasselhoff: Actor and singer known for *Knight Rider* and *Baywatch*.

Laurence Olivier (1907–1989): Famed English actor and director.

"Raise the Spirit": A 2007 song by Grant Lee Phillips.

Episode 7.19: It's Just Like Riding a Bike
Written by Jennie Snyder. Directed by Lee Shallat Chemel. Aired April 24, 2007.
Luke helps Lorelai shop for a new car. Jackson stays with Lorelai while his kids recover from the chicken pox.

Ryan O'Neal (1941–2023): Actor known for *Love Story* and *Paper Moon*, as well as for his turbulent personal life, which included a marriage to actress Farrah Fawcett (see earlier entry) and a 2007 incident in which he was arrested for shooting at his son, allegedly in self-defense. The charges were eventually dropped.

DeLorean, *Back to the Future*: *Back to the Future* is a 1985 science-fiction film starring Michael J. Fox as a teenager accidentally sent back in time to 1955 in a time-traveling DeLorean automobile with the assistance of his eccentric scientist friend portrayed by Christopher Lloyd. The DMC DeLorean was a two-seater sports car manufactured in the early 1980s.

Batmobile: The fictional automobile driven by the DC Comics superhero Batman (see earlier entry).

Blades of Glory: A 2007 sports comedy film starring Will Ferrell and Jon Heder as a pair of banned figure skaters who team up to compete.

Jack Bauer: Fictional protagonist of the TV series *24* portrayed by Kiefer Sutherland.

Craigslist: Classified advertisements website founded in 1995.

Episode 7.20: Lorelai? Lorelai?
Written by David S. Rosenthal. Directed by Bethany Rooney. Aired May 1, 2007.
Rory stresses over her impending graduation. Zack receives a tempting offer.

Franklin Delano Roosevelt, Yalta Conference: Roosevelt (1882–1945) was president of the United States from 1933 to 1945, including during World War II, which is the topic of the lecture in the scene. The Yalta Conference is the February 1945 meeting of the heads of government of the

United States, United Kingdom, and Soviet Union—Roosevelt, Winston Churchill (see earlier entry) and Joseph Stalin (see earlier entry)—to discuss the postwar reorganization of Germany and Europe.

Salman Rushdie, Padma Lakshmi, *The Satanic Verses*: Rushdie is a novelist whose works include *The Satanic Verses*, a 1988 book inspired by the life of Islamic prophet Muhammad that prompted assassination attempts and death threats. Lakshmi is a TV personality, model, and author who has hosted *Top Chef* (see earlier entry) and published cookbooks. The two were married from 2004 to 2007.

Lance Armstrong: Former professional road racing cyclist who won the Tour de France multiple times but was stripped of his titles after a performance-enhancing drugs scandal.

John Milton (1608–1674): English writer known for the epic poem *Paradise Lost.*

Bill Keller: Journalist who served as executive editor of the *New York Times* from 2003 to 2011.

Arthur Ochs Sulzberger Jr.: Journalist who was publisher of the *New York Times* from 1992 until 2018, when he appointed his son to lead the company.

"My Funny Valentine": A show tune from the 1937 musical *Babes in Arms.*

"Down with Love": Pop standard written in 1937 by E. Y. Harburg and Harold Arlen.

"Weird Al" Yankovic: Comedy musician known for parody songs like "Eat It" and "Amish Paradise."

Debbie Harry: Singer-songwriter and actress best known as the frontwoman for the rock band Blondie.

Ethel Merman (1908–1984): Actress and singer whose Broadway credits include *Anything Goes, Gypsy,* and *Hello, Dolly!*

***Dead Calm*:** A 1989 psychological thriller film about a married couple isolated at sea.

***Open Water*:** A 2003 survival horror film about a couple who become stranded in shark-filled waters while scuba diving.

***Das Boot*:** A 1981 war film following the crew of a German U-boat submarine.

Titanic: A 1997 epic romance disaster film depicting the sinking of the ocean liner Titanic.

"So long, Farewell": Song from *The Sound of Music*.

Tokyo Police Club: Canadian indie rock band formed in 2005.

Paradise Lost: Epic poem by John Milton (see earlier entry) about the biblical story of the fall of man.

Rev Theory: Rock band formed in Long Island in 2002.

Grizzly Bear: Rock band formed in Brooklyn in 2002.

Star Search: TV competition series in which performers competed in various entertainment genres, including singing, dancing, spokesmodel, and comedy. The original version ran from 1983 to 1995.

Dave Coulier, *Jagged Little Pill*: Coulier is an actor and comedian known for *Full House*. In the early 1990s, he dated Alanis Morissette (see earlier entry) and has long been said to be the inspiration for her song "You Oughta Know" from her breakthrough 1994 debut album *Jagged Little Pill*.

"Friendship": A 1939 Cole Porter song.

"Fever": A 1956 song written by Eddie Cooley and Otis Blackwell. Several artists have recorded it, with a famous version being done by Peggy Lee.

Crooked Fingers: Indie rock band led by musician Eric Bachmann.

The Rosebuds: Indie rock band formed in North Carolina, active from 2001 to 2014.

Bobby Conn: Musician whose songs include "Never Get Ahead" and "No Kids, No Money."

Midlake: Folk-rock band formed in Texas in 1999.

"Do You Really Want to Hurt Me?": A 1982 single by the English pop band Culture Club.

Boy George: English singer-songwriter and DJ best known as frontman of the English pop band Culture Club.

Whitney Houston (1963–2012): Singer and actress whose hits include "I Wanna Dance with Somebody" and "I Will Always Love You" (see earlier entry).

House on Haunted Hill: Lorelai is watching this 1959 horror film at the end of the episode.

Episode 7.21: Unto the Breach

Written by David Babcock and Jennie Snyder. Directed by Lee Shallat Chemel. Aired May 8, 2007.

Rory and Paris graduate from Yale.

Cyndi Lauper: Singer-songwriter and actress whose works include "Girls Just Want to Have Fun," "Time After Time," "True Colors," and the music for the Broadway musical *Kinky Boots*.

Milan Kundera (1929–2023): Czech and French novelist known for *The Unbearable Lightness of Being*.

The Pussycat Dolls: Girl group and dance ensemble whose hits include "Don't Cha" and "Buttons."

Robin Williams (1951–2014): Actor and comedian known for *Good Will Hunting*, *Mrs. Doubtfire*, *Dead Poets Society*, and many other films.

Henry Winkler: Actor and author best known for portraying Fonzie (see earlier entry) on the sitcom *Happy Days*.

Don't Ask, Don't Tell: See earlier entry "Gays in the military."

Unto the breach: Phrase originating in William Shakespeare's *Henry V*, in which King Henry urges his troops to attack the enemy's wall, but used modernly to encourage people to persevere in the face of challenge.

Ray Charles (1930–2004): Iconic and influential singer, songwriter, and pianist.

Episode 7.22: Bon Voyage

Written by David S. Rosenthal. Directed by Lee Shallat Chemel. Aired May 15, 2007.

Rory gets a job following the campaign of a presidential candidate and prepares to depart Stars Hollow.

Jane Pauley: Journalist known for *Today*, *Dateline NBC*, and *CBS Sunday Morning*.

Harry Belafonte (1927–2023): Calypso singer whose hits include "Jump in the Line (Shake, Senora)" and "Day-O (The Banana Boat Song)."

Marisa Tomei: Actress known for *My Cousin Vinny*, *In the Bedroom*, and *The Wrestler*.

About.com: Former website that served as an information repository.

Pomp and Circumstance Marches: A series of marches for orchestra composed by Edward Elgar.

"We've come a long way, baby": Variation on the common phrase "You've come a long way, baby," which originates from a 1960s advertising campaign for Virginia Slims cigarettes. "We've Come a Long Way Baby" is also the title of a 1978 song by Loretta Lynn.

Nick Walker, The Weather Channel: Walker is a broadcaster and meteorologist known as "The Weather Dude." The Weather Channel is a cable television network launched in 1982 and focusing on weather-related content.

Gilmore Girls: A Year in the Life

Episode 1: Winter
Written and directed by Amy Sherman-Palladino. Aired November 25, 2016.
Following a career high, Rory returns to Stars Hollow to contemplate her next move. Lorelai and Michel struggle to find a replacement chef at the inn.

"I Dreamed a Dream": A song from the 1980 musical *Les Misérables*.

Zoolander 2: A 2016 action comedy film starring Ben Stiller as fashion model Derek Zoolander.

Goop: Wellness and lifestyle brand founded by Gwenyth Paltrow in 2008.

Yonah Schimmel's Knish Bakery: A Manhattan restaurant and bakery operating since 1890.

Princess Charlotte of Wales: Member of the British royal family, the daughter of Prince William and Princess Catherine.

Batman v. Superman: Dawn of Justice: Rory references this 2016 action superhero film starring Henry Cavill as Superman (see earlier entry) and Ben Affleck (see earlier entry) as Batman.

Omar Little: Fictional stick-up man from the HBO TV series *The Wire*, portrayed by Michael K. Williams.

Leonard Cohen (1934–2016): Canadian singer, songwriter, poet, and novelist.

Uber: Ridesharing and delivery company launched in 2009.

"Winterglow": A 2008 song by Grant Lee Phillips.

The Talk of the Town: A section of *The New Yorker* magazine.

War on Christmas: Colloquial phrase used to describe the controversy some feel about replacing traditional Christmas terminology with more inclusive terms like "holidays." For example, in 2015, conservatives called out the coffee chain Starbucks for failing to use religious imagery on its annual holiday cups and instead using a solid red design.

Lena Dunham: Writer and actress known for the HBO series *Girls*.

Trainspotting: A 1996 film based on the 1993 novel of the same name by Irvine Welsh about a group of heroin addicts living in an economically depressed area of Edinburgh.

Condé Nast: Mass media company founded in 1909.

Diane Sawyer, Mike Nichols: Sawyer is a broadcast journalist who has anchored *ABC World News Tonight*, *Good Morning America*, *20/20*, and other programs. Nichols (1931–2014) was a film and theater director who was married to Sawyer from 1988 until his death.

Marvel Cinematic Universe: Media franchise consisting of a series of superhero films based on characters from Marvel Comics, as well as various TV series and literature. The franchise began with *Iron Man* in 2008.

Sadness, *Inside Out*: *Inside Out* is a 2015 coming-of-age animated film that follows the inner workings of the mind of a young girl through a group of personified emotions. Actress Phyllis Smith voices the character of Sadness.

Restless Virgins: A 2013 TV movie starring Vanessa Marano about a sex scandal at a Massachusetts prep school.

Deadly Honeymoon: A 2010 TV movie about a newlywed couple's disastrous honeymoon cruise.

Lifetime Movie Network: Cable TV network airing Lifetime TV movies that launched in 1998.

Killer Crush: A 2015 TV movie about a mentally disturbed medical student.

Mini's First Time: A 2006 film starring Alec Baldwin (see earlier entry) about a rebellious girl who hooks up with an escort agency.

Accidental Obsession: A 2015 TV movie about a lawyer who befriends a strange woman following a car accident.

Murder in a College Town: A 1997 TV movie about a woman investigating her son's disappearance.

Crimes of the Mind: A 2014 film about a woman attempting to rescue her brainwashed daughter from a cult.

Fatal Acquittal: A 2014 TV movie about a woman acquitted of her husband's murder only to then be terrorized by the real killer.

Not with My Daughter: A 2014 TV movie about a defense attorney whose client soon becomes a threat to her family.

Baby Sellers: A 2013 TV movie about infant trafficking.

Unfinished Betrayal: A 2013 TV movie about a family's dealings with a suspicious contractor.

The Boy She Met Online, The Girl He Met Online: TV movies about online dating released in 2010 and 2014, respectively.

Deadly Vows: A 1994 TV movie about a woman seduced by a married man.

Lying Eyes: A 1996 TV movie about a thirtysomething lawyer's relationship with an eighteen-year-old girl.

Lies He Told: A 1997 TV movie about a man who fakes his death in order to marry another woman.

My Nanny's Secret: A 2009 TV movie about a nanny who lies to protect her robbery-suspect brother.

Kardashian family: Prominent family in entertainment, business, and other arenas popularized in pop culture in part by the reality TV series *Keeping Up with the Kardashians*.

Eastern Promises: A 2007 gangster film directed by David Cronenberg that includes a scene involving an ambush in a steam room.

Gail Collins: Journalist and columnist known for her work with the *New York Times*.

Rock of Ages: A jukebox musical built around classic rock songs from the 1980s.

"Wrapped in plastic": Rory is quoting a line from the TV series *Twin Peaks*, in which a character discovers a dead body wrapped in plastic and describes it as such to the police.

Roy Choi: Korean-American chef who gained fame through his taco truck Kogi Korean BBQ.

Twitter: Social media microblogging platform launched in 2006 and now known as X.

Wino Forever: A reference to the tattoo on the arm of actor Johnny Depp. It originally read Winona Forever, in honor of actress Winona Ryder whom Depp was dating at the time. He had it altered after their breakup.

Anthony Bourdain (1956–2018): Celebrity chef, author, and travel documentarian known for *Anthony Bourdain: No Reservations* and other works.

April Bloomfield: Famous British chef and restaurateur.

Alice Waters: Chef, restaurateur, and author.

David Chang: Celebrity chef, restaurateur, author, and TV host.

Dan Barber: Chef, restaurateur, and author who owns Family Mill at Blue Hill in New York.

"Top of the World": Kirk sings this 1972 single by the Carpenters (see earlier entry).

Cyrano de Bergerac (1619–1655): French novelist, playwright, and duelist who was the inspiration for the part-biographical, part-fiction Edmond Rostand play *Cyrano de Bergerac*. In the play, Cyrano is in love with Roxane, but fears his big nose makes him too ugly to woo her. She, meanwhile, is in love with Christian, who is too tongue-tied to express his feelings. Cyrano begins writing love letters to Roxane pretending to be Christian.

Mario Andretti: Championship race car driver.

Peter Jackson, Argonath, "You shall not pass!": The Argonath is a fictional monument in *The Lord of the Rings*, consisting of two enormous statues of warriors. Jackson is the filmmaker who directed the trilogy of *Lord of the Rings* films, as well as *The Hobbit* trilogy. "You shall not pass!" is a famous line from the first film in the trilogy, spoken by the wizard Gandalf.

"Play for pinks": A phrase referring to illegal street racing where the winner takes possession of the loser's car, pink being a nod to pink slip or ownership papers.

Babe Paley (1915–1978): Famous magazine editor and socialite.

"The British are coming!": See earlier entry on Paul Revere.

Niña, Pinta, Santa Maria: Ships used by Christopher Columbus on his first voyage across the Atlantic.

"Ave Maria": An 1825 Franz Schubert song.

On the Road: A 1957 novel by Jack Kerouac (see earlier entry).

Llewyn Davis: Fictional young and struggling folk singer portrayed by Oscar Isaac in the 2013 film *Inside Llewyn Davis*.

Mathematical Principles of Natural Philosophy: A 1687 book by Isaac Newton.

Buffy the Vampire Slayer: A supernatural TV series about a vampire-hunting teenager that ran on The WB and UPN from 1997 to 2003. It is based on a 1992 film of the same name.

Yelp: Directory service and online review forum launched in 2004.

Neil Patrick Harris, *Gone Girl*: Harris is an actor best known for *Doogie Howser, M.D.* (see earlier entry) and *How I Met Your Mother*. He also appeared in the 2014 psychological thriller film *Gone Girl*, based on the 2012 Gillian Flynn novel of the same name, about a man who becomes the primary suspect in the disappearance of his wife.

John McPhee: Author and pioneer of the creative nonfiction form.

"What happens in Vegas": Catchphrase of Las Vegas, Nevada, which states that whatever happens in Las Vegas, stays in Las Vegas.

Pablo Escobar (1949–1993): Colombian drug lord dubbed the King of Cocaine.

Zoella: Media personality and author who rose to fame as a YouTuber in 2009.

"Archives": A 2008 song by Louise Goffin, who sang alongside her mother, Carole King, on the *Gilmore Girls* theme song.

Def Leppard: British rock band whose hits include "Pour Some Sugar on Me" and "Hysteria."

Brett Ratner: Film director and producer whose credits include the *Rush Hour* film series.

Benicio del Toro: Actor known for *The Usual Suspects* and *Fear and Loathing in Las Vegas*.

Fridays on ABC: The ABC television network was long known for its Friday night programming block known as TGIF (Thank Goodness It's Funny), which consisted mostly of family-friendly and teen-focused sitcoms.

"I'm the Man": A 1979 song by Joe Jackson.

Marie Kondo, *The Life-Changing Magic of Tidying Up*: *Tidying Up* is a 2011 book by Kondo, a Japanese author, TV presenter, and organization consultant.

Billy Squier: Musician whose hits include "The Stroke" and "Lonely Is the Night."

"Valley Winter Song": A 2003 song by Fountains of Wayne.

EPISODE 2: SPRING
Written and directed by Daniel Palladino. Aired November 25, 2016.
Lorelai and Emily attend therapy together. Rory and Paris return to Chilton.

Penn & Teller: A duo of magician entertainers consisting of Penn Jillette and Teller, known for their act that combines magic and comedy.

"Ironic": A 1996 single by Alanis Morissette (see earlier entry).

Huffington Post: Progressive news website founded in 2005.

Brexit: A reference to the 2016 United Kingdom (UK) European Union (EU) membership referendum that resulted as a vote in favor of the UK leaving the EU.

Aeschylus: Ancient Greek tragedian often called the father of tragedy.

Harrods: Department store in London, England, opened in 1905.

Liza with a "Z": A 1972 television concert film starring Liza Minelli (see earlier entry).

Law & Order: A TV franchise consisting of a number of series, which began with the original *Law & Order* in 1990.

Blue Bloods: Police procedural TV series starring Tom Selleck that aired on CBS from 2010 to 2014.

Jessica Chastain: Actress known for *The Help*, *Zero Dark Thirty*, and *The Eyes of Tammy Faye*.

Jack Black: Actor and musician known for *School of Rock*, *Kung Fu Panda*, and other works.

Cate Blanchett: Australian actress known for *The Aviator*, *Blue Jasmine*, *Notes on a Scandal*, and many other works.

Daniel Radcliffe: English actor known for the *Harry Potter* film series.

Jennifer Lawrence: Actress known for the *X-Men* and *Hunger Games* film series.

"Squirrel!": A line from the 2009 animated film *Up*, yelled by Dug the dog whenever he would spot a squirrel, which would distract him from whatever he was currently focusing on.

Mickey Rourke: Actor and former boxer known for *9½ Weeks*, *Once Upon a Time in Mexico*, and *The Wrestler*.

Natalie Portman: Actress known for *Closer*, *V for Vendetta*, and *Black Swan*.

Skrillex: DJ, record producer, and singer.

Eraserhead: A 1977 horror film by David Lynch.

Alexander Graham Bell, Thomas A. Watson: Bell (1847–1922) was a Canadian-American inventor and scientist credited with patenting the first telephone. Watson (1854–1934) was Bell's assistant. Bell's first call on his invention was to Watson, where he summoned him from the next room.

Rachael Ray: Cook, TV personality, and author who has hosted shows on the Food Network and her own daytime talk show.

"I cannot remember the books I've read any more than the meals I have eaten": Paris recites this famous quote by author Ralph Waldo Emerson.

The Atlantic: Magazine and multi-platform publisher founded in 1857.

Old Faithful: A geyser in Wyoming's Yellowstone National Park.

Beach Blanket Bingo: A 1965 beach party movie, part of a beach-themed film series, starring Frankie Avalon and Annette Funicello.

Airbnb: Online platform for short-term homestays and experiences, founded in 2008.

Igor Stravinsky (1882–1971): Russian composer and conductor.

"Tiptoe Through the Tulips": A 1929 song by Al Dubin and Joe Burke, popularized in the 1960s through a cover by Tiny Tim.

Blake Shelton: Country music singer and TV personality who appeared on *The Voice* from 2011 to 2023.

LinkedIn: Social media networking website for professionals, launched in 2003.

"Take a powder, Baby John": A line from *West Side Story* (see earlier entry).

Confucius (551–479 BC): Chinese philosopher.

Queen Latifah: Rapper and actress known for *Living Single*, *Chicago*, a daytime TV talk show, and other works.

Esa-Pekka Salonen: Finnish conductor and composer.

Bombing of Dresden: British and American aerial bombing of the city of Dresden, Germany, during World War II that killed up to 25,000 people.

A History of Violence, **David Cronenburg**: *A History of Violence* is a 2005 action thriller film directed by Cronenburg and starring Viggo Mortensen (see earlier entry) as a diner owner who becomes a local hero after thwarting a robbery. Cronenburg's other works include *The Fly* and *Eastern Promises*.

Cloud Atlas: A 2004 novel by David Mitchell combining metafiction, science fiction, historical fiction, and contemporary fiction.

Citi Bike: Bicycle sharing system launched in 2013.

NY1, Pat Keirnan: NY1 is a cable news network focusing on news happening throughout New York City. Keirnan is a TV host who has appeared on the network since 1997.

Cronut: Pastry resembling a doughnut but made from croissant-like dough, invented and trademarked in 2013 by French pastry chef Dominique Ansel.

Air Jordan: Line of basketball and sportswear shoes produced by Nike for basketball player Michael Jordan during his time with the Chicago Bulls, beginning in 1985.

Wookiee: Tall, hairy species from the *Star Wars* franchise.

P. J. Clarke's: Restaurant and pub in New York City established in 1884.

Millennium Falcon: Fictional starship in the *Star Wars* franchise.

Outlander: Historical fantasy novel written by Diana Gabaldon, first published in 1991. It spawned a successful TV series adaptation that debuted in 2014.

The *Washington Post*: Daily newspaper published in Washington, DC, founded in 1877.

Get Shorty: A 1995 gangster comedy film starring John Travolta and Gene Hackman.

EPISODE 3: SUMMER
Written and directed by Daniel Palladino. Aired November 25, 2016.

The town plans a production of *Stars Hollow: The Musical*. Rory begins working at the *Stars Hollow Gazette*.

The Returned: French supernatural drama TV series about a small town where people who have died suddenly reappear. It aired from 2012 to 2015.

Matilda the Musical: Musical with lyrics by Tim Minchin and book by Dennis Kelly, based on the 1988 children's novel by Roald Dahl.

White Walker, Khaleesi: White Walkers are fictional humanoid antagonists in the fantasy novel series *A Song of Ice and Fire* by George R. R. Martin and its accompanying TV adaptation *Game of Thrones*. Their weapon of choice is a crystal sword. Khaleesi is the title bestowed upon the character Daenerys Targaryen.

Kinky Boots: A 2012 stage musical with lyrics by Cyndi Lauper and book by Harvey Fierstein, based on the 2005 British film of the same name, about a shoemaker who forms an unlikely partnership with a drag queen to produce high-heeled boots in an effort to save his family's factory.

The *Boston Globe*: Boston's daily newspaper founded in 1872.

"My wife is crying upstairs": Line spoken by Marlon Brando as Don Vito Corleone in *The Godfather*.

Five-O: Reference to law enforcement, stemming from the TV series *Hawaii Five-O*.

Aaron Sorkin: Screenwriter, playwright, and director whose credits include *The West Wing*, *Sports Night*, and many others.

MS-DOS: Microsoft computer operating system initially released in 1981.

Halt and Catch Fire: Period drama TV series that aired on AMC from 2014 to 2017 focusing on the personal computer revolution and development of the World Wide Web in the 1980s and 1990s.

Abacus: Ancient, hand-operated calculating tool.

Perry White: Fictional editor of *The Daily Planet* newspaper in the DC Comics/Superman universe.

VE Day: Victory in Europe Day, May 8, 1945, commemorating the end of World War II.

Pat Lafrieda: Meat wholesale company founded in 1922 specializing in steak and burger patties.

There Will Be Blood: A 2007 epic period drama film directed by Paul Thomas Anderson (see earlier entry) about a silver miner-turned-oilman during the California oil boom. The milkshake line is a famous quote from the film.

The Jungle Book: A 2016 fantasy adventure film produced as a live-action remake of the 1967 Disney animated movie, itself loosely based on the Rudyard Kipling story collection of the same name.

Michael Bay: Filmmaker whose credits include *Armageddon*, *Transformers*, *Pearl Harbor*, and others.

Bataan Death March: A 1942 Japanese war crime involving the forcible transfer by the Imperial Japanese Army of American and Filipino prisoners of war from the Bataan Peninsula to Camp O'Donnell.

Baby Monitor: Sound of Fear: A 1998 TV movie about a woman who learns of her husband's affair with their babysitter.

***Co-ed Call Girl*, Tori Spelling**: *Co-ed Call Girl* is a 1996 TV movie starring Tori Spelling as a college student who becomes involved with an escort service. Spelling is an actress best known for her role on *Beverly Hills, 90210*. In 2015, she fell backward into a hot grill at a Benihana hibachi restaurant resulting in serious burns.

Industrial Revolution: Period of rapid technological change taking place from 1760 to 1840.

James Naismith (1861–1939): Inventor of basketball.

Hamilton: A 2015 biographical stage musical by Lin-Manuel Miranda based on the life of Alexander Hamilton.

Magneto: Fictional Marvel Comics character with the ability to control magnetic fields.

Jeff Koons: Sculptor and painter whose works often deal with popular culture.

Occupy movement: Socio-political protest movement that expressed opposition to social and economic inequality, lasting from approximately 2011 to 2016.

Nostradamus (1503–1566): French seer and astrologer.

"Waterloo": A 1974 song by the pop band ABBA.

Simba: Fictional protagonist in Disney's *The Lion King*.

School of Rock: Rock musical by Andrew Lloyd Webber based on the 2003 film of the same name about a rock musician who pretends to be a substitute teacher at a prep school.

"Hasa Diga Eebowai": Song from *The Book of Mormon* stage play, a parody of *The Lion King*'s "Hakuna Matata."

Edward Albee (1928–2016): Playwright whose works include *The Zoo Story* and *Who's Afraid of Virginia Woolf?* (see earlier entry).

Joe Allen: A New York City restaurant.

Busta Rhymes: Rapper, singer, and actor.

Trish: Factory worker character in the stage musical *Kinky Boots* (see earlier entry).

Benny Andersson, Björn Ulvaeus: Musicians best known as members of ABBA (see earlier entry).

"I Feel the Earth Move": A 1971 song by Carole King.

The Federalist Papers: Collective of articles and essays written by Alexander Hamilton, James Madison, and John Jay.

Duncan Phyfe (1768–1854): Leading cabinet maker in the nineteenth century.

Matlock: Murder-mystery TV series that ran from 1986 to 1995 starring Andy Griffith (see earlier entry) as a crime-solving lawyer.

PBS: Public Broadcasting Service, a public broadcasting network founded in 1969.

Henry Wadsworth Longfellow (1807–1882): Poet and educator whose works include "Paul Revere's Ride" and *The Song of Hiawatha*.

David Carr (1956–2015): At the newspaper office, Rory has a photo by her desk of this journalist, author, and editor who covered culture for the *New York Times*.

Lou Grant: Drama TV series starring Ed Asner as the titular newspaper editor. A spinoff of *The Mary Tyler Moore Show*, where the character first appeared, Lou Grant ran from 1977 to 1982.

Dave Eggers: Writer, editor, and publisher whose works include the 2000 memoir *A Heartbreaking Work of Staggering Genius*.

I Feel Bad About My Neck: And Other Thoughts on Being a Woman*:* Rory paraphrases the title of this 2006 book of humorous essays by Nora Ephron (see earlier entry).

"I could've been a contender": Famous line from the 1954 film *On the Waterfront*.

The Mysteries of Laura: Police procedural TV series starring Debra Messing as a detective that aired on NBC from 2014 to 2016.

Jack the Zipper: Director known for pornographic and erotic films.

"Gold Digger": A 2005 song by Kanye West.

The Manhattan Project: World War II research and development project led by the United States focused on producing nuclear weapons.

The Ghost and Mrs. Muir: A 1947 supernatural romantic fantasy film starring Gene Tierney and Rex Harrison.

Narcos: Crime-drama TV series that aired on Netflix from 2015 to 2017.

Sandra Lee: TV chef and author whose hosting credits include *Semi-Homemade Cooking with Sandra Lee*.

Wild: A 2012 memoir in which author Cheryl Strayed chronicles her 1,100-mile hike of self-discovery on the Pacific Coast Trail. A film adaptation was released in 2014.

Episode 4: Fall

Written and directed by Amy Sherman-Palladino. Aired November 25, 2016. Lorelai's plan to recreate *Wild* doesn't go as planned. Luke and Lorelai finally tie the knot. Rory makes a surprising announcement to her mother.

Doctor Who: British science fiction TV series about an extraterrestrial time traveler that debuted in 1963. Various actors have portrayed the doctor since the show's debut.

Eat, Pray, Love: A 2006 memoir by Elizabeth Gilbert chronicling her trip around the world following a divorce. It was adapted into a 2010 film starring Julia Roberts.

"By the pricking of my thumbs, something wicked this way comes": Famous line from William Shakespeare's *Macbeth*.

In Omnia Paratus: Latin phrase meaning "ready for anything."

Yentl: A 1983 romantic musical drama film starring Barbra Streisand.

La Dolce Vita: A 1960 film by Federico Fellini about a journalist who journeys through the "sweet life" of Rome.

Ryan Gosling: Actor known for *The Notebook*, *Crazy, Stupid, Love*, and *La La Land*.

Mr. Bean: British sitcom airing from 1990 to 1995 and starring Rowan Atkinson as the titular oddball, described as a "child in a grown man's body."

The Call of the Wild: A 1903 adventure novella by Jack London.

"Now I know I have a heart because it's breaking," "I think I'll miss you most of all": Famous lines from the 1939 musical film *The Wizard of Oz*, spoken by the characters as Dorothy is departing from Oz to return to Kansas.

Mr. Toad's Wild Ride: Dark ride at Disneyland, opened in 1955.

The Hurt Locker: A 2008 action thriller film about an Iraq War bomb disposal team.

Chemin de Fer: Brand of jeans popular in the 1970s.

An Unmarried Woman: A 1978 film about a woman coming to terms with her divorce.

Christian Bale, *The Machinist*: Bale is an English actor whose works include *American Psycho*, *The Dark Knight* trilogy, and *The Machinist*, a 2004 psychological thriller in which he plays a machinist struggling with paranoia and delusion after being unable to sleep for a year.

Christopher Hussey (1899–1970): British historian and architecture writer.

Ian Schrager: Entrepreneur and hotelier credited with co-creating the boutique hotel.

Rolf Gruber: Character in *The Sound of Music* (see earlier entry), a Nazi delivery boy in love with one of the von Trapp children.

Chloë Sevigny: Actress known for *Boys Don't Cry* and *American Psycho*.

Whoopi Goldberg: Comedian, actress, and TV personality whose credits include *Sister Act*, *The Color Purple*, and co-hosting the daytime talk show *The View*.

Katy Perry: Singer and TV personality whose hits include "I Kissed a Girl" and "California Gurls."

Beelzebub: A name for the devil.

"My Sharona": A 1979 single by the pop band The Knack.

Candy Spelling: Author, theater producer, and philanthropist who was married to Aaron Spelling from 1968 until his death in 2006. She is the mother of actress Tori Spelling, with whom she has had a complex and, at times, strained relationship.

The Adventures of Priscilla, Queen of the Desert: A 1994 Australian road comedy film that follows two drag queens and a transgender woman on a bus trip. It was adapted into a 2006 stage musical.

Desnudas: Seminude topless female performers covered in body paint who can be found in Times Square in New York City.

Serena Williams: See earlier entry on the Williams sisters.

Serena: Fictional witch on the TV sitcom *Bewitched* (see earlier entry).

Tracy Anderson: Celebrity fitness entrepreneur and author known for the Tracy Anderson Method.

Barbara Sinatra (1926–2017): Model, showgirl, and socialite who was the fourth and final wife of Frank Sinatra.

Bob Seger: Singer-songwriter whose hits include "Night Moves" and "Turn the Page."

Deanna Durbin (1921–2013): Singer and actress who appeared in musical films in the 1930s and 1940s.

Kirk Douglas (1916–2020): Actor whose credits include *Lust for Life*, *Spartacus*, *Lonely Are the Brave* and others.

Eli Wallach, *Baby Doll*, **Carroll Baker, Elia Kazan**: Wallach (1915–2014) is a film, TV, and stage actor whose credits include *The Magnificent Seven*, *The Good, the Bad and the Ugly*, *The Godfather Part III*, and *Baby Doll*, a 1956 comedy film directed by Kazan (1909–2003). Wallach co-starred in the film with Baker, who received an Academy Award nomination for the film. Her other credits include *The Big Country* and *How the West Was Won*. Kazan is one of Hollywood's most beloved directors.

Chloe O'Brian: Lorelai's mention of Chloe is a reference to this character from the TV series *24* (see earlier entry), portrayed by Mary Lynn Rajskub. Lorelai recites several quotes from the series, which starred Keifer Sutherland (see earlier entry).

Five by five: Rory references this line from the TV series *Buffy the Vampire Slayer* (see earlier entry), meaning "perfectly fine."

Beats by Dre: Consumer audio products company known for headphones and speakers. It was founded in 2006 by rapper and music producer Dr. Dre and producer Jimmy Iovine.

Mr. Bernstein: See Woodward and Bernstein.

***Jerry Maguire*, "Show me the money!"**: *Jerry Maguire* is a 1996 sports comedy film starring Tom Cruise as a slick sports agent. "Show me the money!" is a line that became a popular phrase after the film's release.

Starz: Cable TV network founded in 1994.

Dorian Gray: Fictional character from the 1890 Oscar Wilde novel *The Picture of Dorian Gray*. In the book, Gray remains young and beautiful while a portrait of him ages.

Bugsy Siegel (1906–1947): Mobster and driving force in the development of the Las Vegas Strip.

Well hooray for the bulldog: Line from the film *Citizen Kane*, spoken sarcastically by the wife of Orson Welles's character when he tells her the bulldog, referring to his newspaper, has gone to print.

Wolfgang Van Halen: Musician who is the son of rockstar Eddie Van Halen and actress Valerie Bertinelli.

Sméagol: Fictional character in *The Lord of the Rings* (see earlier entry), a monster who was corrupted by the One Ring.

Little House in the Big Woods: Autobiographical children's novel by Laura Ingalls Wilder published in 1932.

"Welcome to the Jungle": A 1987 single by the rock band Guns N' Roses.

Rooster Cogburn: Sookie's rooster is named after this fictional character who first appeared in the 1986 Charles Portis novel *True Grit* and was portrayed on screen by John Wayne.

Panama: Sookie refers to the US invasion of this Latin American country in 1989 under the presidency of George H. W. Bush in an effort to depose General Manuel Noriega, who was wanted for racketeering and drug trafficking.

Jonestown, Kool-Aid: Jonestown is a South American commune overseen by cult leader Jim Jones where over 900 people were killed or took their own lives in 1978. While actual Kool-Aid is a brand of flavored drink mix introduced in 1927, the phrase "drinking the Kool-Aid," which means accepting and believing a deranged ideology, is closely associated with Jonestown.

Log Lady: Michel calling Sookie a "crazy log lady" might be a reference to this eccentric character from *Twin Peaks* who always carries around a log with which she seems to share a psychic connection.

Right Said Fred: English pop duo known for the 1991 song "I'm Too Sexy."

Rande Gerber: Businessman who founded the tequila brand Casamigos with George Clooney.

"Relax," Frankie Goes to Hollywood: Frankie Goes to Hollywood is an English new wave band formed in 1980. "Relax" is their debut single.

"Hey Nineteen": A 1980 single by Steely Dan (see earlier entry).

"Karma Chameleon": A 1983 single by Culture Club.

Edward Scissorhands: A 1990 film by Tim Burton starring Johnny Depp as a humanoid who has scissor blades instead of hands.

Jerry Orbach (1935–2004): Actor whose credits include starring on the TV series *Law & Order* (see earlier entry) from 1992 to 2004.

References Index

Episode Title Index

About the Author

Matt Browning is a television and pop culture aficionado. His 2021 book *The Definitive Golden Girls Cultural Reference Guide* is an episode-by-episode encyclopedia of that show's pop culture references. For twenty-five years he operated a website devoted to the *Golden Girls* spinoff series *Empty Nest* and continues to manage its social media presence. He lives in Charleston, West Virginia, where he owns Plot Twist Books, an independent bookstore and vacation rental space. His other works include *Chicks and the City*, an award-winning children's picture book, and *Bookstore Explorer: West Virginia*, a travel guide to the state's independent bookstores. Learn more at MattBrowning Books.com.